life:
connected

A devotional journal for
getting real with a very real God

by
Suzanne Rentz

To: Tina
God loves you so
very much—Thanks
for all you do!
Psalm 139:1-18

Life: Connected
ISBN: 978-1-60683-193-9
©2011 by Suzanne Rentz

Published by Harrison House Publishers
P.O. Box 35035
Tulsa, OK 74145
www.harrisonhouse.com

Contents

Sound Familiar?

The alarm clock goes off and it is still dark outside; you stumble over yesterday's dirty clothes, making your way into the bathroom. As you look in the mirror, something scary is staring straight at you! Your feet slowly drag down the hallway. The clock in the kitchen has to be fast; is it that time already? You grab a cold Pop Tart and head out the door. Another day has officially begun. Will this day be like all the rest? Maybe, school isn't what it used to be or work has lost it's charm. You wonder, *Is there more to life? Or is this all there is?*

Why do deep questions like these echo in our minds? As young women, why do we feel deeply, love intimately, and hope blindly? When I was young, I believed that if I lived exactly the way God wanted me to, the result would be a picture-perfect life, without disappointments or pain, all my dreams would come true, and I would live happily-ever-after — yeah right! Unfortunately, this is not reality. There is no such thing as a problem free life! Life is a complex, ongoing journey filled with steep hills to conquer (or should I say crawl over) and flat terrains where you get to coast a bit and catch your breath. There will be those steep downward slopes, coming out of nowhere, causing life to suddenly spiral out of control.

At times, you will travel with your friends and family, laughing and talking; life couldn't be better. But there will also be times when you will travel alone, when the only sound you will hear is the sound of your feet crushing the rocks; the laughter and the voices will no longer be heard — just silence. Just when the silence seems overwhelming, you will sense God's sweet presence urging you on.

As you read the pages of this book, it is my prayer that God will become very real to you! Every chapter is filled with great insight, God's life transforming Word, and remarkable stories from young women who share your pains and triumphs. Wherever you find yourself in life, God wants you to know that you can make it! He has designed the journey set before you. He knows your past and your future. You can trust Him completely.

God believes in you! Not only does He want you to make it on this crazy journey called life, but know that He is with you every step of the way. He will never leave you. Pursue Him and let Him guide you. Be satisfied by Him and Him alone. God desires for you to live your life to the fullest: full of purpose, love, adventure, and most of all, full of Him!

Section I

God = Fire Insurance

"Does GOD hear me when I PRAY?"

LOVING GOD

"…the Bible has so many rules…"

"Is God even real?"

Reading my Bible

When I try to single out one experience where I grew deeply in my relationship with the Lord, it seems virtually impossible, not to mention a bit cheap. Life is full of ups and downs and mine has certainly had its share. For me, being a woman who desires God is about what I do in all phases of life. Whether up, down, or somewhere in between, the question I have come to ask of the Lord is, "what do You want of me?" I have tried to pursue the Lord through all kinds of methods: from getting up in the morning to read the Word or doing it at night, to journaling, to prayer walks and so many other ideas that have been sent my way. Through it all, what I have found is that the Lord truly does know me better than I know myself. He knows exactly what avenue of pursuit I need to focus on at any given time.

Most recently when I sat with the question of how to grow deeper with the Lord, His answer was for me to read the Word both in the morning and at night. I have always had a difficult time being consistent with just one or the other, but attacking a chapter or two from the Old Testament in the morning and another chapter from the New Testament in the evening did the trick this time. He knows what we need in order to grow better than we do. Music and prayer are two other areas that He has asked me to be diligent in because He knows I am wired in such a way as to meet Him in those places.

As I have grown in my relationship with the Lord, I have found that desiring and knowing God is really all about His Word - the Bible. The more time I spend in it, the more time I want to spend. To me, it is not just some "manual" or "instruction book for life." Instead, it is the very place where I find the Lord - His heart and character. It is also the place where I discover more about who I am - who He says I am and who He has called me to be in this world. The Bible is an intimate story and I am part of it! The more I dig into that story, the more I find myself in it. Since I have been on this journey, it has become so intoxicating that desiring God no longer needs a second thought, for He has become my very breath.

Erin

chapter 1

DESIRE

Rebecca Simmons

Grow

As I sit here in the café area of my favorite grocery store, collecting my thoughts, a young father walks in with his daughter. She must be about 20 months old. I'm immediately drawn into the scene unfolding before me and can't help but sneak a few peeks. She toddles just in front of her dad. The fur-lined hood of her pink coat is pulled up over her head. With white-mittened hands covering her eyes, she gingerly forges ahead, playing "shy" with the strangers she passes. After nearly bumping into a table, Dad instructs her to uncover her eyes. She obliges and beams up at me as she passes by. Just when I thought our momentary interaction had ended, she crawled into the booth beside me, pointed at me and exclaimed, "Mommy!" Dad quickly corrected her, reminding her that Mommy was next door getting her nails done.

I laughed inwardly. No, I'm not her mommy. I'm not anyone's mommy yet, but I've been around kids enough to know a thing or two about them. One thing I know is that they don't stay young forever. As adorable and delightful as this little girl is right now, she will inevitably grow up – and that's a good thing. God designed us this way. If her parents feed her and care for her well, she will eventually reach a point where she can take care of herself. Isn't that what parents want for their children? As much as they love us and, hopefully, enjoy our company, they want to see us grow into responsible adults who can contribute something valuable to the world. And then they want grandbabies!

I suppose the cycle never ends, and it shouldn't. God's design is beautiful. Parents raise their children to be mature, responsible adults who can care for themselves and later raise their own children. But what if things weren't this way? What if there was a kink in the design? What if people suddenly stopped growing and developing at age five? Sure, naptime and play-dough sculptures would be fun for awhile, but who would fly the airplanes, perform life-saving medical procedures, or cook dinner? Think about it. Do you really want a five-year-old working on your car or, better yet, cutting your hair?

Just as we are created to grow physically, we are designed to grow spiritually. 1 Peter 2:2-3 tells us "Like newborn babies, crave pure spiritual milk, so that by it you may grow up in your salvation, now that you have tasted that the Lord is good." (⋮⋮⋮) Why grow spiritually? So you can become the dynamic woman God created you to be and lead others to Him through your life and testimony.

Is It All About Rules?

At this point, you might be thinking, *Oh, here we go again. I know what's coming next.* You're probably expecting me to tell you how important it is to grow closer to the Lord and that, to do that, you need to pray, read your Bible, and attend church regularly. While that's all true, I'm not going to tell you how long and often to pray, how much or what to read of your Bible, or how many times a week you should attend church. If only our relationship with the Creator of the Universe was that simple and easy.

There is a certain security and satisfaction in rules. But Christianity is not about rules. God's purpose in creating you and placing you on this earth was not so you could live a mediocre, cookie-cutter life. No, He created you because He knew you would be unique and that, once He put the finishing touches on your tiny frame and sent you to (let's say) Bob and Betty Johnson in Bloomington, Minnesota, He would fall passionately in love with you. He gave you a free will, hoping you would choose Him and grow to love Him with the same intensity and passion. He has already chosen you and invited you to be a part of His story – the greatest story ever told. It's exciting, dramatic, and action-packed. What role will you play? Will you be part of the crowd? You could live a safe existence that doesn't cause enough trouble to call attention, yet doesn't make an impact worth remembering. Maybe that appeals to you. Maybe you prefer to fly alone, live for yourself, and look out for number one.

While looking out for ourselves may feel good for a time, it will ultimately leave us feeling unfulfilled, frustrated, and even bitter. I dare say most of us do not wish for an average life. Why are we so intrigued by movie stars or the rich and famous? Why are *American Idol* and other such reality shows among the most highly rated programs of our day? We love fame and fortune. We crave it. We want to know what the stars wear, how they style their hair, where they shop, what they eat . . . the list goes on. There are racks of magazines at every store checkout line, ready to dish the latest gossip. Why do we even care? Because we want to be like them. We want to be great.

Greatness

You were created for greatness. Genesis 1:27 tells us that "God created man in His own image, in the image of God He created him; male and fmale He created them." (⋮ ⋮ ⋮)⋮ You were created in the image, or likeness, of God. If that doesn't scream "greatness," I don't know what does. Can you think of anything about God that isn't great? I can't. As a young lady who bears the image of her Creator, who possesses the same spiritual / emotional DNA of her heavenly Father, that same greatness is already within you. It runs through your veins, beats with the rhythm of your heart, and shines brilliantly each time you flash that bright smile He carved out on your beautiful face.

So, I can't give you a formula for growing in your relationship with Christ. I can't tell you that if you do A, B, and C, you can become the next Beth Moore, Joyce Meyers, or CeCe Winans. That may not even be your thing. Maybe you're more of a Rachel Ray, Oprah Winfrey, or Condoleezza Rice type. There is only one you. I know you've heard that before. Mr. Rogers reminded us of that every day in his song, "Won't You Be My Neighbor?" and it's true. You are unique, special, one-of-a-kind. God would not have created you and graced this earth with your presence had He not placed within you something our world needs – something only you can offer – YOU!

Although we each possess greatness within us, we must learn how to cultivate it and reveal it. That has to be the most miraculous part of how God created us. He did not create finished products. He created works-in-progress. He designed us with the ability to learn, grow, and develop. Remember kindergarten? We walked into a classroom full of tables and chairs, colorful carpets, cubbies, art supplies, fat pencils, gray paper with wide lines, and lots and lots of books. Flipping through those books at the beginning of the year, the words may as well have been a foreign language. We couldn't decipher "apple" from "astronaut" unless it was the only word next to a picture. Ahhh . . . the pictures. Remember books with pictures? Those were the days! But before I get too far off track, let me get back to the point. By the end of kindergarten, we could read, at least a little. Words meant something. Our brains had found the key that unlocked the door to a whole new world of learning and discovery. It didn't end once we could identify "apple," "ball," and "cat." Otherwise, you wouldn't be reading this book! We kept practicing when we moved on to first grade and, by second or third grade, we were reading chapter books.

God created us with the capacity to learn, grow, and develop into something better than what we are now. From the day we are born until the day we die, we have the ability to change. The opportunities are endless. Are you ready to embrace the adventure and begin to unleash the greatness that lies within you?

My Journey...

As we embark on this adventure together, let me tell you a little about my journey. I'm certainly not "there." I don't claim to be an expert. In fact, I find that I have more questions than answers. I am on this journey with you and, like you, I want to grow closer to my heavenly Father and fulfill His purpose in my life. I've been on this journey almost my entire life – twenty-two out of my twenty-six years. The first four, I don't remember. Over these years, I've grown and changed quite a bit. The adventure becomes more exciting every day. I hope that something I have discovered, by this point in my journey, will inspire and encourage you on your journey into the wild, exciting life God has called you to.

Remember those old Sunday School achievement charts? You got a sticker by your name every week you were present and, sometimes, more stickers for bringing your Bible or reciting a memory verse. There was always one kid who left everyone else in the dust. This kid's row of stickers stretched five times longer than anyone else's, forcing the teacher to constantly post new charts before the rest of the class could experience the satisfaction of completion. Didn't you ever feel annoyed, frustrated, or lackadaisical because of that kid's glorified over-achievement? Or, maybe like me, you were that kid.

I did not grow up a PK (pastor's kid), though people often assumed I did. My sister and I coined the title DK (deacon's kids) to explain our extensive Bible knowledge and proficient use of Christian-ese. We could throw down "sanctification," "redemption," and "discipleship" with the best of them. We were those kids who knew the answer to every question before the teacher even finished asking. When you spend your childhood going to church three times a week and attend a Christian school, you've heard more Bible stories than you can count, and you've heard them all multiple times. In fact, to keep from going crazy with boredom, you start listening for discrepancies in your teacher's story so you can correct her the moment she misses a detail. Yep, we were brutal. Not only did we annoy our friends and classmates, I'm sure we aggravated many teachers as well.

It was my parents' fault really. They were the ones who made sure we were always at church and then quizzed us about our lessons at home. The one question we could count on every Sunday afternoon was, "What did you learn in Sunday School?" Oh, and did I mention my dad's signature Sunday morning song was "Everybody Ought to Go to Sunday School"? From my earliest memories, church was about learning – learning about God, discovering how He wants us to act, and to obey. Failure to do so was met by disapproval, reprimand, and, if needed, discipline. Neither my sister nor I were inclined toward rebellion. Apparently, we were not the strong-willed type. We preferred to keep the peace and make Mom and Dad proud.

So, as a young child, I was externally motivated to attend church, read my Bible and learn about God --all things we do to grow closer to the Lord. Can you do all those things and not grow in your relationship with Christ? Absolutely! I did not begin to understand all this relationship stuff until sometime around junior high. God did not just want me to know about Him; He wanted me to know Him.

Getting to KNOW Him!

It's easy to learn about a person, especially someone famous, like Oprah. I could tell you how old she is, where she lives, who her best friend is, how many dogs she has, and even the brand name of her favorite jeans. If you want to know about Oprah, all you have to do is read her magazine or watch her show, just like millions of other people do all around the world. And where does that get you? Do you know Oprah? Will that knowledge about her get you past her bodyguards so you can knock on the door of her dressing room and pop in for a little pre-show chat? Probably not, unless you happen to be Gayle King, Oprah's best friend and the editor of her magazine. You see, Gayle knows Oprah. Maybe even more importantly, Oprah knows Gayle.

Relationships go both ways. Have you ever tried to be in a relationship with someone who doesn't want anything to do with you? It doesn't work very well. You become a stalker and they become the avoider. It reminds me a little of the Road Runner and Wiley Coyote. Did Wiley ever catch that speedy Road Runner? If he did, I missed that episode. Every one I saw ended with Wiley under an anvil or at the bottom of a ravine while the Road Runner sped off into the sunset.

The good news for us is that God has already initiated a relationship with us and He's not going anywhere. If anything, we are the ones who sometimes reflect the Road Runner. We run off to sports practice, the mall, our friend's house, and get home just in time for dinner. Then it's time for homework. A friend calls. You check email and get caught instant messaging until your mom personally escorts you to bed because that's the only way she can tear you from the computer. We are busy – insanely busy. If we want, we can be in contact with people 24/7 through our Blackberries, cell phones, and computers. In some ways, we are now more connected than we've ever been before. But with so much demand for our attention, it's easy to neglect the most important relationship we will ever have. We speed through our day's activities, talking or typing to someone in every spare moment, and crash in bed just to wake up the next morning to start the whole cycle over again. Where did God fit into the picture? Did you read a chapter in your Bible or pray for a few minutes?

Before you start making calculations in your head and placing yourself in the "Super-Christian" or "scum-of-the-earth" categories, let me stop you. My point is not to make you feel guilty or proud or even to challenge you to schedule more "God-time" into your day. I want to talk to you about this thing we call a "relationship."

It's More Than a Crush

Have you ever been around two people who are madly in love, or even madly in like? They can't stop touching each other, smiling, or sending little messages with their eyes. Depending on where you are on the romance map at the time, you might find it absolutely adorable or utterly disgusting. Yet, regardless of how you feel about it, you are basically powerless to stop it. Try, and you will find yourself fighting a losing battle. Your girlfriend can't help but talk about "her guy" every second of the day. If she's not talking about him, it's because she has ditched you completely to be with him. You might feel annoyed and frustrated, but somewhere deep inside, if we are brutally honest, isn't there also a hint of jealousy? We all want to feel the blissful excitement of being in love. It's more than a crush. A crush is fine for awhile, but it eventually gets old. We long to experience the thrill of someone being as "into" us as we are to them – to know that we are infinitely important in someone else's world.

I am a huge fan of romantic comedies. After a few laughs and some twists of fate, you are essentially assured the girl gets the guy, or vice versa. Don't you just love the way Tom Hanks and Meg Ryan finally meet atop the Empire State building in "Sleepless in Seattle"? Apparently, it was so good that the same pair went for a repeat performance in "You've Got Mail" before Meg Ryan met up with George Clooney in "One Fine Day." You can't go wrong with a romantic comedy. For ninety minutes to two hours, you get to live vicariously through a beautiful heroine and be swept off your feet by the perfect Prince Charming.

The Main Character, Lucy

One of my favorite chick flicks of all time is "While You Were Sleeping." I first saw it when it came out in the mid '90s. I was only fourteen or fifteen at the time and, though Bill Pullman was not my first choice of leading men, the Sandra Bullock character gripped my heart. Her name was Lucy.

Lucy lived alone in a Chicago apartment. Her only real companion was her cat, "Mow." Like all of us, Lucy longed for a relationship. She yearned to love and be loved. Yet, each day, she sat in a booth, collected tokens for the train, and went home again to her empty apartment. She dreamt of falling in love. In fact, one of the regular passengers caught her eye and she began to write him into the story of her life as her Prince Charming. Sadly, he didn't even know she existed.

Through a crazy series of events, this passenger (who we come to know as Peter) ends up in a coma and his family thinks Lucy is his fiancée. Suddenly, she has a family. It doesn't even matter to her that it's all based on a misunderstanding. Peter's family embraces her as their own, filling a void of loneliness she carried for years.

While Peter remains in a coma, Lucy allows the charade to continue. A family friend convinces her that it's better for the family to believe Lucy is Peter's fiancée because it gives them a sense of connection to Peter. When Peter wakes up, this friend says the family will be so ecstatic they won't care that Lucy lied.

Sounds good, right? Yep, except for one thing . . . Peter has a brother. While Peter lies unconscious in the hospital, Jack and Lucy innocently begin to spend time together. Jack sees her as his future sister-in-law, so, any contact they have is platonic and completely unromantic. As a decent man and loyal brother, Jack wouldn't want anyone to accuse him of stealing his brother's fiancé. Lucy, however, is well aware that she is not engaged to Peter – that she doesn't even know him – and Jack begins to pique her interest.

Even if you haven't seen the movie, you can guess what happens next. After all, it is a romantic comedy, and how can Lucy truly fall in love with a man in a coma? That is precisely my point. Relationships go both ways. How can you fall in love with someone who doesn't even know you exist? Developing a relationship requires both people to open up and share a bit of themselves. It involves risk, honesty, and discovery. The more you share of yourself and discover about the other person, the more your relationship can grow.

Getting back to our juicy story . . . why did Lucy begin to fall for Jack? Jack (Bill Pullman), in my opinion, was not nearly as handsome as Peter (Peter Gallagher), nor as rich. Lucy could have maintained the illusion of a future with Peter, but she didn't. Jack captured her attention because he sought to discover her. Peter, as Lucy would later realize, was only concerned for himself. (Only a self-absorbed person would fill his wallet with posed pictures of himself!) What girl doesn't want to be discovered as the priceless treasure she truly is? Jack sees that in Lucy, but feels helpless to pursue her, believing she is in love with Peter.

The Real Thing

Eventually, the truth comes out. Lucy objects at her own wedding, revealing that she is not in love with Peter, but with Jack. Peter is exposed as the selfish, immoral counterfeit he has always been when his real fiancé storms into the wedding confusion, followed by her husband. It's a mess. But, finally, Jack knows how Lucy feels about him, and he is free to love her back. In the last scene, Jack and Lucy ride the train off into the sunset with a "just married" sign and cans hanging from the caboose. As Lucy narrates her story in this final shot, she dotingly claims, "Jack gave me the world." Jack saw and celebrated the real Lucy. Isn't that what every woman wants?

There is nothing better than knowing we are enough – that we are loved, cherished, and appreciated – just as we are. And that is exactly how God sees us – how God sees you. God's unconditional love frees us to be the women He created us to be. You are enough, just as you are. You don't have to be prettier, smarter, or more talented to win His attention. You already have it. He is captivated by you. He created you for His pleasure, so He could have a relationship with you. But the choice is up to you. Will you choose Him? He invites you to a life of adventure and total fulfillment. He offers you the world.

Lucy could have forged ahead with Peter, but "the world" or the life that choice would have afforded her was merely a gross counterfeit of the fulfillment she could have in following her heart and choosing Jack. In the closing scene, Lucy reflects on Peter's question to her: "When did you fall in love with Jack?" She answered, "It was while you were sleeping." Sometimes we need to put to sleep old loves before we can fully embrace the life God has called us to. What has captured your attention, distracting you from recklessly pursuing Christ? Is it your quest for popularity, sports, a hobby, or another relationship? Lucy had to choose Jack over Peter. She knew she could not have the real, intimate, and loving relationship with Jack that she desired until she closed the door on any hope of a future with Peter. Her "relationship" with Peter was a counterfeit anyway. It did not fulfill her heart's cry to be adored, cherished, loved, and known. Jack offered what she truly desired. That's why she could claim, "He gave me the world."

"My" Thoughts:

1. Think of your closest relationship right now. Maybe it's with your mom, dad, sister, or a best friend. What do you do to cultivate and maintain that relationship?_____

_____

_____

How can you apply those same principles to your relationship with God?_____

_____

_____

2. What rules or expectations have you believed you must achieve to be a "good Christian"?_____

_____

_____

How did you feel when you met those expectations or failed to meet them?_____

_____

3. If Christianity is not about rules, how do we know whether or not we are succeeding – that is, how do we know if we are growing closer to Christ?_____

_____

_____

4. Just for fun . . . were you the over-achiever kid or the kid who felt like she didn't even have a chance, so why try?_____

_____

_____

_____

5. How does knowing that God is passionately pursuing you change how you feel about spending time with Him?_____

_____

_____

I just Wanted to feel Loved!

When I was younger, I suffered a lot emotionally. My parents never hit me, but my mother found a way to hurt me at least once a day. I never realized why, I never did much to make her mad, so I grew up thinking she liked being mean to me. At times, a thought would pop into my head; *Maybe she doesn't love me.*

When I was in 7th grade, I began to contemplate running away or even ending my problems the "easy" way. Then, I started to look toward guys; maybe they would give me what I was missing. I wasn't sure what that "something missing" was but I was determined to find it. Guy after guy…it seemed like it was impossible to find what I desired. It was like looking for buried treasure; I didn't know what I would find, or where to start looking. Little did I know that soon enough, I would find whatever it was that my heart desired.

That's when God stepped into my life and flipped it right side up! He showed me all the wonderful things in my life and a love I had never known or seen before. That's when I realized, I didn't need a guy to feel loved, all I needed was Jesus. I didn't always need to have a boyfriend tell me he loved me, or my family, either, because as long as I was loved by Jesus Christ, it was okay. He filled my heart with warmth and love; He mended my broken heart and filled the empty hole I had with His eternal love! If I had known that all I needed to be happy was Jesus, then life would have been so much easier.

When you are loved by Jesus and you love Him, you will be so happy. You will feel like you are at peace and everything is ok.

Angelica

chapter 2

ESSENCE OF DESIRE
Rebecca Simmons

Desires of Your Heart

Psalm 37:4 says "Delight yourself in the ⁞⁞⁞ and he will give you the desires of your heart." (⁞⁞⁞ This verse is both a promise and a fulfillment rolled into one. God wants to give you the desires of your heart. He wants to fill your life with good things. He wants to give you the world. And He will give you the world, fulfilling your deepest desires, when you delight yourself in Him.

Almost ten years ago, when I wrote a chapter for the first *Daughters of Heaven* book, I had no idea how this verse would play out in my life. I thought I knew what I wanted – what would make me happy. Now, I'm going to be a bit candid with you here. If you had asked me what I desired, where I hoped to be in ten years, I probably would have said, "I'd like to be married to the most amazing, handsome, and Godly man on the face of the earth, have twin toddlers running around – a boy and a girl, live in a nice, quiet neighborhood, drive an SUV (I've always been a bit anti-mini van), and be doing some type of ministry with my husband."

Well, things have not turned out quite like I planned. I'm not married. I'm not even engaged, and all the children in my life belong to other people. All those things I thought would spell "happy" and "fulfilled" to me, at this point in life, have not yet happened. I've discovered that I don't need those things to be happy or fulfilled. Sure, I still desire them (And I've decided I can be a little flexible on the details!), but I am completely content in my little apartment, ministering to my young flock, and I would be just as happy living in a hut in some remote African village, if that is where God called me. My joy, my satisfaction, and my peace are found in Him.

You might be thinking, *Yeah, that sounds good, but get real.* I'm not asking you to abandon all your hopes and dreams because, really, all you need is God. I'm not saying you should join a convent or sell everything you own and become a missionary to Siberia. If God calls you to do that, great, but most of us will grow up, get a job, marry, and maybe start raising the next generation. If your delight is in the Lord – in knowing and honoring Him - then each one of those events will be far more exciting and fulfilling than you can even begin to imagine.

What Does It Mean to DELIGHT in Someone or Something?

According to *Webster's Dictionary*, to "delight" means "to give or take great pleasure; to rejoice; to gratify or please highly." It's a verb. "Delight" can also be used as a noun. It can imply action or the result of action, but here, in Psalm 37:4, "delight" is a verb. As I sit here, writing, an old DC Talk song runs through my head. Actually, just one line from the song: "Love is a verb." True, authentic love is more than a feeling. It's action born out of commitment. "Delight" works the same way.

Before you start thinking of this as a chore or a way to trick you into doing the right thing, let's take this a step further. This is not like the time your mom tried to give you cherry cough syrup and told you it was candy so you'd swallow before the bitter aftertaste caused your whole body to shudder. To this day, I can't stand anything cherry-flavored, but that is beside the point.

God is not that way. He is not going to trick you into loving Him or delighting in Him. Yes, He wants you to seek Him and obey Him but, ultimately, it's your heart, not your actions that concern Him most. Remember King David, the adulterer, the murderer, who took another man's wife and had that man killed to cover up his sin? Oh, David made mistakes. He made big mistakes. God knew David would make those bad choices even before He set David on the throne, yet He still called David "a man after his own heart" (1 Samuel 13:14). This same man, this king, is the psalmist who penned Psalm 37:4. David, like us, was far from perfect. Still, he was a man after God's own heart, a man who delighted himself in the Lord.

We are going to make mistakes and fall flat on our faces sometimes, but that doesn't change the way God feels about us or acts toward us. He is always loving and forgiving. He is the compassionate and gracious God, slow to anger, abounding in love and faithfulness (Exodus 34:6). What more could you want?

The Pursuit Is On

God, the Creator of the Universe, our Savior and Friend, the One who formed you in your mother's womb and knew you before you were born (Psalm 139:13-16), is out to win your heart. A man who is in love will stop at nothing to win the heart of his beloved. He will pursue her with a vengeance because she is his passion. How does he win her? He tells her how beautiful, lovely, and captivating she is – that there is no one else in the world who stirs his heart the way she does. He takes her out, buys her flowers, and sends little emails or text messages during the day to show her how much he cares.

Not long ago, I received a special letter in the mail with purple petals pressed into the hand-written note. "He" knows purple is my favorite color. The letter re-affirmed what I hear every day – that he values me, respects me, and cares deeply for me – that I am special to him. He could have said all that in an email or over the phone, but it wouldn't have been the same. Girls, you know what I mean. Emails, text messages, and phone calls are all great, but to know that someone took the time to hand-write a personal letter, press your favorite flowers in it, and send it in the mail just to brighten your day? Well, that's something special. In fact, I think it deserves a great, big "awwwwwwww!"

Did you know that God himself penned the greatest love letter of all time? Before you roll your eyes in ambivalence, track with me for a moment. You see, God is not only the Author of this letter we call "the Bible," He is also the Creator of the story and its main character. In fact, He is the very source and goal of life. The story of life, of our lives, goes something like this:

life: connected

God existed. He always is and always was. There was no such thing as time because God didn't need it. He just was. So, where does our story start? In the beginning . . .

I'll spare you the details, assuming you are familiar with the creation account. If not, read Genesis 1. Basically, God started from scratch and created the world – the entire Universe, for that matter, and maybe much more that is beyond our current scope of discovery. He designed a lush, flourishing garden in a place called Eden and placed man in the center of it. Adam, or mankind, was the pinnacle of God's creation. "God created man in his own image" (Genesis 1:27 ⠇⠿).

Chapter 2 gives us a more detailed account of exactly how that happened. Adam was created first. God himself breathed life into Adam's nostrils (2:7), placed him in the garden to work and take care of it, and gave Adam his first task: naming all the animals.

"So the man gave names to all the livestock, the birds of the air and all the beasts of the field. But for Adam no suitable helper was found" (2:20 ⠇⠿). And here, ladies, is where we come on the scene in grand style. When God created woman, His work was complete. God saw everything He had made and considered it all "good." Now, God had what He wanted most – relationship.

Sadly, our history took a tragic turn when Adam and Eve ate the forbidden fruit. Sin entered the world, and we were separated from our Creator. While this may sound like the devastating end to a once beautiful story, let me remind you that this is just the beginning. Every great love story has a bit of tragedy. Our story, God's story, is no different. Sin separated us from the greatest Love of our lives, all because of a decision made thousands of years before we were born. But this isn't about blaming Adam and Eve. God, because He's all-knowing, knew before He created Adam and Eve, that they would sin. Still, He gave them that freedom, and their choice broke His heart. The rest of the story chronicles God's relentless pursuit to win our hearts.

We still break His heart. Every day, we make choices that hinder our relationship with Him. You know what I'm talking about. It might seem small, like arguing with your mom, or it may seem bigger, like having sex with your boyfriend. Whatever it is, sin is sin, and it separates us from God. Yet, regardless of what you do, God does not stop pursuing you, and He doesn't want you to stop pursuing Him either. No relationship is perfect – not even our relationship with God. We are going to make mistakes. It's what we do when we make mistakes that will determine the depth, closeness, and passion in our relationship with the Lord. Like David, will we have a "broken and contrite heart" (Psalm 51:17) when we sin? Will we ask for mercy, turn from that sin, and keep pursuing God? Will you? You can be a woman after God's own heart. He is already eternally committed to winning yours.

If you want to know just how hopelessly in love the Creator is with you, read His Word. You won't be disappointed. Every account from Adam and Eve through Christ's sacrifice, the Apostles' mission, and the birth of the early Church tells of God's relentless pursuit to win your heart; it's not just an account of all those people you read about. Sure, it's their story, but it's your story, too.

I used to think reading the Bible was boring. All those laws in Leviticus can be difficult to get through; and how many times do you really need to read Jonah? But I don't feel that way anymore. The deeper I go in my relationship with the Lord, the more excited I get reading His Word. And the more I read the Bible, the more I discover who God is and I grow closer to Him. Remember how I told you I wouldn't tell you what or how much to read in your Bible? The promise still stands. If you read your Bible because you feel like you have to, you're not going to get much out of it. But if you embrace it for the love letter that it is, you won't be able to put it down. In fact, you will find yourself asking questions and digging deeper in your quest to know the Lover of your soul.

When I received that letter in the mail with purple petals pressed into the page, I couldn't wait to read it. I knew it was written just for me by someone who thought the world of me. I wasn't satisfied to read just one line. I read the whole thing. Truth be told, I read the whole thing through, over and over again. As you read God's love letter to you, you will discover just how wild He is about you. Every story will tell you something about His character. Each account screams of His faithfulness, His ultimate plan for all creation, and His relentless pursuit to win your heart.

Great Grandma's Ring

Have you ever received a gift that touched your heart so deeply it left you utterly speechless? I have. Over the years, I've received many gifts that have touched my heart in a special way. There is the tube of pink Chapstick, given to me by a little boy in my swim class. His mom gave me the go-ahead to dunk him one day, after he had continually refused to put his head under water. I did and he cried. I felt horrible, thinking I had traumatized this sweet, little five-year-old. The next day, he arrived at swim lessons with that pink Chapstick – a gift for me. His mom had taken him to pick out a prize for having put his whole head under water, finally (though not by choice), and he insisted on choosing a gift for me instead. Can you feel the guilt? In my defense, it was a quick dunk and I comforted him afterward. Still, he was a bit shaken.

Another favorite gift came from my best friend, Jenny. She spent one summer in Alaska on a mission trip and brought me home a pair of socks with moose and pine trees. Jenny died tragically in a car accident the spring of 2000. She was only twenty-one years old. Though she had given me many things over the years – we were best friends since we were seven – those socks are special. I wear them and think fondly on my many happy memories of her.

My favorite gifts are usually handmade or small and silly – something that reminds me of the person who gave it to me. My desk and refrigerator are covered with drawings and paintings from the kids I teach. I treasure each one. Among the many precious gifts I've received over the years, one, in particular, stands out in my mind. It's a ring I wear nearly every day, so I am constantly reminded of that special person who gave it to me. (No, it's not from a guy!) Though she did not give it to me directly, the ring came from my Great Grandma Ashley. When she passed away, at ninety-one years of age, my grandma, (her daughter) became partially responsible for distributing her jewelry to the women in our family. It was my great grandmother's wish. You see, she loved jewelry and had collected a great deal of it over the years.

When my grandma came to visit, shortly after Great Grandma Ashley's passing, she brought a spread of jewelry for my mom, my sister, and me to choose from. I don't remember what my mom and sister chose, but Erin probably picked out some pieces that were funky and black or red, and I think my mom may have passed on it altogether. She's not a big jewelry person. I, being the sentimental sort, picked out a unique watch with multi-colored gems set in the silver band, a dainty gold ring with a small pink stone, and a silver ring that crossed into a bold, yet delicate knot on top.

It's this silver ring I wear nearly every day. Something about its unique yet simple design resonates deep within me. That knot reminds me of my proud heritage – my family's love for God and each other. It was not always this way. In fact, my dad was the first believer on his side of the family. My great grandma committed her life to Christ sometime later, after seeing the change in her grandson (my dad) who was also the catalyst in leading his parents to Christ (great grandma's daughter and son-in-law). I never witnessed that side of the story. As far as I was concerned, my family was always committed to Christ and each other – always loyal and loving.

I envisioned Great Grandma as a type of matriarch over our family. Though her stature and demeanor never demanded it, the family's deep respect afforded her that position. At only 4'10" tall, Great Grandma was all sweetness and strength, wrapped in one, tiny package. I only saw her once, that I remember; and I was only four years old at the time. Most of what I know of her came through the mail.

When we were young, Great Grandma sent my sister and me gifts of collector's edition books, like *Anne of Green Gables* and *Little Women*. As we got older, her gifts became more personal and were often hand-made. Great Grandma was a phenomenal artist and craftswoman. Even arthritis failed to stifle her talent. One Christmas, she made stockings for my whole family. Although she had not been around my sister and I to know what would suit our very different personalities, she nailed us. My stocking was made of pink, silky fabric and delicate lace, cut in the design of an elegant Victorian boot. Erin's, on the other hand, was rounded and chunky. While made of the same pink fabric and a thicker lace, it possessed a certain blunt and playful quality that is my sister. To this day, I have no idea how Great Grandma figured us out so well. Somehow, she just knew.

Although I only saw her once and almost never spoke to her, Great Grandma was a real and active part of my life. When I became deathly ill and had to spend months in the hospital, Great Grandma wrote me the most heart-felt and inspiring letters. She quoted God's Word and echoed His promises with her own conviction that all would be well. Her beautifully scripted words and elegant penmanship, shaky as she struggled to write with ninety-one-year-old arthritic hands, inspired hope within the darkest recesses of my soul. She passed away during my recovery. As I became healthy and realized the purpose God had yet for me to fulfill on earth, she went to be with Jesus.

But, I still have Great Grandma's ring. I will cherish it forever. The silver knot reminds me that I am complete; I am loved; I am grounded. I know my great grandma's love is a mere reflection of God's love for me. I'm sure that if she could have taken my place in that hospital bed and faced the threat of death in my stead, she would have. But she couldn't. Instead, she inspired hope and life in me until God took her home. She fulfilled her purpose; and Christ fulfilled His. He did die so I could live. There is no greater love than the love He demonstrated through His sacrifice on the cross.

One day, as I was fingering Great Grandma's ring, I noticed an imprint inside the band. Upon closer inspection, I could make out the word, "Avon." *No way!* I thought. *You've got to be kidding me!* I felt a strange mix of irony, humor, and foolishness all at once. Here, I thought I had inherited this wonderful heirloom – not that I had expected it to be expensive, but at least "real" – and it was from Avon? I called my grandma to tell her of my discovery, but she was not in the least bit surprised. "Oh yes," she knowingly claimed, "your great grandmother loved Avon." So there it was – the plain, naked truth. My family heirloom had been ordered through an Avon catalogue.

But, you know what the most amazing part is? That knowledge did not change how much I value Great Grandma's ring. I still wear it every day and treat it with just as much respect and sentimentality. After all, it is Great Grandma's ring. Avon can't change that. Some people may think I'm silly for ascribing such value to a simple, plain, factory-made ring, but it's not really their call to make. The ring was a gift to me, and I get to determine its value. Sure, it may be worth only a few dollars on the market, but, to me, it's priceless.

God has given each one of us a gift, unique and priceless, but how much we value this gift and how we treat it is up to us. Your salvation is not just a free ticket to heaven. It's an invitation to the most intimate, fulfilling, and exciting relationship you will ever have. Many people will not understand. They can't get past the "Avon" mark. When they hear the label "Christian" they automatically think of religion, rules, and restriction. They miss the whole point. It's about relationship – the most important relationship of your life.

Just Say "Yes"

Picture, for a moment, the jumbo screen at a ballpark. I must confess -- I think this method of proposing is terribly over-used, but it provides a fitting illustration nonetheless. The camera scans the crowd, and then zeroes in on a young couple. Just as the girl notices their good-fortune at being caught on the screen, she points excitedly. Meanwhile, her boyfriend reaches deep into his pocket and bends down on one knee. Her expression turns to confusion, then shock, and finally, pure joy as he flips open the box, revealing a sparkling diamond ring. She clasps her hands together, jumping and squealing in delight as he stands to his feet. Before he even gets his bearing, she throws herself into his arms. The deal is sealed! The entire crowd, interpreting her response as an emphatic "yes," erupts with cheers and applause.

Girl, you've been offered a ring. Have you received it? If so, how is the relationship going? Maybe I should say, "How is the relationship growing?" Sadly, if it isn't growing, it's dying. Just as many marriages today end in divorce, many commitments to Christ become derailed. We become seduced by other loves – money, education, careers, appearance, popularity, ungodly or unhealthy relationships – abandoning the greatest Love of all for a gross counterfeit. Receiving the ring is just the beginning. It will take a lifetime, maybe more, to discover the depths, wonder, and ever unveiling beauty of the Lover of your soul.

Have you seen anything more precious than an elderly couple walking hand-in-hand? If you watch too closely, you will feel as though you are intruding on a deeply, intimate experience. They shuffle through the park, focusing closely on the path so as not to stumble. He uses a cane while she patiently matches his pace, glancing up to watch a squirrel scamper off toward some trees. A bird chirps happily above and flits from branch to branch. She tilts her head upward; he remains focused on the concrete beneath his feet, deliberately setting one foot in front of the other. They come to a bench and gingerly lower their frail bodies onto the hard, wooden slats. Calmly, almost reverently, they take in the scene around them. A small child plays in the sand. Two more clamber up the face of the slide, only to slip back down again. The old couple chuckles softly. Wrinkled skin creases into familiar smile lines as thin lips curve up at the corners. Maybe they are remembering days past – times they had witnessed their own children or grandchildren embrace the joys of childhood. Not a word is spoken. Just a glance and a gentle touch passes between them, and you know there is no greater love. Time, love, commitment, and loyalty have melted the two into one. Looking at them now, you can hardly tell where one ends and the other begins. They appear to be one and the same – one life, one love, one heartbeat!

It's not about rules; it's relationship . . . and the best is yet to come!

"My" Thoughts:

1. When I think of "delight," I picture a kid rushing downstairs on Christmas morning or walking through the streets of Disneyland for the first time. What does "delight" mean to you? Write your own definition below._____

_____

_____

2. What are some of your greatest delights? I love doing cartwheels through fresh grass, jumping in piles of crunchy leaves, and splashing through big rain puddles. In those moments, I think, *God, you are so good to create this amazing world for me to play in.*_____

_____

_____

God created you with the capacity to enjoy life and created the world for your playground. What do the things or people you delight in say about your relationship with Him?_____

_____

_____

3. Like it or not, you are part of God's story. He wrote you in, when He created you. However, what role you play and the impact you make is largely up to you. How do you want to be remembered in God's story?_____

_____

_____

Read Hebrews 11, then write what you want people to say about you when you are gone._____

_____

_____

4. If you treasured your relationship with the Lord more than everything and everyone else, how would your life be different?_____

_____

_____

Read Psalm 139 as your guide and paraphrase God's love letter to you.

Which parts mean the most to you?_____
_____
_____
_____

5. Now ... write your own love letter. (Don't you dare skip this because you think it's corny!)

Dear God,_____
_____
_____
_____
_____
_____
_____
_____
_____
_____
_____
_____
_____
_____
_____
_____
_____
_____
_____
_____
_____
_____
_____
_____
_____

                              Forever Yours,

God is With me During Difficult situations

    I have grown up in a Christian home my entire life and I have lived a pretty comfortable lifestyle. I have never really had to deal with a lot of change, but this year I did. Our family decided that we were going to move to a different city because we felt like God wanted us to. I was completely shocked because I never would have thought this was going to happen. Sure we have thought about moving before but it was never a real thing. When I found this out I was so upset and so scared but I didn't let anyone know it- not even my best friend of 5 years. I became upset at God and I didn't understand why He would do this to me. I had a feeling something was going to happen before because I was starting to drift away and was having some friend problems.

    One day I finally broke down crying to my mom and she was telling me that God does have a plan and He wouldn't throw me away and forget about me. It really helped me because I did realize that God would not leave me. So we did move and it was really hard. Even though we did move, God has been a part of my life and has helped me. I went into a school where I knew no one at all and it was really hard from going to having a lot of friends to having none. I would pray for hours at night, crying out to God asking Him to help me. I started reading my Bible more often and just asking Him for help. God does always helps and He definitely did help me. He brought some friends who have been good friends to me. I am so thankful to God that He has been a part of my life and has been really helping me through difficult situations.

Jessica

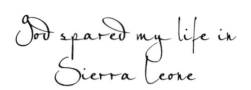

God spared my life in Sierra Leone

Boooooooomaaaaash!!! Boom!! Boom!! WAR!! TERROR! EXPLOSIONS! The vibrations could be felt in the ground along with the sights and smells from the explosions. Worse yet were the cries full of terror all around me! Every time a bomb dropped I wondered who it was this time. Is it someone I know, someone I love? Me? I really didn't know if it had happened to me or my next door neighbors. Has my luck finally run out; is this my time? I felt so numb I didn't know if I was happy to be alive, afraid of not surviving the next round of bombs, or feeling the total disappointment that I still had to endure my circumstances. Every moment was another chance that my family and I would die inside a crowded basement, feeling hopeless, without food and being able to barely breathe in that tiny space.

Every time the bombing started in my area I would go to a corner and roll myself up in a little ball. I would cover my ears and close my eyes wishing I could just disappear; that it would all go away! I wished that everything would be fine and we could all be happy again. But when I opened my eyes from dreaming nothing had changed. I wondered *Why am I still here when so many are not?*

Then I looked up and realized the answer was God; nothing else, no one else but Him. When I was locked up in a little basement with no air and no hope, He was there to supply me with hope.

Now, years later, I am sixteen and I live in America. God is with me but in a different way. When I am locked up in my room with tears fogging up my eyes, He is still there with me. When that jerk I was dating decided the new girl was better-looking and he dumped me, God was there to show me His love. From a life and death situation, to a "should I date that guy?" question, God has been there to lead my way, shining the right path with lights so bright and beautiful that I won't miss it. All I have to do is open myself to Him, look at the size of my problem, then look at the size of my God. There is no comparison, God is so much bigger.

I know that if God could save me from a war that many died from, He could save me from anything. And with God by my side I will always have hope! When I am surrounded by impossibilities, I know with God everything is possible! NO matter what circumstances I face, no matter how scary or big, God will never, ever let me down!

Ada

Section II

"Does God really love me?"

"Why can't I be more like her?"

WHO AM I?

Who defines you?

"I don't seem to fit in!"

"Something is missing..."

I was hungry for the glory of God

As I sat and listened to the minister preach about "the glory of God," I knew the Lord had something else He wanted to show me. I went home and, over the next month, a deep hunger began to arise in my heart as I looked up the scriptures about Moses and how he asked to see God's glory. I spent time in prayer asking the Lord to show me His glory. At the time, we were at a ministry called Christ for the Nations and their annual worship conference was coming up. It amazed me to find out that the theme of the conference was "Show Me Your Glory." I felt like I had been following the path God had ordered for me.

When the conference came, I was so excited. I love to worship the Lord more than anything and the thought of sitting in the Lord's presence for hours was just awesome! The first night was incredible! The Lord was there in such a powerful way that, at times, it was hard to stand because of the weightiness of His presence.

Upon arriving home that night, I went to the bathroom to get ready for bed. I looked at myself in unbelief as I noticed light coming from my eyes! Could it be possible? Certainly, I must be seeing things! I thought about how Moses had been in God's presence so long that the glory of God radiated from his face. I went to bed after this strange experience; I didn't mention it to anyone because it was too weird.

The final night of the conference was equally amazing. I worshiped, danced, and wept in the Lord's presence. He was there in an awesome way. When I came home that evening, my husband... still awake, was standing in the kitchen. As our eyes met, he said, "Honey, light is shining from your eyes!" I said, "Really? I saw it last night but I thought I was just seeing things!" It was true! The Lord's glory was indeed shining out of my eyes. I had been hungering to know Him "in His glory" just like Moses. Did I expect my eyes to shine? No, I just expected to be with Him and I was not disappointed. So, what are you hungry for?

Kathy

chapter 3

MADE IN HIS IMAGE
Shereen Christian

I praise you because I am fearfully and wonderfully made; your works are wonderful, I know that full well.

Psalm 139: 14

Who Defines YOU?

Everybody has a personal belief system of who they are and what defines them. This chapter is all about getting to the truth about image, (Girl, you have been MADE!) Let's debunk the myths, and develop a rock-solid, healthy, and positive outlook based on who you really are in Christ Jesus.

What Is Self Esteem?

Breaking it down … Whether it is flawed, distorted, or grounded in truth, every person has one: A Self-Image! Face it; we could fill an entire mall with all the books out there talking about self-image. Not only can you find a gazillion psychology books on the subject, there's a colossal supply of how-to manuals on stand-by, ready to teach us how to repair and improve it. So, to save us from spending our summer vacations researching the mounds of information available, let's start with the basics – What exactly does "self-image" mean?

> **self-im·age** (sĕlf'ĭm'ĭj) , n.
>> The conception that one has of oneself, including an assessment of qualities and personal worth.

In other words…

Self-Image= What I believe about who I am and what I am worth.

Your self-image is the impression you have of your whole self--looks, personality, strengths, and weaknesses. It's how likeable you are, how loveable you are, and how much you are worth as a person. [Worth: value, merit, significance, attraction, importance] It's sizing yourself up, basically.

Where did you get an idea like that?

Family, friends, teachers, church…we all get a sense of who we are from somewhere. There's an endless supply of stuff that can shape what we believe about "who" we are. Today, with all the technology available 24/7, the flood of opinions coming at us can be overwhelming.

SPAM

The other day, I was checking my e-mails: I couldn't believe how much junk e-mail was in my mailbox! It was the most annoying thing EVER, sifting through massive amounts of stuff, trying to determine which e-mails were legitimate. For the most part, I usually don't have to deal with all of that. My junk e-mail is filtered out by a spam blocker before ever making it to my box. However, on that particular day, I was bombarded! Clearly, something had happened to my settings to let that much junk get through. So, there I was, resetting my security levels to block the spam when it came to me: self-images need spam blockers! Think about it! Filters to sift out the deception and receive genuine information – how great is that?!? [genuine: real, authentic, true, undisputable]

BTW: Spam=flooding the internet with a ton of copies of the same message, in an attempt to force the message on people who would not otherwise choose to receive it.

Where In the WORLD?

Let's face it: the world is full of major "spammers"; the most blatant being the media industry. For the record, I am not slamming the entire media world, and we'll touch on this later in the chapter; but, there is no denying the barrage of irresponsible, ungodly advertising, marketing, and entertainment targeting young women!

Talk about forcing a message. Even girls who see themselves as loved, valued, and having purpose are being confused (and sadly, influenced) by the never-ending ambush, telling them who they should be and how they are supposed to act, think and live. It can be totally discouraging!

Most of the standards for beauty and worth through the "eyes" of the media are unrealistic, dangerous, and degrading. No person and no thing have the right to make you feel like you don't measure up. The right jeans, shoes, even hangin' with the "right crowd" will not make you any more valuable and deeply loved than you already are. No in-your-face hotel heiress, pop singer or pant size holds the key to your value, personal worth, and importance in this life.

The IT Girl

Beautiful girl, take a good look around you...magazines, billboards, commercials, and clothing in your favorite store at the mall. Notice anything? Do things look the same as they did last year? What about the year before that? Probably not—one minute it's HOT and the next, it's NOT!

What was "it" yesterday may be ancient history tomorrow. The point is that they are not dependable. They are constantly changing. Building our identity around this stuff is like building a house on shaky ground. It may stand for a while, but, eventually, it will come tumbling down.

The only standard for true beauty and worth in this world is the Bible. God's Word is a solid rock: a firm foundation that will never erode or fade away. It's not going to change on you whenever the winds of popularity shift direction, and it's never going to abandon you for anything or anyone else. When it comes to you and your Lord Jesus, you are it, girl! You are exactly who you are supposed to be! God has placed gifts, talents and desires inside of you that He, himself, lovingly chose for you, for His Glory. They are uniquely yours, and they're not made to fit into anybody else's box or mold.

When you break out of the mold this "day-and-age" is trying to lock you into, you will shine with all the brilliance God intended, and you will shine for Him!

Listen, if you are caught up in the hype, you may not even realize the damage it is doing to your sense of self-worth. Buying into what these "messages" are selling devastates a young woman's image of herself. Trust me on this, I know from experience. Please remember, the goal is to sell you something. Sooner or later, there's a price to be paid. I am convinced that, for every good and perfect gift God desires to give us, the enemy invents a "decoy." At first glance, it looks like it holds the same promise, but its only intent is to mislead, misguide, and entrap. Remember: the enemy came to rob, steal, and destroy, but Jesus came that you may have life and have it to the full! (John 10:10.) The enemy wants you to "buy" into his propaganda to keep you from the knowledge that Jesus has already "paid a price" for you.

Who Are YOU and Where Did You Come From?

Even if a young woman has a positive self-image, if she is not rooted and established in God's love for her, she will never experience true fulfillment. [fulfillment: contentment, satisfaction, peace, success, pleasure, happiness] Do you wanna know WHY?

[Reality] Stuff happens! We all face challenges, setbacks, and difficult times. Life continues to change: friends may move, parents may disappoint, and the standard for "beauty" will swing from one extreme to another. But God's love for you and your value in Him will remain constant. He is Unchanging, Unfailing, and Unfaltering. He is stability and reliability at their finest. God is Love!

REAL LOVE is what this whole life "in Christ" is all about! Not that we loved God, but that He FIRST loved us, and while we were still sinners, Christ died for us. (1 John 4:19, Romans 5:8.) It's not about what we can do to earn our identity, but what He did to buy us a new identity in Christ Jesus. It is not about anybody in this world choosing, for you, "who" and "what" you are going to be. It's not even about you choosing for yourself. It's about God choosing you FIRST. Loving you FIRST. And, then when you respond to his call, it's about your "new identity" in Christ Jesus. So, don't worry about the rest of it. God's got it all under control, and He will show you the way!

"image." Dictionary.com Unabridged (v 1.1). Random House, Inc. 26 Jan. 2007. <Dictionary.com http://dictionary.reference.com/browse/image>

"My" Thoughts:

Answer these questions as openly as you can. Don't worry...this is not a test and there are no "wrong" answers.

1. What do you think of when you hear the word "image"?_____
_____
_____

2. Where do you think you get your self-image?_____
_____
_____

a. What, if anything affects it positively?_____
_____

b. What, if anything, affects it negatively?_____
_____

3. Is the image you have of yourself the same as the image you want to present to others?_____
_____
_____

4. What makes you, "YOU"?_____
_____

Personal Challenge:

Reread Psalm 139:14 (found in the beginning of this chapter)

Write it down here: _____
_____

What does this mean to you personally?_____
_____
_____
_____

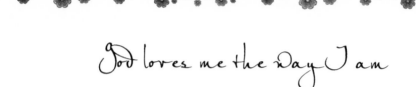

God loves me the way I am

God loves me the way I am! In my life I've had times where I've said to myself that I'm not pretty. No matter how many people said I was I didn't believe them. I had so many doubts in myself. But God made me, actually He made each and every one of us and He made us just as He wanted us. Saying that I am ugly is like saying that God made a mistake. Sometimes, I think on this, God is the all power-ful, perfect being of the universe! How could He make a mistake? Everyone was made by God and was made just the way they are supposed to be. Also, everyone is a bit weird in their own special way. God gave me my personality and I should not think for one second that it is bad! That is what sets me apart from every other person in this world. God loves individuality. One time, I talked to someone I could trust about my thoughts and they told me God did not make a mistake on me. Whenever I begin to think that I am ugly, I just know that beauty is in the eye of the beholder and God made me just the way I am.

Clare

chapter 4

MADE vs. MADE UP:
The Showdown

Shereen Christian

So God created human beings in his own image.

–Genesis 1:27 ⠿⠿

You were created to LOVE God and BE LOVED by God.

You are not an invention of the media. You are not a product of your environment. And you are not invisible. You are a representation –a likeness and reflection of God himself. CREATED on-purpose, CREATED with purpose. Sweet girl, you have been MADE! Made in the image of a very real, very much alive, loving God.

God made you, sized you up, and determined your value to be immeasurable. Every girl needs to get this truth deep-down in her heart. Your Heavenly Father loves you, cherishes you, and His thoughts toward you are good. Your identity and worth come from who you are "in Him." The ungodly things in this world will tell you the opposite if you let them! So, don't let them have the last word! The more you fill your mind and heart with Scripture, the more powerful your "spam blocker" will become. God's Word living inside you will filter out the junk-mail. The less junk, the easier it will be for you to receive what God says about whom you are and what you're worth. Let's get started on that whole spam-blocking thing right now. Consider a priceless painting, say, the Mona Lisa– its value is beyond estimation; no amount of money can determine its worth. Do you have a good mental view of a masterpiece? Now, think about another work of art, one written about a long time ago by the apostle Paul:

For we are God's masterpiece. He has CREATED us anew in Christ Jesus, so that we can do the good things he planned for us long ago (Ephesians 2:10 NLT, emphasis mine).

You, child of God, are a masterpiece. You are MADE by the hand of the Master himself and priceless beyond measure. Take any message that you accepted in the past that says differently and send it to the trash bin where it belongs.

Don't copy the behavior and customs of this world, but let God transform you into a new person by changing the way you think. Then you will learn to know God's will for you, which is good and pleasing and perfect (Romans 12:2).

The Problem with worldly views of image [made-up]:

Constantly CHANGING.

Very unstable and insecure.

Will never be enough to fulfill or satisfy the need to be loved and to belong.

The BEAUTY of God's word on image [made]:

Stays constant no matter what we're going through.

We can rest in the security that we are who He says we are.

Can truly satisfy.

The world will tell you that you have to "do" to be worthy. God says that you are worthy because your worth is in Him.

The world will tell you that if you want to be part of the chosen few, you better have the right clothes, the right car, and the right look. God says you already are chosen—He chose you, called you by name, and you are His.

The world will tell you that your image is something you can make-up. God says that you are created in His Image.

The world will tell you to change your personality and alter your appearance to be loved and accepted. God says He loves you just as you are.

R.E.S.P.E.C.T.

self-esteem 'selfi'stim, 'self-[self-i-steem, self-] –n,

> 1. A realistic respect for or favorable impression of oneself, self-respect 2. An inordinately or exaggeratedly favorable impression of oneself.

I love these two definitions for self-esteem; what a perfect example of MADE vs MADE UP! The first definition describes the young woman whose beliefs about herself and God are grounded in the truth: realistic and favorable.

Self Esteem and Your Choices

Your choices can reveal 3 important things about what you really think of YOU:

1. Who or what you ALLOW to define YOU (identity).

2. Who or what gives you a sense of worth (value).

3. Who you think YOU are to GOD (purpose).

If there is any area of your life where you are not looking to God, for whatever reason, you are missing out on His very best for you. Trust me on this! Like I have said before, I know what I am talking about!

Self Esteem and Purity

When we compromise our purity by our choice of clothing, language, or behavior, or if we trade it for a sexual relationship with a guy who's not our husband, it WILL affect the way we see ourselves.

God has a plan for your sexuality; and it is a good and worthy plan, designed to build you up, not demean you or tear you down. God's ways will always lead to life and peace.

If you have compromised in this area of your life and are experiencing the loss and devastation, please hear me on this: God can make all things whole, all things clean, and all things pure. And, if for one second you are asking yourself, *Yeah, God can do all that, but is he willing to do it for ME?* Yes, sweet girl. He is willing. And He is waiting for you to ask.

Self Esteem and Obedience

Have you ever been forced to obey somebody that you did not respect, did not really know, and did not trust? If your answer is yes, I want you to know that I have been there, too. There are very few places that feel more like a prison than that. But you know what? There is only one who came to enslave and imprison, and it ain't God! Jesus came to set you free, not to enslave you with impossible-to-follow rules, regulations, and burdens. He came that we may have life and have it even more abundantly. You know what enslaves? Sin does! But God is a loving and trustworthy guide. Doing life His Way ensures our safety, peace, and success in everything we do. His laws and precepts are boundaries meant for our benefit. I believe with all my heart that God delights in blessing his "precious daughters." Trusting Him and obeying Him is one of the smartest choices you will ever make. Do it because He loves you with a perfect love. He will never leave you. He will never turn His back on you!

Smile... GOD LOVES YOU!

Do you believe (know, really, truly know, deep-down beyond the shadow of any doubt, out of the reach of anything that can touch it) that you have a Heavenly Father who values you, loves you, and created you anew in Christ Jesus to be a stunning success? Do you know (really, truly know) that you are cherished and adored? Do you believe that your God is for you?

If not, I want you to know that I have been there and I can totally relate. For the longest time, it was very hard for me to see myself as one of God's very own, beloved children. In fact, the opposite was pretty much true. I saw myself as an unwanted step-child; I felt sure that God spent more time being annoyed with me, and was quickly losing patience with me, than He was actually loving me and wanting to give me His very best.

I had some pretty tough times when I was a kid. On the outside, though, everything looked great, but behind closed doors was another story entirely. I was not raised in a family that knew the love of God through Christ Jesus. All I knew of Him was condemnation and judgment. My parents went through a pretty nasty divorce when I was about twelve. These experiences left me feeling that no matter what I did, it would never be good enough; I would never be good enough.

When I was in high school, I decided to change all that. I tried anything and almost everything to earn other people's approval and love. I tried to be prettier, smarter, hang out with the right people, wear the right clothes, you name it—I did it. Oh, sure, for a while all my efforts actually worked—or so I thought. I was popular, dated lots of guys, and since I didn't see love modeled in my home nor did I know how loved and valued I was by God, I pretty much thought that all this attention was equal to love. I was going to hold on to it no matter what the cost. I didn't see the temptation as a trap and walked right into the snare. Every time I turned around, it seemed like the stakes were getting higher and higher. Soon, being pretty wasn't enough; girls were expected to be sexy. Dressing "in-style" became more and more provocative and revealing. Before I knew what was happening, I was so caught up in trying to be what everyone around me wanted me to be that I completely lost myself in the process.

As I got older, my "if-onlys" changed a bit; "if-only" I met the right guy, had the right career, drove the right car - but one thing remained the same: I was still willing to do everything and just about anything to earn people's approval and love. The sad thing was that I was convinced nobody could love me if they knew the "real" me, so, I just continued on with this charade, being this person I knew I wasn't, but too lost to remember who I was.

By now, my life looked a lot like the home I grew up in. Great on the outside: I had a handsome husband, a beautiful home, and a great career. On the inside, though, I was filled with emptiness, loneliness, and pain. All these years of trying to fill the void, all the choices I made, they all seemed to add up to nothing. And even though to the world it looked like I had it all, I had a sinking feeling in my heart that this counterfeit existence was all there was.

It was right about that time when I was invited to attend a church service with a really good friend of mine and her fiancé. I said, "Yes," before I had a chance to really think about it. By the time Sunday rolled around, I really didn't want to go, but I already told my friend I'd meet her there, so I got in my car and went. That church service changed the course of my life forever. I couldn't tell you a word the pastor said, or even a line from one of the many songs that we sang. All I knew was the love I felt when I walked into that building. I didn't know what it was that all these people believed, but I knew with everything inside me that they had found something good, something right, and something true. I wanted to know this God, this Lord Jesus, this Savior, Redeemer, and Friend that they were there to worship. That morning, I did the bravest thing I've ever done. I opened my heart to God, asked Him to forgive my sins, and accepted Jesus as Lord of my life.

It has been about ten years since that Sunday, and God has been "with me" and "for me" and "faithful to His Word" every single step of the way. What the enemy used to destroy my life, God used to bring healing to me and the young women I share my testimony with whenever I have the opportunity.

So, now that you know a little bit about me, I want to ask you one more time: do you believe (know, really, truly know, deep-down beyond the shadow of any doubt—out of the reach of anything that can touch it) that you have a Heavenly Father who values you, loves you, and created you anew in Christ Jesus to be a stunning success? Do you know (really, truly know) that you are cherished and adored? Do you believe that your God is "for you"?

If you don't, there is a void in your life that only God's love can satisfy. Please be honest. If you doubt God's love toward you, now is the time to deal with it. Let go of anything else you are doing to fill that void, cover that pain, hide that shame, and find out who you are, what your purpose is, or how to heal a broken heart. Stop all of it for now. Let God transform you and renew your thinking with the truth about His love, His goodness, His kindness, and His grace. Look up the many scriptures about God's unfailing love for you and His commitment to you. I've provided some for you at the end of this chapter. Allow God's word to re-align your thinking, to expose any lies that may have embedded themselves in your heart, and to heal you and make you whole. Then, and only then, will you begin to see yourself as God intended: a masterpiece--created, chosen, and dearly loved!

"self esteem." Dictionary.com Unabridged (v 1.1). Random House, Inc. 26 Jan. 2007. <Dictionary.com http://dictionary.reference.com/browse/self esteem>

"My" Thoughts:

Write down some Negative Media "Messages" that influence your Self-Image.

For example:

1.   What "pretty" looks like.

2.   Being "sexy" is important.

3.   Purity is for losers.

4.   _____

5.   _____

6.   _____

How do you feel about yourself after having one of these "messages" in your face? Ever "sized yourself up" after viewing a TV commercial or flipping through a magazine?_____

_____

_____

What choices have you made as a direct result of a message you received through media (positive or negative)? _____

_____

_____

What choices have you made that reveal your sense of self-worth?_

_____

What choices have you made that reveal your sense of purpose?___

_____

_____

[DISCLAIMER]: We are all capable of really blowing it once in a while! Everybody makes mistakes—so, don't be too hard on yourself when you do. The idea here is to look for "patterns" in our choices. Do you always choose the guy who treats you disrespectfully, or the one who values what you have to say? Do you wear the shirt you love, or the one that's totally uncomfortable just 'cuz it gets attention?

Personal Challenge:
Time for a makeover from the inside-out

1. Ask God to reveal to you anything that may be influencing your view of Who He IS.
2. Ask God to reveal to you anything that may be influencing your view of who you are in HIM.
3. Spend time with God as you read your Bible, and ask Him to reveal His Truth to you in all the places where you may be believing a lie.

Out of the following scriptures, choose your favorite. Circle it and then write down the reason why you like it.

This is real love-- not that we loved God, but that he loved us and sent his Son as a sacrifice to take away our sins (1 John 4:10).

I will never fail you. I will never abandon you (Heb 13:5).

See how very much our Father loves us, for he calls us his children (1 John 3:1).

I am writing to all of you...who are loved by God, and called to be his own holy people (Romans 1:7).

Then Christ will make his home in your hearts as you trust in him. Your roots will grow down into God's love and keep you strong. (Ephesians 3:17).

God created human beings in his own image. In the image of God he created them; male and female he created them (Gen 1:27).

I picked the following Scripture:_____

_____

It means a lot to me because ..._____

_____

I am His Favorite!

In January of my sophomore year in college, I saw an ad in my school newsletter that said, "Wanted: beauty pageant contestants." I had always had an interest in being in one, as a young girl, and I thought it sounded like fun. After asking the Lord about it, I felt peace in my heart so I signed up. At the first meeting, we were told that, of the 30 girls trying out, only 10 contestants would be chosen to participate in the pageant. It was a whirlwind experience filled with rehearsing, practicing "the walk", and refining our talent. Having determined from the beginning that I wanted to shine His light, I found the perfect song to sing that was a lively and fun Christian song with a message that would fit the occasion. When the selection time came, I was chosen as one of the 10, which made me very excited. The time seemed to fly by as we prepared and, before I knew it, the pageant day was here.

The Saturday morning of the pageant I had the interview with the judges. I thought that everything went just fine until I spoke with another girl in the competition. All her answers sounded perfect and I realized that mine sounded pretty dumb. This shook me up quite a bit so I took some time out to pray and seek the Lord. I felt His comfort and gained courage from being in His presence, so, I knew I could face the night. That evening, everything went wonderfully and I felt like I had done my best. As I was waiting behind the curtain, in the excitement of the moment, listening to the ending act before we were to mount the stage for the last time, the Lord spoke so clearly to me that I will never forget it. He said, "You did not place, but I am pleased with you." In that moment, His joy flooded my heart and I knew that I had won the pageant, not in the world's eyes, but in my Father's eyes. He was pleased with ME! I was not expecting this from Him; He just told me because He loved me! I felt like His favorite child! How amazing that the God of the universe would take the time to speak to His daughter in the middle of a beauty pageant, none the less! Needless to say, I walked out on the stage with my head held high and a huge smile on my face. Oh, and just like the Lord said, I didn't win a thing, except for the most important thing, His approval!

Kathy

Section III

"Forgive and forget, yeah right!"

"I just don't know if I can make it anymore…."

BREAKING FREE

"Why can't I let go?"

"… I just need to move on with my life!"

Breaking free from Drugs

My name is Roxanne and I was born in Sacramento. Because I was molested by my grandpa for years, beginning at an early age, it left me feeling completely dirty and ashamed with a gigantic "hole" inside of me that desperately needed to be filled. This is where my addiction started.

I allowed this man's sin to become a starting block for all my sins. My life became a fast paced, out of control race on a path of destruction. I had one prize in sight. My prize was drugs and alcohol! When I had my first taste of alcohol, it was great. I felt numb and happy; I had confidence and I wanted more. I was filling that "hole" inside of me. But, as most of you know, drugs and alcohol are just a temporary fix, a "false" sense of reality that makes you feel great — for a little while, until you become its slave!

When I was 12 years old, I started drinking and skipping school. I also lost my virginity. I thought if I slept with this boy, he would love me forever. My thinking was twisted and irrational.

When I was 16, I was introduced to methamphetamines; they soon started taking over my life. I had this "false" sense of control. I was riding high on the world's biggest uphill roller coaster. Life was exciting and fun! But, as you know, what goes up must come down. I entered into a world of darkness and desperation. I learned how to lie, cheat, and steal more than I ever thought possible.

From there, I was in and out of different programs: Kaiser CDRP and Campobello. I would stay clean for awhile. I remember the one time, when I had left Campobello two days before Halloween, and then, two weeks later, I found three vicodin pills hidden in the middle compartment of my truck. I held on to those pills for two days; I thought I was in control! But, in the morning of the third day, I called in a refill for the Soma. I had awakened a sleeping tiger!

I finally ended up entering Teen Challenge. Everyone was pulling for me! This is where the miracle happened. My past became my past and my future began. I no longer felt dirty and ashamed. As the days went by, my faith grew. God loves me, He forgives me, through Him and His Word, I learned how to forgive myself. After Teen Challenge, I entered Calvary Ranch.

God has saved me and I now believe that drug addiction and alcoholism is a choice and a sin. It is not a disease. It is true that once I use them, I am out of control and I can't stop. But, I have a choice; not to use. I have a choice not to pick up that "first time." I have also learned that I used the molestation as an excuse to use. I should have asked for help, instead I choose to use. Besides myself, the victims were the people I loved the most.

I now live a life, clean and sober! I don't know what my future holds. But I do know this, the Bible tells me in Philippians 1:6 that God has begun a good work in me and will carry it on to completion until the day of Christ Jesus. And, according to Romans 8:31, if God is for me, who can be against me?

Roxanne

Breaking free from Depression

I remember it was a struggle. Life! Just living was a struggle. To brush my teeth, to write my name on my homework, even waking up in the morning. Just the process of existing was a chore. The simple things that everyone did daily without thinking were completely exhausting.

I had a lot of friends at school. We had fun and laughed a lot, but everyday when I went home, my life was consumed with unending tears and sleeping. I hated school. I hated life. I hated existing. Thoughts of Heaven always filled my imagination. The words, "I just want to go home to be with Jesus" rolled throughout my head, and then tears. Tears would flood my eyes and my soul.

I began going to a Christian counselor who made life a little bit easier to live. My whole life, I had felt like the forgotten child with no voice. I told the Lord, "I don't care if I have to pay $90 an hour to get someone to listen to me." I just needed a friend, someone who would nod his head and understand. The counselor and I decided it would be best if I went on anti-depressant medication, although, after a while I noticed it was not doing anything. I was still stuck in the midst of deep sadness, with no emergency exit.

At one point, my mom told me she heard of this great preacher who was also known to have a prophetic gift. I loved listening to preachers so I went by myself to hear him speak. At the end of the service, the speaker pointed to my seating section and said, "Someone in this section is here with their family and is in their third stages of cancer." After a moment of silence, a man stood up weeping because the person the pastor was speaking about was his father. Just after prayer for healing with that family, the speaker pointed to the seating section on my right side and said, "There is someone in this section with severe depression." No one stood up, but I knew at that moment the Lord wanted to speak to me. He said softly to my heart, "Happiness is a choice my darling." That night I chose to stop taking anti-depressants. Over time, through many, many hard choices of happiness, my depression dwindled.

Years later, I still find myself in seasons of depression. One thing the Lord keeps showing me is that whether I am on medicine or off, I need to keep making choices to believe truth. This means taking captive of all of Satan's lies and telling him that Jesus owns my thoughts and my life. One major key I have found is to write lists of things I am thankful for and speak those out loud to the Lord. Usually depression is a consummation of the tragedy or situation of our own life. If we step outside our own problems and help someone whose problems are greater than ours, the heavy weight gradually becomes lighter; we are then forced to face the reality that others have life worse than we do and, if they can get through it, so can we. That is the freedom of Christ! Praise God!

Shiloh

Breaking Free from Self Mutilation

When I was fifteen, I was at the end of my rope, struggling with depression and suicide as a result of my parents' divorce and the memories of childhood sexual abuse. In order to express the emotions that I could not verbalize, I started cutting myself in order to "feel." I cut pretty regularly throughout my high school years and It was not until my senior year that I, finally, had the will power and support to overcome this challenge.

My youth pastor and Young Life leader played huge roles in empowering me to stop cutting through teaching me in the Word about who I am in Jesus Christ. I started to identify myself more as a redeemed child of the living God, instead of just a victim.

I wish I could say that I was never tempted to cut again after that year, but that would be lying. I doubt a week has gone by where I have not been tempted. Once you let Satan have that foothold, he knows how to get to you in your weakness. I have not cut in almost four years, yet, I still need the support of close friends and, occasionally, therapy in order to keep from succumbing to the temptation.

One of my favorite Bible verses is Psalm 119:32, "I run in the path of your commands, for you have set my heart free." God has truly set me free!

Kristine

Breaking free from an Eating Disorder

"I could never be anorexic." Those were the exact words I spoke to my mom after watching Tracy Gold's graphic portrayal of her own battle with anorexia in "For the Love of Nancy." I couldn't fathom how or why anyone would starve herself nearly to the point of death. Little did I know that just a few years later, I would be in my own life and death struggle against anorexia.

No one, myself included, understood why I stumbled into an eating disorder. You see, I had the perfect life…or so it seemed. I had a great relationship with my parents, who had raised me with a solid Christian foundation, and I had a sister who was, and still is, my very own "built-in best-friend." I did extremely well in school and I excelled in sports. I got along with everyone. In fact, I was voted "Best Christian Character" at my small, private school when I graduated from both the 8th and 12th grades. When I wasn't at school, playing sports, or working, I was ministering. I frequently spoke during children's services, I ran a sidewalk Sunday School program, and I interned with the children's pastor at my church. My life was incredible and I thoroughly enjoyed it.

However, everything changed the fall of '98, when I left for college. I made a great choice in the school to attend, packed all my belongings, and headed half-way across the country. I could hardly wait to begin this new adventure – to make my mark on the world. To my dismay, I soon discovered that I did not know who I was. I found myself in a vast sea of new faces, faces that did not know where I had come from or what I had accomplished. Soon enough, I gained recognition for something: running. Yep, I was quite the runner. People saw me all over town. Running became my anecdote, my stress-reliever, and, eventually, it became my obsession. Who would have thought that something so wonderful, so healthy, could go so terribly wrong, spiraling out of control? People noticed something else about me. I was a healthy eater. Not really . . . but by their standards, I suppose it appeared that way. So, I became "the runner" and "the healthy eater." It wasn't much in the way of an identity, but it was something. I latched onto the new "me" and, in no time at all, found myself depressed and losing weight at an alarming rate.

My parents pulled out all the stops when I came home for Spring Break. They took me to our doctor, who then referred me to a psychiatrist. I could hardly be-

lieve my ears when I heard the psychiatrist tell my parents, "If you let her return to school, she will either be hospitalized in less than a month or sent home to you in a box." His words sent chills through my parents. I, on the other hand, was furious! How dare he tell me I couldn't finish out the semester! To this day, I remember his name — Dr. Diebol. I thought it should be "Dr. Devil." He was, however, right. I was extremely sick — sicker than any of us realized.

You may think this encounter put me right on the road to recovery. I wish that had been the case. Unfortunately, things got much worse before they began to get better. I was in and out of out-patient treatment programs and hospitalized twice before I was sent to Remuda Ranch in Arizona. Remuda was my parents and my last hope. By the time I arrived, I was so sick I could hardly walk and my face and body were emaciated beyond recognition. After three months of intense treatment at Remuda, I was finally on the road to recovery . . . a very rocky road that I continued to walk for nearly six years before my body and mind reached a healthy state.

So, what saved me from death? Surrender — complete surrender, with no strings attached. For me, surrendering to God in this area meant trusting the professionals and following their instructions, no matter how terrifying it seemed to me at the time. Believe me, it was not easy. It never is. Relinquishing control of any stronghold in our lives is never easy, but painful and frightening. I lived with a feeding tube stuck down my esophagus for two months, cried through meal after meal, and ate foods I could not stand to look at, much less eat! But with each bite, each small act of obedience, I moved one step closer to health and wholeness.

God gave me a verse during that time, one I clung to in the most difficult times. Deuteronomy 30:19 says "…I have set before you life and death, blessings and curses. Now choose life…." Which will you choose?

In our media-driven society, we are bombarded by images that tell us what the world thinks we should look like. Every day we have a choice. We can live in freedom and appropriately give our bodies what they need to be healthy (and, yes, this requires self-control to maintain balance and not over-indulge) or we can micromanage our diets to achieve a certain image, thereby starving ourselves of the richness of what God wants to accomplish in us and through us. The choice is ours. I pray you will join with me and choose life!

Rebecca

chapter 5

FREE
Suzanne Rentz

God knew that you would pick up this devotional, wherever you find yourself in this journey called "life!" If you feel you have failed Him one too many times, or if you have lost any or every desire to serve the Lord, God still loves you! If you are waiting for a lightning bolt from heaven to zap you, consider it done! This chapter is God's wake up call and the alarm is just about to go off!

I know first hand what it is like. It is as if this "God" everyone is talking about exists, but yet He doesn't exist for you; now the feelings and emotions are gone. Like a triangle turning, you once felt the Holy Spirit's nudge but after ignoring that nudge, the edges have dulled and you no longer feel the pain of sin. As a matter of fact, you really don't feel much at all. Every once in a while, you remember what it was like, but then the memory fades off into the distance. Where have the dreams gone? Why is your heart so hard? Why does God seem a million miles away?

This was my story. I was trapped in an unhealthy relationship with a "kinda" Christian guy. I had just graduated high school and was very young and successful at a job with a promising future. I had to work on Sundays, which to me was okay; I didn't have a choice, or did I? I was just going along, "somewhat" serving God from a distance. In the Bible, Paul describes my condition perfectly;

People will be lovers of themselves, lovers of money, boastful, proud...
lovers of pleasure rather than lovers of God—having a form of godli-
ness but denying its power. Have nothing to do with them.
2 Timothy 3:2-5

I had a form of godliness, but I was denying its power. On the outside, I looked okay and I professed to be a Christian, but on the inside something was missing. And that "something" was my close relationship with God.

What I didn't understand was that I had invisible chains around me. I was in a self-induced prison! The choices I had made brought me to the state I was in. In my heart I knew I needed to get right with God but my emotions and my feelings were null and void.

God sent his son Jesus to deliver a strong message about freedom. All you fellow prison inmates, read on. It is found in the book of Isaiah:

> *The Spirit of the Sovereign LORD is on me, because the LORD has anointed me to preach good news to the poor. He has sent me to bind up the broken-hearted, to proclaim freedom for the captives and release from darkness for the prisoners.*
>
> Isaiah 61:1-2

God desires to set you free! Do you want to change? Do you want to fall in love with Jesus all over again? Maybe you have never really known God in an intimate way; do you desire that? If you want to break free from your coma-like prison, you can, but it involves change!

God's Freedom Is Like a Fountain of Chocolate!

One time, my family was attending an ordination service. After the service, they had a formal dessert reception. My three boys were dressed in their Sunday best. I ran into a longtime friend, so, I let them go ahead of me while I chatted. When I walked in the door, I could not believe what I saw. It was an absolutely horrifying sight. My three darling boys were knee deep in chocolate heaven! In the center of the room was a beautiful chocolate fountain; and they had jumped in line the moment they arrived. They dipped fruit, cookies, cakes, themselves, you name it—they dipped it. The worst part of all was that the room was decorated with white linen tablecloths. I would have loved to disappear and pretend those milk chocolate-covered children belonged to anyone but me, but I guess my dessert for the evening was humble pie!

From their perspective, my boys didn't realize that their manners were not socially acceptable. All they could think of was how good and luscious the chocolate looked and how delicious it smelled and tasted. The chocolate was theirs for the taking.

If we could just see God that way! If we could be so consumed by how good He looks and smells, our surroundings might just disappear and we might end up covered in Jesus. Wouldn't that be awesome?

True freedom is only found in Jesus Christ! God wants you to come closer to Him, to bask in His holiness, to go deeper and farther than you have ever been! God wants to reveal himself to you and He wants to set you free!

My boys were in a chocolate induced state of euphoria but you see, in God's presence, you will be so completely satisfied. Nothing compares! God satisfies your deepest desires, your inner longings, and any and every one of your cravings will be met.

For he satisfies the thirsty and fills the hungry with good things
Psalm 107:9

God wants to quench your thirst and satisfy your hunger; seek after Him!

As you hunger for God's presence, you will find true freedom. And it is in the shelter of the Most High that you will find the sweetest deliverance. A love so profound that it will shatter the chains of sin that have imprisoned you and give you a peace that at times will overwhelm you!

Freedom Begins with Commitment

I was at a church service when I rededicated my life to Christ. Some people can recommit their lives and *bing, bang, boom* - they are immediately delivered. For others, like me, once the decision was made and the prayer was prayed, the real work began. God forgave me the moment I asked Him to, but my heart lay there in ruins and it was up to me to get healthy again and rebuild the walls around my heart.

Above all else, guard your heart, for it is the wellspring of life
Proverbs 4:23 ⬚⬚⬚

I wanted the dreams, the treasures, and the freedom back. But, unless the walls were built and securely in place, the devil could steal, plunder, and destroy me all over again.

For me, it was a church service, but you can rededicate your life to Christ anywhere or anytime. Maybe you are reading this book and God is speaking to you right now! Don't wait … set the book down and cry out to God and ask for forgiveness. I love the Bible verse that I used to hear as a little girl:

'Come now, let us reason together,' says the LORD….' Though your sins are like scarlet, they shall be as white as snow…'
Isaiah 1:18 ⬚⬚⬚

God will cleanse you no matter what you have done. Jesus loved you so much that He died on the cross for you even when you were still a sinner. He paid the ultimate price so you could be free!

It Is Time to Let Go!

The first step I took after recommitting my life to the Lord, was to break the ties that kept me connected to my boyfriend. If someone is trying to escape from prison, don't you think it would be silly for them to continue to hold on to the bar of the cell once the door has been swung open? They may take a few steps, but, as long as they are holding on to that bar, they'll not get far.

What about you? What are you holding on to? Even if you are clutching it with your pinky finger, that tiny little grasp could mean the difference between freedom and captivity. Breaking all the ties is what my kids would call "Ginormously" (Gigantic and Enormous combined) important! If you are trying to get out of a relationship with a guy, be ready and willing to break all contact with him.

I had dated my ex-boyfriend for four-and-a-half years, during that time he had bought me a Shar Pei puppy, named Princess. We traded her back and forth. I had let him use some of my furniture for his house, and I was in love with his family. At one point, we had broken up and I was determined to make it stick; that is, until I got the phone call that "Princess had puppies!" He just wanted to show me the puppies, that's all! Well, that little puppy visitation caused me to spiral downwards, right into his arms. He promised that he was going to change this time! Three more months (of captivity) later, I still remember sitting in the restaurant with my "new" Christian friends at my "new" church that I was trying to plug into. They didn't even know I knew him, but his name entered the conversation, and not in a good way. He was taking out this girl who was only 15 and, here I was, in my early 20's. He was wining and dining her, while he was trying to make things work with me.

The next time I broke up with him, I knew in advance that Princess and her puppies now officially belonged to him and him only. I wanted my furniture back, and I no longer trusted myself, so, I took a Christian guy friend with me to get it. At first, I backed off of my relationship with his family, but later his family and I grew close again! They actually thought the break up was a good thing.

Your prison may not come in the form of a six-foot-two, blonde-haired guy; maybe, it's partying, drugs, or alcohol. Is it an eating disorder or witchcraft that has kept you in bondage? Prisons can take on all types of forms and sizes, but, nevertheless, the principles are the same! You have to get rid of that tiny, little bottle of pills hidden under your dash board, and you have to throw out the small bottle of beer stuck in the back corner of the fridge. If it is witchcraft that you are escaping from, throw out any games, books, music, or anything that feeds that bondage. Whatever prison you are in, break every tie that binds you to it! Don't go back to that dark, gloomy jail cell; it's not worth it!

Don't Try and Do It on Your Own!

Satan would love nothing more than for you to isolate yourself. When the church is having a service – you need to be there. You are at a very vulnerable place and every step you take needs to be the right one. Get healthy in a spiritual way. Remember, it is not about feelings! You may not get a warm, fuzzy sensation when you first breeze through the church doors. You might get the exact opposite feeling, maybe even a few cold stares. But that's okay, just don't let it stop you. Whenever the church doors are open, make it a priority to be there.

Ask God for new Christian friends to replace the unhealthy friendships. Find a smaller group where everyone knows your name. You need to be accountable. You need prayer support. Bible studies can be an excellent way to connect with other Christians!

I remember receiving counseling from a Christian counselor. It was a big help to me. I also took some classes on self-esteem and a class called "Reconciling Yourself with God." I did anything and everything that I could do to strengthen my walk with the Lord! I knew the more active steps I took, the sooner I would become healthy. Whether it was just a little baby step or a huge Michael Jordan step, the important thing was I was becoming free!

Change Your Mindset

Because of my new, healthy choices, I was finally getting a taste of freedom. But I had to make changes in a different way, if I really wanted the results to be permanent. I had to change my mindset and the way I thought.

As young women, we base so much in life on our feelings and emotions. But our feelings and emotions can be very deceiving, and we can't make any important decisions based on them alone. Sometimes, we have to go in the exact opposite direction of our feelings. Your emotions may be screaming, "Go back!" but what you really need to do is run, and run fast and far away! I know when I broke up with my boyfriend for the final time, it was as if someone took a knife and tore into my heart. I felt raw inside. A spiritual fog siphoned into my brain, and, consequently, nothing was clear. I remember saying to myself, "I will obey God; I choose to obey God. No matter how I feel!" At that moment in time, every baby-step I took was based on faith and trust!

If you can identify with the foggy brain syndrome, that is not all that you will experience. I will tell you in advance, you will have sad, lonely, and discouraging times ahead. There will be times when thoughts of failure and self doubt will come at you like a flood. During these "tuff" times, I promise you that if you go to God and read His Word, those overwhelming and depressing feelings will start to fade. You will soon discover the sweetest place of intimacy with God! God will do a deep work in you and it will bring permanent results.

Read, meditate, and memorize God's Word. Yes, God will heal and restore you in a powerful way. Your thoughts will change and your life will turn around! You will not be the same!

Freedom at Last

They say it takes 30 days to break old habits. I wish I could promise you that this quest for freedom could be accomplished in 30 days! Really, there is no guaranteed time frame. But as you choose obedience and you take steps in the direction of freedom, you are laying the ground work for God to fill your heart up with good things. The emotions and the feelings will come back in full force, but this time the emotions will be happiness, joy, and true peace. The hardness...finally gone!

Although God is doing a new work in your heart and life, your pursuit of Jesus and the precious freedom that comes from knowing and loving Him is a lifelong pursuit! I know, for some, there will be times when you will feel the pull of sin, trying to lure you back. The Bible says that in our weakness, He is made strong. God will strengthen you as you depend on Him.

Don't let the devil have any place in your life; break every tie to that cold, dark prison! Don't go it alone, get involved in church, be accountable, and surround yourself with Godly, caring friends. Memorize and meditate on God's Word, develop your prayer life so you can win the battle raging in your mind. God desires for you to break free and to walk in that freedom!

My life is a testimony of God's grace, mercy, and His amazing restoration power. I have a wonderful, Godly husband and the best kids ever. In my home, God is the center, and we are all involved in and serving at our church. In recent years, I have had the privilege to write, speak, and minister to many young women. If God could use my life, let me tell you, God certainly will use yours! The most important part of this equation is that I have a close and intimate relationship with Jesus. I have been right where you are, so I can tell you first hand, "freedom" is yours for the taking!

If the Son sets you free, you will be free indeed.

John 8:36-37 ⠿

"My" Thoughts:

How would you describe the condition of your heart?_____
_____
_____
_____

What is imprisoning you?_____
_____
_____
_____

What ties do you need to break?_____
_____
_____

What "healthy" choices can you start making?_____
_____
_____
_____

Proverbs 4:23 tells us, "Above all else, guard your heart, for it is the
wellspring of life." What does this verse mean to you?_____
_____
_____
_____
_____
_____
_____
_____
_____
_____
_____
_____

Personal Challenge:

Does God want you to live free? Read, meditate, and memorize these powerful scriptures on freedom!

It is for freedom that Christ has set us free. Stand firm, then, and do not let yourselves be burdened again by a yoke of slavery.

Galatians 5:1

Then you will know the truth, and the truth will set you free.

John 8:32

In him and through faith in him we may approach God with freedom and confidence.

Ephesians 3:10-12

Now the Lord is the Spirit, and where the Spirit of the Lord is, there is freedom.

2 Corinthians 3:17

Breaking free from the Internet

When I was in high school, I had a lot of friends who had AOL instant messenger, or MSN messenger, or Yahoo messenger. So, I had to make sure I had one of those on my computer to chat with my friends. My parents got AOL which I was fine with, because I got to create my own name and password where my parents wouldn't be able to get into my stuff and see who I had been talking to.

One day, I thought I would experiment with "chat rooms" to see who would be in there talking and what they would be talking about. I just wanted to get a feel of what it was all about. I thought I "got lucky" when I found a Christian chat room! And, I said to myself, "Great! I am going to find some nice guy FRIENDS to talk to." It had been about a week that I had been in there chatting with people in my area, and I liked it. I thought it was a lot of fun. I never met these people in person; they had only seen some pictures of me online through e-mail. We were just "online" friends.

Then, I ended up meeting this one guy, and we really clicked. I felt like he knew me really well, and I knew him really well. We sent pictures back and forth on e-mail for a couple of weeks. I was talking with my friends saying, "I would really like to meet this guy, but not alone!" I wanted them to go with me! Of course, they said, "Sure, let's do it!" The guy gave me his cell number and I gave him mine. We talked for a few days and planned where we wanted to meet, and how we would recognize each other. Finally, we figured out where to meet and set a date and my friends would come with me! It was Friday afternoon, and we decided to meet at a coffee shop for lunch. I was so nervous about it that I couldn't figure out what to wear, so I just put on a cute skirt and shirt. My friends and I waited there for him wondering when he was going to show up because he was already 20 minutes late. Well, he finally showed up and it went okay in the beginning, except that he looked a lot older in person than in his pictures. I found out that he was really 30 years old and had 3 little girls! We talked about our age difference and how I knew he was way too old for me to date. I thought, well, we can just be friends. At least, for a couple of weeks, until I figured out that he wanted to be more than friends.

At that time in my life, I was struggling with some things and very vulnerable, so, I got sucked in; one night, I called him up and told him let's go out somewhere alone, and, of course, he said, "Sure!" I lied to my parents; I told them I was going

out to the movies with some friends. But something inside me said not to go; and I had a flash back of myself "signing my contract between me and God" which stated that I was going to save myself for marriage. If I went along with this date, everything in my future could change! I then immediately called him and told him not to come get me; that I couldn't do it, but he kept insisting and tried to change my mind. I told him I wouldn't be there to meet him and to never call me again. After that night, I blocked him from everything on my computer and stopped meeting people I didn't know.

Since that happened, I realize that things could have turned out much worse. I could have met up with a rapist or a child molester. I stopped chatting online and trying to meet guys just to fill the void in my life that only God could fill.

During my senior year of high school, I met my soul mate, Daniel! We dated for four years and finally decided to tie the knot. Through the whole trying-to-meet guys online thing, I really learned that trying to find a guy to just fit in with the crowd, or filling the void in your life, is not worth a broken heart. But, waiting for the right prince (God's best) to come into your life is priceless!

Angy

Breaking free from Same Sex Attraction

As a child, I remember thinking that since I was a Christian I had some sort of immunity from sin or even from the desire to sin. Well, okay, so I wanted to sin, but not "big" sin, just "little" sin. By asking Jesus Christ into my heart at six years old, I felt that in some way, I had received a spiritual vaccination shot. Nothing could penetrate this heart.

I grew up in a wonderful Christian home with a loving father, mother and a sister who was three and a half years older than me. I always knew as a little girl that I was different. My favorite toy was a gun and holster set that I had gotten for Christmas. I was often lovingly referred to as a tomboy. I remember thinking, *What's a tomboy? Who is Tom and why do I have his name?* I knew that being a tomboy didn't mean I was a boy, but it also didn't mean I was a girl. I was a tomboy . . . what's up with that?

Around the age of 10, I really began to see how extremely different I was from other girls my age. I had different interests. I knew I wasn't a boy, but then again, I just didn't feel like a girl. Now that I look back, I realize how important feelings really are. They are not necessarily good or bad; they just are. It's what you do with your feelings that are important. As a teenager, I would often reach out to my mother who would reassure me that I would change, that at the right moment, *poof*, I would transform. It was only a phase I was going through and, once I hit puberty, all would be well.

As I grew up, I had a lot of perceptions that weren't correct. For example, I continually felt that I wasn't accepted by the women in my family. We were worlds apart. It was never really them who pulled away from me, but my own rebellion to not fit into a role that my sister had already claimed, which distanced me from them. Growing up, my sister was a "diva." Her nickname was "princess." She was a "girly" girl. The last thing I ever wanted to be was like her. I wanted to forge my own way, have my own claim to fame and find my own place among the family. My God-given personality is strong, yet kind. I've never had a hard time saying what's on my mind. I enjoy people, but I enjoy them more when they clean up after themselves and drive without talking on their cell phone. You get the picture!

So, I was Daddy's Girl. I was often told how much I was like my father. When you begin to hear the same thing over and over again, you begin to act as you're expected to. However, now that the Lord has led me through a healing journey, I realize that I have a lot of my mother in me, which is an answer to prayer.

I was left with this huge need, as a little girl, to feel accepted by my own sex. I remember going to kindergarten and picking new friends. Naturally, the friendships I formed at that small age were with boys. Who would want to play house during recess when you could play Star Wars on the blocks with the boys? Besides, you can't use a light saber when playing house. As I entered adolescence, these needs didn't go away: the need to fit in, to be accepted, and to be one of the girls. Psychologists agree that, as you enter puberty, you take your needs with you and they become sexualized. As a child, I had no idea how important it was to my sexual identity to identify more with my mother or that it was extremely important for me to play with those of my same-sex.

The last thing I ever wanted was to have my need for female acceptance sexualized. I remember the many nights I would lay awake, terrified, knowing that I was dealing with something I never wanted to admit to anyone. *But, wait a second, I'm a Christian; I can't struggle with homosexuality. I can't be attracted to my same-sex. I accepted Christ when I was six years old; I got the vaccination shot. Did I need a booster? I know this has to be the devil. The devil did this to me, and if I just pray more and read my Bible more, these thoughts and feelings will go away, and everything will be alright again.*

I had read and re-read what the Bible said about homosexuality and I knew if I didn't change my thoughts, I was going to hell. Do not pass go, do not collect $100. How could this be happening to me? I loved the Lord with all my heart. I felt a call to the ministry at a young age and I knew the Lord had a great plan for my life. My grandfather was the pastor of the church, my father was the head deacon, and my mother taught Sunday School. How could this be happening to me? What I didn't realize at the time is that no one chooses who they are attracted to, but they do have the ability to choose their response to their attractions.

Years later, after a lot of healing and counseling, I began to notice that everyone in the body of Christ has weaknesses. The last thing we like to do is admit our weaknesses, especially to each other. Most of us go through life acting as if our prayer of salvation inoculated us against sin, so, therefore, we are holy! I praise

the Lord for His mercy and grace, and that He kept me from ever leading a gay lifestyle or even experimenting in this area. Yet, I've come to realize, when I look at the bigger picture, that my goal in life is not heterosexuality, but holiness. My number one desire is to make Jesus the focus of my life rather than to try and rid myself of every bad thought or desire. I love how the Bible says that only He can take what is crooked and make it straight.

As I grew up and entered into Bible College, I had the option of dealing with my issues or pretending they would go away. When we bury our feelings, we soon find out that they really are buried alive. What we thought was long forgotten has a way of resurrecting itself. Believe me; the path to healing was not easy; it was extremely difficult. I had to repent of the many vows I made as a child that held me in bondage now as an adult. I had to forgive those who had hurt me and I, also, had to forgive myself. I had to allow Christ to come and love every part of me, even the parts I hated.

As a young person, my prayer requests would often go unspoken. How do you ask for prayer for your sexual identity? Little did I know that the word "unspoken" would represent a ministry years later that helps young people who struggle with their sexuality as I did. Unspoken Ministries is a non-profit organization that is answering the unspoken needs of today's youth. I'm able to equip youth pastors and youth workers with the knowledge that I have gained from this experience. How was I to know that I would eventually become a human vaccine helping to stop the spread of homosexuality?

Char

Breaking free from Witchcraft

When I was in Junior High, I had dreams of playing bass guitar in a heavy metal band. For my 13th birthday, my dad bought me a bass guitar and an amp. In my sophomore year in high school, a girl named Crystal approached me about being in a band that she and her boyfriend, Jerry, were putting together. I said, "Sure." She began to tell me about how her boyfriend just recently got out of a devil worshiping occult but was now just practicing "black magic". I was a little concerned about it, but she reassured me that he wasn't into sacrificing people or anything like that.

When I went to Jerry's, I noticed in his room that he had a big pentagram painted on a piece of wood sitting against the wall, all kinds of black magic books, incense, and a lot of occult figures laying around. I was so curious about everything. I knew worshiping the devil was wrong, but I figured that if it was "just" witchcraft it would be ok. I started talking to him and told him that, when I was a little girl, I lived in a house where a lot of strange things used to happen. And, as I got older, I would overhear my mom tell her friends about how strange things happened to her, too, and how she found witchcraft books in the attic, left there by previous renters. I, sort of, grew up intrigued by the whole thing. He began to tell me about how he had similar experiences growing up and how he used to summon demons when he was a devil worshiper. He said that they never left but that he still used them to cast spells and had control over them. I thought, *Wow, I don't want to go that far!*

But as I kept coming back to his house, I found myself wanting to know more. Eventually, I thought that I could dabble a little bit but stay far enough away to where I wouldn't get hurt. He talked to me about meditation and said that if we meditated together, I might be able to see spirits (demons). I was scared but at the same time too curious to say no. As we began to meditate, I felt such darkness and evil around me; I was so scared and I kept gasping for breath and closing my eyes. Eventually, I asked him to stop.

He began to tell everyone in the room how he saw me in my past life and went on and on about it. For some reason after that, I felt like I had power, that I could maybe control things with magic if I wanted to. I liked the feeling of being able to

get revenge on people and no one would know. I justified it by saying to myself, "It's not like I'm worshiping the devil or anything."

We started hanging out every weekend; and all we did was talk about it. We played Dungeons and Dragons and the Ouija board a few times, but I wanted to start getting into other things. I began to almost feel "called" to do this, like I had a psychic gift I was born with and I needed to start using it. I bought Tarot cards, began to study dreams, astrology, numerology, and Crystology. I was seduced by the feeling of power that it gave. When I would talk to people about it, I would just suck them right in, and I would take them to Jerry's house to introduce them to what I was into. It seemed like everyone was immediately curious about it and they thought I was "so great." I even had one girl tell me, "I'm so glad I met you." Like she found the "answer" she was looking for.

One day Crystal and I went to Jerry's house and we noticed that all of his black magic stuff was gone. We were like, "What happened to you?" He said, "I became a Christian, I just couldn't take it anymore." He said he started having anxiety attacks and it was just too much to handle. We just kind of looked at him like he was crazy. He said that the demons would threaten him at night but he wouldn't listen. All of a sudden, I had this weird feeling that these demons were going to attack me; I knew that I had opened myself up way more than I meant to, and, now that Jerry was no longer available, I was a target.

Sure enough, one day while I was doing my Tarot cards, an evil presence came into the room. The presence was so thick and evil; I felt like I could see it with my own eyes. I began to dread going home at night. Every time I would try to go to my room, I would sense an evil presence. After a few weeks, I got so desperate that I told my parents. My mom believed me, but my step-dad tried to tell me, in a gentle way, that I had something mentally wrong with me. As I was waking up the next morning, I heard something scream in my ear so loudly that my ear drum closed up. I didn't start hearing voices or seeing anything, but I knew I was in trouble. I thought that, if I just did my Tarot cards and astrology, it would eventually leave, but the evil presence continued to torment me every night. I couldn't even sleep with the light on, so, I would stay up until the sun came up. If I fell asleep, I would have horrible nightmares and see demons in my dreams or sometimes, I would wake up feeling like I was having an out-of-body experience.

One night it was too much. I had to sleep! I wanted to cry out to Jesus but was so afraid of what would happen to me if I did. I remembered that my mom told

me one time that Satan couldn't read our minds. So, I said in my heart, "Jesus, please help me." That night, Jesus was in my dream, to keep it brief, at the end of my dream. He was holding me in His arms like a baby, just looking down at me. I NEVER felt such love and peace like that before; there's no way my mind could have come up with that. When I would tell my friends about it, I would start crying. But I didn't stop doing what I was doing; I didn't know better. I thought, as long as I didn't worship the devil or practice black magic, I was ok. I had another dream where Jesus showed me that His hands were tied and He couldn't do anything for me because I wouldn't stop. I had no one to guide me to the truth, but I knew He wanted to help me.

Later that year, while I was partying, I took 2,000mg of pain killers and was getting drunk. The next night, while I was smoking pot, I had an anxiety attack and started throwing up. I would have the most horrible, demonic dreams and the attacks would last for at least 5 days. I was 17 years old and I felt like my life was over.

About a week later, I was riding in my brother's truck and he started talking to me about Christianity. I grew up partying with him, so, I was totally confused. Then he said, "I don't know, Jacquelyn, I just want to go to heaven." I thought, *Me, too!* Then the Holy Spirit began to reveal to me that it wasn't "just worshiping the devil" that would take me to hell, but unless I gave my whole life to Jesus, I wouldn't be saved. No one told me that; I just knew it. I went to church that Sunday with my brother and I received everything the pastor said. As we were driving away, I felt this sort of tingling around my eyes… like my eyes had just opened for the first time and I could see like never before. The Lord spoke to me and said, "I just removed the blinders that Satan had on your eyes. You can see now." I didn't even know if that was a scripture, but I knew it was God speaking.

I still had things to overcome from that point on. Satan did not want to give me up because I was becoming more and more on fire for God. One day I grabbed a big garbage bag and threw everything away: rock magazines, worldly music, crystals, some of my art that reminded me of the occult…everything, and I burned my Tarot cards. From that point on, the Lord began to teach me about faith and who I was in Christ and how to speak His Word. I was set free from the powers of darkness, healed of panic attacks, and slept with the peace of God. Just like it says in Psalm 91, God continues to be my refuge and my fortress.

Jacquelyn

Section IV

"Why can't my family just be normal?"

"… my parents are so unfair!"

Get CONNECTED…the FAMILY plan

"I just want a little freedom, that's all!"

"My dad left me when I was little…"

Going through a Divorce

I remember the first time I felt abandoned. It was the spring of my third grade year; my parents had just gotten in a massive fight. I remember sitting on my dad's lap, just bawling my eyes out while begging him not to leave. I felt like my world was falling apart. Little girls look to their fathers for comfort, because he is the only man in her life in her younger years. I've experienced my parents splitting up many times before that, but, in that particular moment, I felt completely help-less for the first time. My dad was gone for the majority of the summer; I don't recall seeing him until the school year got underway.

My dad finally came around, sometime before Thanksgiving, even though I don't remember it. I began to block out parts of my childhood. I figure that the portions I can't remember were around the time frame that he was gone. I had grown into a very bitter middle school student by the time sixth grade came around. I was always angry! I didn't have very many true friends even though I was one of the more popular kids in my grade. I pushed people away. I figured that if my own dad would let me down, then there surely couldn't be a friend in the world that wouldn't either.

Morgan was one of the few people who never let me down. Now that I think about it, she was the only person who wasn't part of my family who didn't. We met in kindergarten and were pretty much glued to the hip over the course of the next several years. We fought quite a bit, but the majority of it was because my frustra-tion was getting the best of me. I think by that time, I was so hurt that I couldn't handle myself. I was always the type of kid who didn't like people to know that I had a weakness, and I still am that way to some degree. Instead of communicat-ing my issues or sharing my hurts, I'd lash out, or yell. I'd get really mean and I'd boss people around. She was the only one who never stopped being my friend.

Morgan and her mom were both the biggest influences on me. I remember my sixth grade year being the hardest. It was the summer after fifth grade that my parents got a divorce. My mom started dating someone new; my dad had already had someone new around for awhile. I felt that I had been forgotten. I started try-ing to find my self- worth in guys. I spent all my time liking one guy after another. It was all innocent but, none the less, I didn't rely on God to find my identity. My lowest point came when I liked a guy that Morgan liked. I was always more outgo-

ing than her; so, I did what I could to get him to notice me. It destroyed trust in our relationship. I did to her what I felt like my father did to me. I had lost any real friends that I had ever had. Even though I had finally got what I wanted, I was so unhappy.

An opportunity arose later on that year to go on my class missions trip. That was the best decision I could have made at that point in my life. I had learned valuable lessons, even though I had learned them the hard way. I was able to rekindle old relationships, let my wound heal, and forgive.

Forgive, that was the hardest one! It did take me a long time to get past the fact that my dad had left my family, but the biggest obstacle that I had to get past was that I felt like God had abandoned me. It hurt so much, at first, to think that God had allowed so much pain and division in my family. With the help of my mom and a few other influential people in my life, I learned that it is never God's will for His children to hurt. I was able to forgive God and let Him do a work in me. It was so hard at first, but I kept pushing through because I knew that if I put my trust in God, He could heal the wounds and help me put my anger aside. He even opened the door for me to sit down with my dad and tell him the things that I had always wanted to tell him.

My dad and I have an awesome relationship now. God has really intervened and mended wounds. From the outside looking in on the situation, most people would probably feel sad for me because in their eyes I come from a broken home, but that isn't true. Some people would say we have a blended family, but I call it a mended family because God has truly come in and mended the hearts of the broken and turned out every area for the good, as so often God does. Let it be an encouragement. Hope is never lost when you're on God's side.

Britni

Breaking free from Molestation

When I was a young girl about eight or nine years old, my biological father molested me for a period of about 6-9 months. Because I was so young when it happened, I'm unsure of the exact length and period of time this went on. The Lord protected my virginity; however, I was violated sexually, which in turn meant that I was violated, not only, physically but also mentally, emotionally, and spiritually. One sunny afternoon, I came to my dad and said, "It has to stop." In denial, he asked me, "What has to stop?" I told him, "You know what I'm talking about." He then pleaded with me not to tell my mother and reassured me that he could go to jail for what he had done.

Several years later, the physical abuse had stopped but the verbal and emotional abuse had worsened for my whole family. I grew angry with my dad one afternoon, and, while he took my brother and sister to a movie, I spilled everything out to my mom. At first she didn't know if she could believe me, knowing that I was angry with my dad. But when I told her I wouldn't know anything about these kinds of things unless it had happened to me, her eyes were opened to the truth.

My mom contacted the pastor of our church who put her in touch with a marriage counselor my parents had previously seen. When this counselor learned of my dad's crime, he told him that he would lose his license if he didn't report this. Dad's option was to turn himself in or be turned in by this counselor. Dad never expressed anger toward me for ratting him out, only fear. God's hand of grace was on me in this manner, as well.

After an unnerving encounter with the sheriff, I learned that Dad would be sent to jail. This was not what I wanted. I simply wanted him to be out of the house, away from us. In my time of distress, God became more than just a Sunday School story to me. For the first time, that day I opened my Bible, not for a "Bible drill" or to satisfy a teacher's questioning, but to seek out the God who knew what my heart was feeling better than I knew what I was feeling myself. After opening it, my eyes fell directly to these verses, "May our Lord Jesus Christ himself and God our Father, who loved us and by his grace gave us eternal encouragement and good hope, encourage your hearts and strengthen you in every good deed and word" (2 Thessalonians 2:16,17 NIV). By reading this, my heart was stilled, even though the whole rest of my world was spinning.

My grandpa on my dad's side paid for his $22,000 bail. My whole family wrote letters to the judge asking him to have mercy on our family. Knowing well that our family would suffer greatly financially without Dad's income, the judge sentenced him to house arrest (in a separate home) for a period of time, as well as high fines to the city, periodic drug tests, and he was assigned a parole officer. For the next four years, I was to have absolutely no contact with my father, whatsoever. No phone calls. No letters. No visits. I could write him letters, but he could not write me back. Sometimes I would be in the car in a parking lot somewhere around town and see him from a distance. If he saw me, too, he would instantly turn and leave as fast as he could. He feared being caught near me. When I saw him react this way, it made me feel like I was unlovable or that I was a disgrace to him. I missed having a daddy, but did not miss him!

My sister and I had agreed, as young girls, two things about our wedding days. First, that we would both be each other's maid of honor and, second, that neither of us would have our dad walk us down the aisle.

This pact that we had informally made with each other came up one evening during my senior year of high school when Mom and I got into an argument. She said to me, "Angie, I wish you wouldn't say that you don't want your dad to walk you down the aisle on your wedding day, because that's like saying that God can't do a miracle in your life."

When she said that to me, the Holy Spirit opened a door in my heart to allow for the change that He was about to bring. As I lay in bed that night, I prayed like I'd never prayed before. I asked God how I could forgive my dad. It was beyond me how to get rid of the bitterness that had grown in my heart over the years. I began to have flashbacks of when I was really little. My mind flashed back to a time when my parents were always fighting and Dad was packing his suitcase to leave. I went in to him crying, pleading with him not to go. He cried too and stayed home because I asked him to. Then I saw a vision of my wedding day. My vision did not reveal who the groom was going to be, but emphasized my dad walking me down the aisle. These visions brought on by the Lord caused a deep longing in me to be re-united with my dad. But the bitterness in my heart toward him was warring against the pull to recover our relationship. I wrestled with God in prayer that night. The Holy Spirit spoke to me and basically said, "I view every sin the same. You are a sinner and so is your dad. You are no better than he is. He struggled with this sin; you struggle with your sins." I cried out in a heart wrenching prayer, "God I forgive him!" I felt the release of bitterness leave my body just as evidently as breathing out a sigh of relief. I cried and cried. And the angels rejoiced over me in my freedom.

The next two weeks I tested myself to see if I had truly forgiven my dad. I believed that I had, but, if bitterness were still there, it would become evident as soon as I saw a father and daughter holding hands. The weeks went by and I sensed no bitterness upon seeing those kinds of sights. I wrote a 13-page letter to my dad explaining to him the process I went through that led to my forgiving him. I told him how important father-daughter relationships are and how badly I felt we both needed each other. I explained to him that I was taking measures to legally reunite us through his parole officer. At this point, I was eighteen years old, which made the process much quicker. He had not asked for my forgiveness, but the healing came to both of us because of it. Two weeks later, we saw each other again for the first time in about four years. I went straight up to him and said, "I love you, Dad." And, I really meant it! We both cried! Mom was there, too, and she cried as well! This time they were tears of joy.

On June 29, 2002, my dad walked me down the aisle of the church, where my groom waited to receive me. Dad humbly accepted the position. Ken, my husband, proudly accepted his new position.

Today, almost five years after my wedding day, Dad & I carry on as friends. Anyone who meets the two of us together would never guess that we went through the turmoil that we did. When I give my dad birthday cards, I usually have a difficult time picking the right one. Hallmark doesn't make cards that say, "Dad, I forgave you for all the terrible things you put me through, so let's just be friends. And, oh, by the way, happy birthday!" Instead, I choose a "thank you" card for how hard he has worked over the years to financially support our family or I choose an "I'm so glad we're friends" card. These are truths that bless his heart much more than any sappy birthday card could.

Statistics show unhealthy results for a young girl who has been molested. They have proven time and time again that a girl will, on one hand, become timid and withdrawn, expressing at least a strong distaste for any physical affection even when displayed appropriately. On the other hand, a young girl who has been molested may become loose, seeking one dating relationship after the other trying to satisfy her deepest longing for true masculine love. Some even go as far as stripping and prostitution. I give praise to God! I grew up to become neither of those extremes, but grew into a healthy relationship with my boyfriend who is now my dear husband. But for the woman who finds herself identifying with one of those problems, I just want to say that God desires to be the complete fulfillment of masculine love in your life. If you are timid or withdrawn, God desires to love you in the most appropriate of ways. He proved the purity of His love when He died for us without asking anything in return. And for the woman who finds herself going through relationships with a quick turnover rate, please know that mankind will always be subject to failure, but God is faithful! He is the same yesterday, today and forever. He has loved you since before you were born and will continue to love you always. This is the power of God!

Angela

I have Aids

I think I began my life like every other kid, just wanting to be loved and cared about by my parents. But, my brothers and I were not raised that way. My dad drank and got mean; my mom was mentally ill. Life with them was one painful, never-ending nightmare of physical, verbal and mental abuse. A bitter and unnatural coldness always filled the air in our house. I grew up knowing pain, hatred, endless guilt and shame. Hearing Mom tell me daily how unwanted, unlovable and totally worthless I was became more than my heart could bear.

When I was thirteen, I was in the hospital for three weeks with a kidney problem and became friends with a six-year-old girl named Karen, who had appendicitis. Karen's mom really loved her. Every day, she would come to see Karen and she was so nice to me. After two weeks, Karen got a high fever and died. I felt so sad. I needed a loving Mom so much, but when I looked at my own mother and saw her mean, empty heart, I just said, "No more!"

I chose an attitude that caused me to die inside. My spirit was broken; my reality collapsed; I unplugged myself emotionally. I began my long journey of alcohol and drug abuse that sent me into emptiness, the neutral zone of everyday existence.

After years of drug and alcohol abuse, I found myself, twenty-nine years old, a single-mother, living on the streets with my six-month-old son. I began to realize that I wasn't responsible for just myself any more. One day, I passed out in front of a home where a group of ladies were having a Bible study. I was taken by ambulance to the hospital and one of the ladies took my son into her home, and then, opened her home to me when I got out of the hospital.

God had just walked into my life, whether I knew it at the time or not. His loving Spirit tenderly embraced my weary, tormented heart and soul. I wanted to raise my son in the environment I'd come to know in this Christian home, though I knew that I had a lifetime of anger, shame and fear to overcome. I didn't know if it was possible.

I placed my son in a Christian foster home while I went into a Christian drug rehab program. Then, I faced the past, went to college, got a good job and an apartment so I could get my son back, to give him a loving home.

For a period of time, life was good for my son and me, but then I got sick with pneumonia. When the doctors tested me for AIDS, I thought, *No way—I haven't done drugs for years.* But, the test was positive. At first, anger surged from deep within and my words to God reflected it: "Why, God, why? You could have prevented this! Is this Your idea of punishing me?" I spent the next hour venting my frustration to God. Despair and loneliness hit me hard! But God showed me that a part of my past that I had considered closed, had come back. He was not the one punishing me and He couldn't prevent it because it was a result of my choices I had made with my own free will. Jesus says in John 10:10, "The thief (Satan) comes only to steal and kill and destroy; I (Jesus) have come that they may have life, and have it to the full" (NIV).

Realizing that I was going to die, to stand before God, I knew that wouldn't be good, because I had been living by the "religious rules," but I didn't "know Jesus." I fell to my knees and prayed, "Dear God, living with this disease and knowing it was self-induced is more than I can bear. My body is weak, my soul aches with guilt, and my spirit is filled with despair. I need Your forgiveness and love. Please hold me, God. Please save me from my sins. I accept Jesus Christ as my Lord and Savior."

God heard my prayer. He filled my heart, soul and mind with His love and the Holy Spirit. This was one of the most beautiful, unforgettable, breathtaking and, definitely, most important events in my life. As a result of having a real relationship with my Lord and Savior, I have laughed more, enjoyed life more, learned more, grown more and I've "loved" to a capacity beyond my imagination.

God has helped me to learn that my attitude does make a lot of difference in the world that I live in. I have a choice to see the bad; darkness and hopelessness, or, I can see the hope in Jesus Christ. With Christ, I can know that, although life is not a bed of roses, God reigns and He is victorious.

> "...in all these things we are more than conquerors through him
> who loved us."

> Romans 8:37

Debbie

chapter 6

PARENTS
Suzanne Rentz

"Hey, Jill, it's me, Suzanne! I am so mad! You would not believe my mom… we just had a big blow out and she just took my car keys away; I can't go out tonight, all our plans are ruined…. She is so unfair! I can't stand her! She always does this to me! I will figure out a way to get my keys back. I refuse to stay home!"

"Suzanne, just say you're sorry …it doesn't matter if you mean it. I don't want to stay home either."

"Whatever… I guess I can say the 'words' but I didn't do anything wrong. I know I yelled, and said a few bad things, but she deserved it. I don't care anymore! I will do whatever it takes to get the car back."

That was me when I was seventeen and I remember that conversation as if it were yesterday. I was very angry that day. I really had blown up at my mom! My heart was so hard that I faked a pathetic apology just to get out of the house.

I really wasn't an angry person. I rarely lost my temper and, normally, I kept my frustrations with my mom to myself. I guess that is what makes this incident so crystal clear. Later that night, as I was lying in my bed, I realized I had a problem. My selfish attitude was so ugly. I expressed horrible thoughts and hateful words that I didn't even know were inside me. What happened to the special relationship I once had with my mom?

Growing up as a little girl, my mom and I were very close. We did everything together; I was her "little buddy." She was fun, and she exposed me to so many opportunities. I tried every sport, ballet, tap dancing and many musical instruments: flute, clarinet and piano. I sang in the choir at my school and my church; I attended every club, whether it was Girl Scouts or 4H. She entered my art projects and drawings every year at the fair. She made me feel as though I could do just about anything. She was very creative and stirred those gifts in me!

Things started changing when I became a teenager. Screeching hormones entered into the picture; I wanted some independence, the kind where you spread your wings a little. She seemed so strict! I felt like my choices were never good enough for her. She pointed out how I could do things better, safer, or smarter. Then, there was the fact that she was always so busy doing everything for everyone! I wanted to just hang out with her (you know – quality time) and I wanted her to listen to me. Listen without talking! It seemed like she felt the need to give me her opinion when all I wanted was for her to nod her head in agreement.

During my teen years, there were good and bad times, but the more I focused on the negative, the more the positive side of our relationship seemed to disappear. And now here I was wondering what happened. Where did we (or I) go wrong? How did something so good become so bad? I knew that I did not want to stay distant and cold anymore and it was at this point that I asked God for help! God definitely answered my prayer, but it was not the way I expected. He did not transform my mother into a perfect mother; I certainly did not become the perfect daughter. God showed me things and gave me a different perspective, one that I had never known before.

How Would You Rate Your Relationship with Your Parents?

Maybe you are reading this and you find yourself frustrated and angry at your mom or dad. Maybe you have an okay relationship, but it could be better. It is time to go above and beyond in the parent relationship department! I want to challenge you to take your relationship with your parents to a whole new level. This challenge is so important that God actually included it in the Ten Commandments.

Honor your father and your mother, as the LORD your God has com-
manded you, so that you may live long and that it may go well with
you in the land the LORD your God is giving you.

Deuteronomy 5:16

It all begins with three simple words: "Honor your parents!" If you truly want to please God, then honoring your parents will put a huge smile on His face! The Bible does not say, "Honor your perfect, elderly, or dead parents." It just says to honor your parents-regardless, period, case in point!

Your biological parents may have checked out but you can still apply this challenge of honor to your extended family. If it is your grandma or grandpa, your aunt or maybe your guardian, or whoever is fulfilling the parental role, they all deserve that place of honor and God has placed you in their care!

What does the word *honor* mean? It means to respect, highly regard, appreciate, and revere. Can you honestly say that you respect, esteem, appreciate, and highly regard your parents?

It is all in perspective, the way you view your parents. When you learn to change the way you see your parents, you will change the very core of your relationship. You will learn to appreciate and respect your parents in ways you never thought possible.

A Star Versus a Square

One way I changed my perspective was to realize my mom was not perfect! She might not ever change. She was who she was. I had a choice. Do I accept her for who she is and make the most of the relationship, or do I abandon the relationship altogether?

My daughter has a favorite toy that she plays with over and over again. She has to drop the correct shape into the correct hole so that it will fall into the little yellow bucket. The only problem is that the "star shape" will not fit into the "square hole" no matter how hard she pushes! I have seen her little face get red with frustration as she kept trying. But she is finally starting to understand how it works and after many attempts, she has finally got it down.

Sometimes, with your parents, you try to make them fit into a mold that they were never intended to fill. If your parents are shaped like a star then you cannot make them into a square. A triangle will never become a circle no matter how hard you try! You cannot change your parents! You might want them to act a certain way, take on a different personality, love you the way you want to be loved, but the bottom line is that you can't make them do anything. Whining, becoming bitter and angry; none of those things work. And let's face it--God gave you your parents. You had no choice in the matter, and although you may have wished you were born into your best friend's family, it just didn't happen. You may never have a mom who bakes homemade bread, shops with you until you drop, or plans a "girl's night out." Your dad may never shower you with encouraging words, buy you thoughtful gifts or listen without giving advice. But, nevertheless, your parents are all yours and your relationship is what you make of it. You can learn to accept your parents right where they are. Acceptance doesn't mean you embrace their every fault. The acceptance I am referring to is to understand and let go of unrealistic (star vs. square) expectations, and accept them for face value, the good and the bad!

Are You Speaking Spanish or French?

How do you express your love? Do you express it through giving gifts, serving and helping out, through your words of encouragement, and quality time, or is it through affection, hugging, kissing, and constantly touching? When you talk about differences, your love language can differ from your parents quite a bit. You may feel that your parents don't love you, but, in fact, you are loved much more than you realize. They just express it through a different language.

My husband and I went on a missions trip with our youth group when we first started out in ministry. There was this one kid on our team named Joey who kept telling us he knew Spanish; he wanted to be the interpreter the entire time we were in Mexico. The funny thing about Joey was that he could not speak a lick of Spanish, but he just didn't get it. We were laughing hysterically at the people as they watched him babble on and on. They had this bewildered look on their faces. It makes me laugh now just thinking about it! Joey was absolutely butchering their Spanish language. We could have delivered the best sermons known to man, but the people would never have understood unless they heard it in their own language. Finally, we did have an actual Spanish interpreter join our team and it was a huge help!

Speaking a certain dialect is an important factor in communicating with words; "love language" is an important dynamic in the way we communicate love. "Love languages" come in all shapes and sizes, nevertheless, they are always present. Some ways of expressing love are not as obvious as others but if you look for them – you will see them! I challenge you to see if you can understand and speak your parents' language.

Gifts (Providing): Some parents show their love by going out of their way, in giving gifts and by providing for their family. They are always giving gifts, wanting very much to give you everything that they missed out on. Dates, anniversaries, holidays; they don't miss anything! A thoughtful card and a $20.00 bill is always just a pocket away.

By Doing (Acts of Service): Some parents express their love by "doing"; they are always in motion. They might not sit and hangout with you but that is because they are too busy doing things, providing opportunities for you, taking you places, etc.

Affection (Meaningful Touch): Some parents express their love through constant affection, hugs and kisses, and back rubs; they are emotional, touchy and feely, and quick to invade your space.

Words (Words of Affirmation): Some parents express their love through words. They might not always back up their words with actions but their intent is to do so. They make promises, express hopes, compliment you; if there is something positive to say, they will.

Quality Time (Hanging out): A movie, shooting a basketball, watching T.V. together - they just want to be with you. They always seem to be in the background and they like to listen. Words may not be many, but a pat on the back goes a long way.

Do you want to be more independent? Celebrate your differences! Your mom or dad may express their love in more than one way, but it may not be your way. Do you see how expressing your love in different ways could cause you to miss each other? If you are extremely sentimental and love to give gifts and your mom or dad forgets your birthday-- Wow, that is a huge blow! Or if you are big with expressing your love through your words and you have a mom or dad who is not overly positive or big on praising you – you end up feeling unloved. In reality they love you very much, but they are just not the cheerleader type. They may be busy providing for you, giving you things, or providing you with opportunities to be a better person. It is critical that you understand that just because they show their love in a way that is different from you, it does not mean that they do not love you. They love you very much but it is in their way.

Personalities Can Get in the Way...

God created each of us in our own unique way. At times, we think, act, and speak so differently! You may be wired exactly the opposite of your parents or guardians. One way is not right and the other wrong; it is just different! You may love to have fun, relax, and let life just happen and your mom or dad may like order, systems, and schedules. Or if you are a deep thinker, moody, and a perfectionist, you may feel that your parents are pretenders, shallow, and superficial.

Personalities are like a double-edged sword: with every good personality trait comes some negative ones. Sometimes, it is hard to understand or relate to what each other is feeling!

My middle son, Drew (at age eight), had a wild imagination and had a colorful vocabulary, often exaggerating when telling a story. He and one of his favorite cousins started having problems getting along. The same situation kept reoccurring. Drew would explain something or tell a story, and his cousin would tell him that he was lying. This happened time and time again, and it started affecting the relationship. Finally, it hit me-- his cousin saw things as black and white, as he was very literal. The truth was the truth and any variation was a lie. Drew was the exact opposite; black and white were boring, many colors made life exciting. I sat down with both boys and explained why they were misunderstanding each other. Even though they were both very young, they realized that neither one was wrong, but instead, just different.

There is usually a common ground that can be reached. There is a way that you can communicate so that each person really gets it.

As a young woman, you have so many emotions, thoughts, and feelings, and you can't just pretend they don't exist. You think that your parents should automatically know or realize what they are doing wrong. But they might not understand how you really feel. You have to learn to communicate. Explain and share your feelings with their personality in mind.

Can You Hear Me Now?

Before you erect a great big wall, like the Great Wall of China, that separates you from your parents, or before you isolate yourself to a far off distant island, miles and miles on an emotional sea - express your feelings! If you stuff your feelings inside, they will metamorphosize into something that looks a lot a thunderstorm. Your feelings will change from simple hurt to destructive anger, and they will do some serious damage.

You need to express how you feel, not in the heat of the moment when your emotions are running wild, but in a constructive way. Maybe you can do this through a letter, maybe while driving in a car, or even lying on your parents' bed. Sometimes if problems are serious enough, a pastor, a youth pastor, or counselor can also play an excellent role in helping you express your feelings. Let them be a neutral third party.

There is a common ground that can be reached. And there is a way that you can communicate so that each person really gets it. When it comes to personalities, many times, it is not a right way and a wrong way but instead, just different ways. Learn to understand your parents' line of thinking, so that when you express yourself, you are communicating in a way that they will understand.

One of my favorite passages that I memorized when I was in Junior High was Psalms 37: 1 - 6. These Bible verses really encouraged me for a number of reasons. I am going to break it down and explain how it relates to you, your choices, and a simple word called "boundaries".

> *Do not fret because of evil men or be envious of those who do wrong; for like the grass they will soon wither, like green plants they will soon die away. Trust in the LORD and do good; dwell in the land and enjoy safe pasture. Delight yourself in the LORD and he will give you the desires of your heart. Commit your way to the LORD; trust in him and he will do this: He will make your righteousness shine like the dawn, the justice of your cause like the noonday sun.*
>
> Psalm 37:1-6

The part of the verse that I want you to focus on is verse three:

> *Trust in the LORD and do good; dwell in the land and enjoy safe pasture.*

Let's pretend for one minute that you are a sheep. What would happen if you ignored the fence and got out of your "safe pasture"? You might get eaten by dangerous animals, or you might get caught in a thorn bush, or even fall off of a steep cliff. The fence helps you determine the "safe pasture," so you know where to go and where not to go. In the game of basketball, are their boundaries? What about football? God gives us boundaries in the game of life. I have a "news flash" for you--God has entrusted you to your parents or guardians, and you need to think of them as temporary shepherds or coaches until you are an adult. They provide a covering over you like an umbrella that keeps you safe and protected from the rain, the storms, and anything bad. Under that umbrella, you will find a "safe pasture."

The concept is simple. If you were allergic to peanuts and you knew you had to stay away from them, would you? Of course! Let's say you blew it and had a huge peanut butter sandwich, knowing full well that you shouldn't and you ended up having a horrible reaction. Could God rescue you? Yes! But first and foremost, did God give you a brain? So many bad consequences could be avoided if we just think about doing what is right! Trust God! Stay under the umbrella, dwell in the land of obedience and understand those fences are put in your life to keep you from harm. Enjoy the "safe pasture!"

My point is that chances are you will have consequences when you cross the boundaries. God strategically put them in your life. Staying under the covering of obedience with your parents is "staying in the safe pasture." As you delight yourself in the Lord, God will give you the desires of your heart! It is a Biblical principle.

> *Delight yourself in the LORD and he will give you the desires of your heart.*
>
> *Psalm 37:4*

And God will bless you with long life. But your part of the deal is to avoid the "unsafe" pasture. Stay in obedience!!! It is a Biblical principle. You need to stay in obedience and in the "safe pasture" if you want God's covering over your life.

One side note regarding obedience; obey with your actions and your heart. You will rob yourself from the blessing if your heart is not in the right place. This is a huge deal to God. He cannot stand grumbling or complaining. As you choose to obey your parents, ask God for His help to change your attitude.

This is God's promise: "If you are willing and obedient, you will eat the best from the land" (Isaiah 1:19).

Understanding Their Past

Understanding your parents' past can make a huge impact on your relationship. Your parents were actually teenagers once. How much do you really know about them? What made them laugh? What challenges did they have to overcome as teenagers? Was your dad a class president? Was he in the Navy? Did your mom leave home when she was young? Did they experience death? Did they experience heartache? Did they get good grades, or did they get in trouble for talking too much? Did they walk to grandma's house uphill for two hours in the snow?

Ask Questions and Get Answers; It Is Actually a Lot of Fun!

The way your parents were raised plays a huge role in the person they are today. So many parents fall back on what is natural or what they saw modeled before them: abuse, alcoholism, molestation, abandonment, the list goes on and on. These sins may have been in the family for years and the cycle keeps repeating itself over and over again. Maybe, the sin isn't as obvious as the ones I just mentioned; maybe, it is more like neglect, depression, fear, or secret sins that have carved a place in your family tree.

Sin Always Seeks Out a Victim!

When elephants are little babies, many zoo-keepers chain them to a pole. As the elephant grows up, the chain stays attached. Once the elephant becomes a mature adult, he doesn't realize that he is strong enough to break the chain (being attached to a chain was all the elephant ever knew). Sometimes, we humans are just like those elephants; we grew up being attached to a chain and we just don't realize that through Christ we have the power to break it. We settle for the same old surroundings, the same old tire to play with, and the same old gray cement when we could break free and experience a life we never imagined. If you want something different, then let it begin with you!

So how do you break that ugly, cold, heavy chain? The answer comes in two parts.

First Part—Destroying the Chain

Why did Jesus die on the cross? For your salvation! The Scripture also says that by His stripes you are healed! (Isaiah 53:5). So your healing is provided for you through Christ dying on the cross. Is it just physical healing? Sometimes, the deepest wounds are the ones you can't see. It is the wound of a broken heart and the pain of rejection. A broken arm can be very painful, but the majority of the pain is only located in the arm. The deep pain you have inside is at the very core of you, and it affects every part of your being.

You may have lived with years and years of rejection. Maybe those harsh words and the painful sting that used to affect you no longer hurt as bad anymore because there is a hardness that has formed much like a scab. Or maybe you would do anything to trade the silence for words; at least then you could deal with the truth.

I have not walked in your shoes and I don't know your situation, but what I do know is that God sacrificed His only Son on the cross so that by His stripes you could be healed. It is the ONLY way you can ever find healing. It is through the precious blood of Jesus! You can't find true healing any other way! You may look for it through guys, popularity, drugs and partying, but they will only be a temporary fix. It is like putting a Band-Aid on a gaping, infected wound. It will hide a little blood and stop the mess temporarily, but it will not deal with the wound.

Think of the blood of Jesus like a powerful acid that can dissolve the chain that has held you and your family captive. A little blood goes a long way. And the blood of Jesus will disinfect by cleansing out the wound. It is powerful and it will be a salve that will give you relief. In His salve, you will find peace, joy, and freedom like you have never experienced.

Yes, God wants to heal you! It can be an instantaneous miracle or it can be a process. Be honest with God and let Him into the dark and painful areas of your life.

Second Part—Shatter the Chain with Pure Blunt Force!

Think of forgiveness as a sledgehammer.

What is forgiveness? In a nutshell, it is letting go and giving the offense to God! He will gently show you how to let go of the hurt, the pain, and all the disappointment and give it to Him.

There are a number of obvious "signs" of bitterness and unforgiveness, but let me mention just a few. You know you need to forgive if…

It plagues your mind...you can't get the situation or the person out of your thoughts!

Your eyes narrow or your jaw sets....(this is actually described in the book of Proverbs).

You have an apathetic, numb, could care less feeling.

Is forgiveness excusing what happened? No way! You are not saying "Its okay – no big deal" but, instead, you are letting go of the offense. You are erasing the debt that the person who wronged you may never be capable of paying back.

Is forgiveness faking or pretending things are fine when they are not? No, but it will mean acting in faith at times when your emotions want to do the exact opposite. At times, we have to defy our emotions and put our feelings aside when it comes to forgiveness. We can only do that through faith, believing and trusting God with the outcome. Forgiveness is a choice, a decision!

Bear with each other and forgive whatever grievances you may have against one another. Forgive as the Lord forgave you. And over all these virtues put on love, which binds them all together in perfect unity.

Colossians 3:13-14

If you do not forgive, the offense will always be with you. It is amazing that people can say something to us and they forget it twenty minutes later and yet, we remember it twenty years later! Unforgiveness is like a bitter root which grows bigger and bigger inside of you, the longer you hold it inside you. And Jesus says that if you don't forgive others, you will not be forgiven.

Over and Over Again

How do you forgive on an ongoing basis? This is the hardest part when it comes to honoring your parents. It is hard and it takes determination, but you can do it! Even though serving the Lord can be "tuff" at times--honoring your parents, walking in forgiveness-it's all a part of loving God.

You are not going to be perfect until you get to heaven. It is an ongoing journey for all of us. You can go along and put on a show at least for awhile. But you cannot compartmentalize your life and withhold part of it from God. God wants all of you!

It is time you get mad, not at your parents, but at the devil who has held you and your parents captive way too long! The blood of Jesus is the liquid acid that will disintegrate and forgiveness is the sledgehammer that has the power to demolish. Either way you look at it, the chains that have held your family captive for years can be broken.

God wants to impact your life, your future, someday your children, and your children's children. Give God the hurts so that He can heal you and teach you to forgive. It is all about surrendering to God. You are growing up and building a new foundation, one without roots of bitterness and anger. It is within your power to decide the outcome. If you don't, you might as well weld that chain back together because you will never get free and that ugly sin that you hate so much will stay forever connected to you.

Don't Settle for So Little

My dad died in a car crash when I was 21 years old. Although I miss him a lot, I don't have any regrets. I made the most out of our relationship despite any of our differences. My dad knew just how much I loved him and I know that he loved me. So much of who I am is a result of the close relationship I had with my dad and his influence, and in that way he will always be a part of me. I am so thankful that I don't have to look back on our relationship with guilt or pain. I know so many girls that would do anything to turn back the hands of time for just one more chance to make it right. It is not too late. Make things right!

As for my mom, she is my very best friend! She has been there through the best and worst of times. She and the rest of my family worked through my dad's death together. My husband, Mark, officiated at the wedding when she remarried, 5 years later, to the most wonderful, Godly man! She has been a huge support to me as a mom, she is an awesome grandma, and we've worked side by side in ministry. She has been there for the birth of every child. Her life has been such an example and amazing testimony of who God really is. Although my dad did play a very important role in who I am, my mom has and still is playing a crucial role. I can't imagine for one moment that I was willing to risk losing her or the relationship I have with her!

Do most teens have a great relationship with their parents? Absolutely not! But the tools are in your hands and you can defy the odds and turn your relationship around. Learn to accept your mom or dad for who they are. Get to know their "love language" and try and understand their personalities and their past. Respect the boundaries that God has placed in your life and stay under the covering of your parents. Let God heal your hurts. Choose to forgive. Spread your wings of independence and become your own person. You can do it! Rise to the challenge of "honoring your parents."

Don't settle for so much less than God's best, especially when it comes to your parents. Yes, the Bible says, specifically, to honor your parents, but, throughout the Word of God it goes on to also say that there are blessings that come as a direct result of obedience. To me, one of the biggest blessings that can come from honoring your parents is discovering a whole new relationship that you never thought possible. God is growing you into something special. You may just change yourself in the process and find out that God did give you the perfect parents after all, perfectly fit for you!

"Honor your father and mother"-which is the first commandment with a promise- "that it may go well with you and that you may enjoy long life on the earth."

Ephesians 6:2,3

"My" Thoughts:

On a scale from 1(bad) to 10(good), how would you rate your relationship: with your mom? _____ with your dad? _____

Love Language...

How do you express your love? (Providing, gifts, hanging out, affection, words) _____
_____
_____
_____

What is your love language?_____
_____
_____
_____

Your mom's love language?_____
_____
_____
_____

Your dad's?_____
_____
_____

Communicating...

When it comes to communicating, do you express how you feel?

Are you a stuffer?_____Are you explosive?_____

When it comes to communicating, it is helpful hints to use words like "I feel" during your conversation. Don't attack the other person and try to avoid using words like "always" and "never".

For example, if trust is a problem:

You don't want to say: "You never trust me ...you are always on my case. I am sick of it. I am not that bad of a kid!"

Instead, you would say: "I am feeling like you don't trust me. What could I do to earn your trust?"

If you feel they are always nagging:

Instead of: "Give me a break! You are always telling me what to do and how to do it. You never stop!"

How about: "Mom or Dad ...I feel like I mess up all the time. Is there a way that you could point out the positive more often? I want to know when I am doing things right. Or, maybe if you want me to do things during the week, you could write them down instead of telling me."

> *Trust in the LORD and do good; dwell in the land and enjoy safe pasture (Psalm 37:3).*

In your own words, define "safe pasture":_____
_____
_____

Your dad says, "Stay away from Jon!"

Which option is the "safe pasture":_____

a. Dad doesn't get it ... Jon's cool. He does not know Jon like I do, Jon needs me and I will find a way to see him!

b. I really want to date Jon but I want to do what is right in God's eyes and obey my dad. I am going to be Jon's friend and maybe through time, and when I am 18, my dad will see Jon the way I do.

What could the consequences be for choosing letter a?_____
_____

What about b?_____
_____

Breaking the Chains...

Take some time and write down some of the sins that have carved a place in your family tree:_____

_____

_____

Do you want to be free? ___ End today's reflections with prayer. Give the hurts to God and ask God for His help. He longs to heal, restore, and break the chains in your life; let Him!

Dear God,

I come to You and I give you the hurt and the pain that I have held on to for so long. Take it from me! I don't want any part of it. When You died on the cross, the Bible says that by Your stripes (beating) I was healed. God, I claim that promise! I need You to heal me on the inside.

God, I also hold on to the promise found in Isaiah 63 that says You sent your Son, Jesus, to set me free, free from the chains that have held me and my family captive for so long. God, you desire to bind up my broken heart and release me from the prison of darkness. God, freedom is found only in and through You!

God, I thank You that You are my Father, God! I am Your daughter! You love me and cherish me. God, I lean on You! You are perfect and You can fill any void that is missing in my life.

I ask You to forgive me and help me to forgive those who have wronged me. God, with Your help I can walk in forgiveness. God, I forgive: _____.

God, I give You my future! I want Your freedom, Your covering and Your blessings over my marriage, my children, and their children. Thank You that as I trust in You, You have plans to prosper me; You desire to give me a hope and a future! Thank You for peace, happiness and freedom.

God, thank You for healing, forgiveness, and freedom! In Jesus' name I pray. Amen!

Love language comments based on information found in the book The 5 Love Languages by Gary Chapman (Copyright 2010 by Gary Chapman, published by Northfield Publishing, Chicago, IL).

If I had just Obeyed!

There I was at midnight, walking through a dark and secluded field with thick trees, and I was all alone, and nobody was around. Nobody, except for a creepy guy lurking in the distance! He seemed to get closer to me with every step I took.

I kept trying to convince myself it was okay to walk home alone. Even though, my mom's words kept echoing in my mind: "You can accept this job as long as you promise to find a ride home every night, no exceptions." This was the first night that I had disobeyed. I was so tired of bugging my friends for a ride. Good grief, this one time couldn't hurt. Or could it? I had promised my mom. Tonight, I broke my promise. I wondered if God would even hear my pathetic cry for help. Why should He? I lied and now, here I was, walking in disobedience at midnight with a strange guy closing in the distance between us.

If only I had obeyed! I wished I could turn back the hands of time! The guy seemed to be gaining on me. I didn't want to run, but I was getting scared and each minute seemed like hours. The apartment complex was now in my sight and, unfortunately, the guy was, too! I could see him clearly, and it made my stomach sick, and my pulse was pounding. I could even hear his footsteps! "God, help me!"

I silently repented and asked His help, "God.... I am so sorry! I need you to help me right now! I am scared to death. Forgive me! I should not have lied or disobeyed my mom. Please, God, make this guy disappear! God, help!!"

All of a sudden, a couple came out of their apartment in Building C. I breathed a sigh of relief. Safe at last! I turned around and, believe it or not, he was gone! "Thank you, God!"

Looking back, I realize the ending to the story could have been very different. I know God came through that night but what a scary wake-up call! I realized that, if I had obeyed my mom in the first place, I would have never been in that situation. Even if I didn't always agree, when I obeyed my parents, there was an automatic covering over my life. If I chose to disobey, I was taking a risk and, quite honestly, that experience made me think twice about chancing my life, my safety, and my future. From then on, I wanted to stay under the "umbrella" of obedience and have God's protection and blessing over my life! Ephesians 1:1-3—

Suzie

My dad died

My dad died. I miss him so much. I was only 10 years old when I first found out that he had cancer. I was devastated! How could this happen? He took treatments but they said there was no hope. He became bedridden and could only get up if someone was there to help him. I was too young to help in that way, however, I loved him so much, and so I did everything I could to be in his room, near him. I picked fresh flowers from our flower garden, arranged them in a jar and brought them to him; I combed his hair, rubbed his sore legs and spent hours reading books and the Bible to him.

He felt bad that he would be leaving us alone and wouldn't be there to take care of his family. He was worried how we could make ends meet without him. I'd hear him talk to my mom about bills and things, trying to figure everything out. Sometimes, I would come into the room and see that he had been crying. I would cry with him. I didn't want him to leave us either. He never complained about the pain, even though I knew he was hurting. My dad put on a show of bravery for us so we wouldn't feel so bad. But, I could feel his pain! I didn't want my dad to hurt or to die, but I didn't know how to stop it. I felt so bad! Sometimes, I thought I'd "cry my heart out"! The only way I could deal with my hurt and pain was to read the 23rd Psalm....I read it so much it became a part of me. I would go outside, crying so hard, holding my little dog, just praying and talking to Jesus. Some days, when I just couldn't handle it anymore, I would stay out there for hours until God's peace would comfort me and I could put on a smile and go back into his room.

After my dad died, I felt such a great loss. I felt deserted and all alone. I didn't want the special times, conversations, and hugs to go away. I had been my daddy's little girl. Now, here it was, my teenage years, he was gone. I really missed not having a Dad to be there for me; all my friends still had their dads. Now, things were different. Who would be there to give me advice, take me places? Aren't dads supposed to be around to protect their little girls? Who would make sure I dated the right boy and got home on time; who would walk me down the aisle? I needed my dad and he was gone! If I could just hear his voice, or see his smile just one more time...

I remember, at the funeral, I couldn't watch them lower my dad in the cold, dark grave. I had to look away. I didn't want people to watch me cry! Later, some-

one said, "The Lord gives and the Lord takes away." Well, I had accepted Jesus when I was seven and I thought, *Why would Jesus take my daddy away?* That bothered me for several years until someone explained to me that it is Satan who comes to kill, steal, and destroy. (John 10:10.) No, it wasn't God's fault my dad got cancer. God wouldn't have taken him away from me!

They say that time heals and for me it did take time for the pain to go away. I had good and bad days. But it helped knowing that my dad was saved and is in heaven now and he's not in pain anymore. I still miss him a lot, but I know that I'll see him again someday.

Something very interesting happened, after my dad died. I slowly started leaning on God in the same way I did my earthly father. I spent more time with God, asking Him for advice, spilling my guts out, sharing my greatest joys. I found a sweet and intimate relationship with God that I had never known before; and that Father/daughter relationship has stuck with me ever since!

I treasure the relationship I had with my earthly dad and I will never, ever forget him, but I am so thankful that God isn't a distant God, I am His daughter, and with Him by my side, I will make it in life. He truly has become my everything!

Marian

I Was Adopted

Some say "blood is thicker than water." Some say "blood is everything." Small-hearted people announce their truth as they see it.

As I listen, I hear "She's not really theirs, she's adopted."

".... yeah.... she's adopted!"

I feel like puking.

Words!

Guess those types of people will always be around.

The Bible I read proclaims Jesus' blood as the blood that is precious. First Peter 1:18 &19 says it is His precious blood that redeems us.

Yep, there will always be those other kinds of people...

Words!

They can hurt. They can cripple. They can tear and gnaw on you until your soul is ragged from the wear of the grinding.

Who was the dummy that said, "Sticks and stones will break my bones but words will never hurt me"?

Right.

Nine. So young...but not so young to not understand that I'm "different" because I'm adopted. At least "different" because "they" say I am. My hands tightly grasp my ears only because I can't grasp my heart. I run full force toward home. To the place I'm loved. To safety.

Some places just aren't safe, you know!

But home is safe. "You were chosen!"

"God blessed us with you. I'm so glad you are my daughter."

O.K., it's better now.

Thirteen. Who is she? She's probably not even alive anymore. Why? Why did she give me away? I wonder what she looks like. I wonder if she looks like me. I wonder if I got these weird toes from her. I wonder if she would like me if she knew me. I wonder if I am like her. She probably hates me; after all...she gave me away. What did I do? Was it my fault? Who's my dad? Did he love me?

I wonder. Somehow all this doesn't make sense to me. Craziness! One plus one is not making two. My friends don't get it...they have "their" parents. Tears roll off the curves of my face, each one dropping down into space like a candle being blown out never to find the flame again.

Sixteen. Today I feel like an alien. This skin...it came from nowhere. It looks like no one. I feel separate. Altogether different. All alone! Hum...yeah...I can see the resemblance of that girl over there and her mom. She looks just like her mom. Cool. I wonder if I look like my mom. I wonder if she feels like an alien, too.

I read truth. Scripture. He adopts.... He makes us sons. Words that bring life to a young heart. Words! Life! Sometimes I feel like He is breathing straight into my heart. Like I was taking my last breath, just struggling to get some air and then... it happens...and I'm revived. Sometimes only a bit. Bit by bit. Although sometimes too slow...yet steady.

Eighteen. Today I will meet her. Nervous is hardly the word. Perhaps scared stiff is the better way to describe this ball of nerves in the pit of my stomach. What should I wear? How should I do my hair? I wonder if she will like me...I wonder if I look like her...

I peek in the rearview mirror and look around. I'm too nervous to open the car door. I think I want to go home. This is probably a bad idea...oh, there's a lady...is that her? I stare in the rearview mirror until I can no longer see the lady passing in the car. I crank the mirror until it won't budge. Oh, I wonder if that's her! She looks nice. She's about my height. Her hair color is the same as mine. No. That's probably not her. Yeah, I think that might be her. Oh, my gosh...what if that's her? I look down. Straight down. What do I do? What now? I am sooo nervous. Oh, stop it! This is ridiculous! Quit shaking! It's no big deal. Just go in there and say "Hi." Just tell her your name. If it's her then she will probably be looking for me, and if it's not her...then she won't. O.K., I can do this. No, I can't.

I grab the front door handle that leads into the restaurant. O.K., just open the dumb thing!

"Hi. I'm Rebecca, are you...?"

Wow...we have the same curl in our hair. I have two brothers! I have a half sister! That's kinda neat.

O.K., I still think I look like an alien though. Everyone who sees the pictures says we look so much alike. It's hard for me to tell. I think when you have been an alien all your life, you just don't know what and who you look like. So, I'm an alien that has skin that came from another alien! So what's all this about blood anyway?

Twenties. I feel thankful for Mom and Dad. The others I love too, but more as a nice aunt and a nice uncle that you meet...ones that you didn't meet until you were older. Mom and Dad are Mom and Dad. That will never change. They are the ones who kissed my scraped knees...who cheered me on in sports...who plastered their walls with my artwork...who listened to my problems and put up with my attitudes.

Older. "Isn't that the most gorgeous baby you have ever seen?" My heart can barely hold all the love I have for my precious, newly adopted child. I feel like I could burst. "Mine...ours..." Can I ever hold more love in my heart for a child? I don't think so.

Four kids. One in heaven and 3 on earth. I start to tell a childhood story about the ones playing around my feet. Suddenly, I am caught off guard by my own words. I hear myself saying, "When I had..." I crack myself up as I hear myself say I "had" my adopted one! There is no difference.

Suddenly, in the quiet of my soul I hear Jesus speak..."I adopted you...out of My good pleasure and will. You are Mine. You are of My blood. You are My real daughter." (Ephesians 1:5.)

I belong. I am blood...and blood is everything. Yeah, Jesus' precious blood is everything.

I'm O.K. It's gonna be O.K.!

Rebecca

My parents don't go to Church

I remember when I was attending my student orientation at my Christian college; they were announcing that there would be a special lunch for the M.K.'s (missionaries' kids) and P.K.'s (pastors' kids). That is when I said to myself, "What about the H.K.'s (heathens' kids)? Where is our special lunch?"

Yes, I am an H.K. I was raised in a non-Christian home. You could just say that my parents' whole purpose in life was to make more money. My dad's family was Catholic, but he never devoted himself even to that. I guess you can say that my dad didn't really know what to believe when it came to God. My mom, also, had a religious background, more on the Presbyterian side. My mom would talk about God and the Bible but she never lived it.

During my childhood, we moved around to many places because of my dad's company that he worked with. At age 12, our final move would be to Sacramento, California. My parents had decided to put me in a Christian school in Sacramento because they heard that you could get a good education there. Little did they know that God had a plan for me to be at this Christian school. You see, at this school is where I learned about Jesus and the Bible. I also became friends with a great Christian girl, Becky, who would be my missionary as I was her mission. I will never forget when she told me that Jesus wanted to be my friend. Believe it or not, I never thought that Jesus wanted to be my friend. I started to hunger to know whom this Jesus was that she always told me about.

When I was 15 years old, my friend, Becky, had invited me to go with her to a Christian summer camp. My first thought was, *What do you do at a Christian camp?* I thought everyone would have to pray all day and do boring things. Boy, was I wrong! The first night that we were there, I saw all these young people my age worshipping God and loving it. After the message, the preacher gave an altar call and I was the first to go up. Or, should I say, "run up"! Let me explain the "run up" part. Like I said earlier, I was raised in a non-Christian home. However, there was no divorce, poverty nor drugs in my family. We were wealthy and would probably be considered an "All American Family." However, I was never close to my dad and had never even had a hug from him or even a little "I love you". There was no joy in our house, and I was always feeling like there must be more to life than this. I became depressed as a teenager and even wanted to give up on life. I guess you

can say when you have everything materially; you have the question of "If I have everything, why do I still feel the need for more of something else?"

(Hint: no matter how much you have, if you don't have Jesus Christ, you have nothing!)

So I kept searching for that "something". I searched in sports, friends, even into some demonic things. So by the time I came to the Christian camp, I was thirsty for that "something" that I had been searching for but still had not found. That is why I ran up to the altar and said, "God if You are real I want all of You and I will give You all of me". At that moment, God's presence was so strong! I think I cried the whole night. God showed up! I was called into the ministry and baptized in the Holy Spirit (spoke in tongues). Or, you could just say that, at age 15 during a Christian camp, my empty cup was filled and my thirsty soul finally quenched. That "Something" was finally found!

Camp was over and now, the reality of going home was real! As a Christian living in a non-Christian home, my parents didn't understand my new convictions, way of life and the passion and fire that I had for Jesus. My parents, for a while, even thought that I was in a cult.

God had spoken to me at summer camp that I was called to full- time ministry to preach the gospel; my heart burned to do just that. I had a very hard time trying to tell my parents (who thought that money was everything) that I was called to preach the gospel. I, also, had to explain how I wanted to go to a Bible college and not a big university. When I eventually told them, they were upset and thought that I was wasting my life away and would never make money. They did not support my decision, but God did. I kept reminding myself that I had to realize that they just didn't understand.

Not only was living in a non-Christian home frustrating and hard, but, also, it was definitely lonely. I know what it was like to go to church every Sunday, alone. I'd invite my parents to come but each time they had an excuse.

To live in a non-Christian home is a very hard thing, however, if you are reading this and you are, also, the only Christian in your family, I want to encourage you. Yes, it is very hard to be the only Christian in your home, but God will always give you the strength to make it (1 Peter 5:10). Instead of seeing your family and your situation as a bad thing, start seeing it as a good thing. Look at your family as God's tool to refine you for His purpose in your life. Having them in your life challenges you to be even closer to God and to live a life of character. You can preach to your family as much as you can, but it is your actions and lifestyle that preach the most.

Remember this, your life is your pulpit! I knew that my family watched every move I made to see if what I was saying was real. This was a blessing for me because it taught me that my actions do speak louder than my words. My home life taught me the importance of always living what you preach and believe. Even to this day, I will not preach on something that I do not do.

The other thing about being the only Christian in my home was the fact that I didn't have the encouragement of a Christian parent telling me to love God, stay pure, do right, etc. Although that was something that I desired to have in my parents, it was actually a "blessing in disguise" to not have it. The blessing was that I had to learn early how to lean on the Lord! I believe that my relationship with the Lord, from the age 15 and on, was so strong because of my family situation. I had to turn to God and learn from Him and Him alone! He literally was my parent, instructor and encourager. I had to learn how to hear the voice of God just to make it through every day. I know that being the only Christian in my family has brought me to an intimate and personal every day relationship with Jesus. He was and is all that I have, and I am so grateful for that.

One last thing I want to mention that is so important to your walk with the Lord, is going to church. You need to pray for God to lead you to a church that preaches God's Word and will be your Christian family, support and encouragement. Join a ministry where you can meet friends and even get involved in leadership, etc. Surround yourself with Christians who can help you out and give you the support that you need. I joined my youth ministry and became a leader in the ministry. Every time the church had something going on, I was there. I wanted to be in the environment of Christians. Don't isolate yourself because you need all the Christians in your life that you can get. Now, years later, I'm still close to my Christian friends that were in youth group with me. Remember God uses people in our lives to give us strength, wisdom and encouragement. So, pray for God to lead you a church to provide lifelong godly friends.

So, what about us H.K.'s? Well, we may not get a special lunch at our college student orientation, but we can know that we have a special God who loves us in a special way. You matter to God, so hang in there and know that God is with

you ALL the days of your life. Read my favorite Psalm—Psalm 139. I have kept this Psalm in my heart, because the more that I realized how much God loved me, the more I knew that He was there with me in my family situation.

Jamie

Section V

"Did you hear her latest blog? Unbelievable!"

"How can I find a true friend?"

Get CONNECTED…the FRIENDS plan

Chicas? "Hangin with the PEEPS."

"…does anyone really care…"

Searching for a best friend

As I was beginning to start school this year, I thought I was going to have a blast with my friends. One of my best friends was coming back to school and I couldn't wait to hang out with her again. I thought that this was going to be such a great year, and my friends and I were going to have tons of fun together. Well, I was wrong. The friend drama started right away. Friends started getting jealous of the time I spent with other friends, people were sharing my secrets, and it seemed like someone was mad at me most of the time.

I felt so lonely and wanted a true friend so badly! Proverbs 25:19 says, "A friend you can't trust in times of trouble is like having a toothache or a sore foot" (CEV). I talked to my parents and to God. I prayed for a long time and asked God to send me a friend I could finally trust. I also prayed that my other friends would stop being so angry and rude. It took longer than I wanted it to, but He answered my prayers. Now, I have more than one friend that I can trust, and my other friends stopped being so angry with me. I'm still pretty careful about what I tell and I try to divide my time between friends. I tried to take what I could from what they said and disregard the rest.

There are a few things I discovered that helped me get through trouble with my friends: I kept a diary or a prayer journal. It gave me a chance to let out what I was feeling. It helped me so much. Sometimes we say things because we are mad. However, I could express my true feelings and discuss them with God in a journal. It was private, so if I said something harsh and later had regrets, I hadn't burned any bridges. Just make sure you hide that journal from your little brother!

I talked to my parents and youth pastor. I couldn't keep it bottled up inside! I'd ask them for advice or tell them my private thoughts. I knew I could trust them not to share my secrets. They gave me good advice, too, because they've been down this road already. Proverbs 17:17 says, "A friend is always a friend, and relatives are born to share our troubles" (CEV).

I talked to God. Sometimes it can feel like God isn't there and that He can't hear you, but I promise you He is listening and He cares for you deeply. He loves us so much. He listens and cares about us. It may take longer than you want it to, but don't give up! He will come through.

I didn't tell my secrets! I know we are girls and it is difficult, but you have to realize that people tell secrets. Again, people tell! I'll put it this way, if you have friends who are telling other people's secrets, most likely they are telling your secrets. Know anyone like that? I do. I learned not to tell them anything. Don't tell anyone stuff that you wouldn't want others to know. As soon as you tell, you no longer have control of the information! Proverbs 11:13 says, "A gossip tells everything, but a true friend will keep a secret" (CEV).

I realized that hurting people, hurt people. Sometimes friends say mean things just to hurt us. However, I understand that people often react out of their own pain. When I really began to look at people's lives, I realized that many of them had insecurities, unhappiness, and self-hate. It helps me to understand that I can just take people as they are, be nice, but don't get too close to them. I try to protect myself and my feelings by recognizing who they really are.

I looked for new friends. I began to search for people who seemed to be people of great character. I don't hang out with people who are mean to other people. It could be just a matter of time before they turn and are mean to me.

Now, it's time to take charge and take action! Don't wait for good friends to come to you. You have to go to them. If someone is sitting alone, go talk to them. Romans 12:15-16 says, "Be friendly with everyone. Don't be proud and feel that you are smarter than others. Make friends with ordinary people" (CEV). Maybe they are lonely too. It can't hurt to try. What have you got to lose . . . other than some bad friendships?

chapter 7

FRIENDS
Jamie Aleman

What is your definition of a friend? Here are some definitions that you might find interesting:

A small boy defined a friend as "Someone who knows all about you and likes you just the same."

Aristotle defined friendship as a single soul dwelling in two bodies.

Raymond Beran defined a friend as someone you can weep with, sing with, laugh with, and pray with. "Through it all—and underneath—he sees, knows, and loves you. A friend? What is a friend? Just one, I repeat, with whom you dare to be yourself."

The dictionary defines a friend as an intimate companion or associate: one attached to another by affection or esteem.

What Is a Friend, Anyway?

I am sure your definition of a friend is just as good as the definitions I just mentioned. The truth of the matter is that, no matter what your definition of a friend may be, friends are a very important part of your life on a day-to-day basis. Did you know that friends are so important in your life that having or not having friends can even affect your health? I know of a study that supports this claim.

Check this out: Leonard Syme, a professor of epidemiology at the University of California, at Berkley, explains just how important being "social" is. Having close social, cultural, and traditional ties can affect your health and disease rate! He said Japan is number one in the world due to these facts. The more isolated you are, the poorer the health, and the higher the death rate. In a nutshell, this professor is saying, friends will cause you to live life longer and healthier! Yikes…have you been feeling sick lately?

Did you know that you have a Creator who has placed in you the desire to have friends and the desire not to be alone? "The Lord God said, 'It is not good for the man to be alone. I will make a helper suitable for him'" (Genesis 2:18). God knows that you need helpers in your life and that it is not good for you to be alone, emotionally and physically. Although this scripture is in a marriage context, as you read the New Testament, you will find that Jesus talks a lot about friendships. I challenge you to look through the Bible and see how many times the words "friends" or "friendships" are mentioned. If you think about it, from the beginning of Genesis to Revelation, God has always been longing for friendships with His people - from the time of Adam, to you and me today. God was and is still longing for friendships!

God so desired to have a friendship with us that he gave His only Son, to die a horrible death on a cruel cross, to restore the friendship that was lost in the Garden of Eden.

> (Jesus said) Greater love has no one than this, that he lay down his life for his friends. You are my friends if you do what I command… I have called you friends…
>
> John 15:13-15

Since you have a creator who desires friendships, and you are created in His Image and likeness, you, too have that same desire. Friendships are very important to God, and to us.

A Few Good Friends?

It is reported that Howard Hughes, when worth approximately four billion dollars, said, "I'd give it all for one good friend."

Wow, that tells you that a good friend is priceless! I remember when I was at college and I was talking to one of my professors about my friends, and about how many of them had been falling away from the Lord. I will never forget what she told me. She said that in most people's lifetime, they will only be able to count on one hand, their "true" good friends. When she told me that, I thought, *No way! I have so many friends that I have known forever; I will have to use my toes, too.* The truth was, I had a lot of acquaintances, but when it came to true, loyal, and committed friendships, I only needed one hand. Good friendships are very rare! Stick out your hand; how many "true" friends can you count on your fingers?

Since good friendships are so rare, what makes them so special? When we have friendships with people who do not live Christ-centered lives, the cords that attach us are usually partying, sin, jealousy, gossip, backstabbing, etc. But, when we have friendships with God's people, the cords usually are made up of love. I believe that a good friendship is, in a way, like God's love attaching each of us to each other.

> *Love is patient, love is kind. It does not envy, it does not boast, it is not proud. It is not rude, it is not self seeking, it is not easily angered, it keeps no record of wrongs. Love does not delight in evil but rejoices with the truth. It always protects, always trusts, always hopes, always and perseveres. Love never fails.*
>
> 1 Corinthians 13:4-8

A good friend is priceless and, I believe, God-given. I have a best friend that I have known for 12 years now. We have had our times of wanting to kill each other (well, not really), but for the most part we have each other's back. I will tell her things that I see in her life that need to be changed, and she does the same for me. We have held each other accountable to live a life of character and Godliness. I have to approve of her husband (not yet found), and she did approve of mine (found). Even to this day, we still keep in touch. Even though I now have my wonderful husband in my life, I'm telling you, there is still nothing like a girlfriend to talk to and lean on. Can I give you a quick golden nugget about life? When you get married, your husband will not want to talk "about whatever" for ten hours on the couch. Men just were not created to talk that long—but girls were! So, hold on to your God-given girlfriends, even when you find Mr. Right, because he will not be able to meet your ten-hour conversational need-to-talk! Hold on to your God given friends and treat them with love. Remember, "Love never fails."

Bad Friends Will Bring You Down and Keep You There!

Two men were out hunting in the northern U.S. when, suddenly, one yelled and the other looked up to see a grizzly charging towards them. The first man started to frantically put on his tennis shoes; his friend, noticing, yelled, "What are you doing? Don't you know you can't outrun a grizzly bear?" The first man hollered back, "I don't have to outrun a grizzly. I just have to outrun you!"

"I would rather have speeches that are true than those which contain merely nice distinctions. Just as I would rather have friends who are wise than merely those who are handsome."[1] Of course, there is the good and the bad in everything. Even though you desire friendships, you have to make sure that the friendship is not bad for you! Take food for example. We all desire and need it physically and emotionally, but there are some things in the food category that are bad for you. Friendships are the same; there are some friends in the friendship category that you just need to stay away from.

I love the typical reaction I get when I warn my youth group about staying away from close friendships with non-believers: I always hear them say, "Didn't Jesus hang out with the sinners and become their friends?" Jesus was known as a friend of tax collectors and sinners. However, as I recall, Jesus never sinned! His purpose for hanging out with the tax collectors and sinners was not to be like them but to save them, not to do what they did, but to change how they lived.

I was a Christian throughout high school. It was funny how the Christians would hang out together during every lunch in their little circle. I, on the other hand, chose to hang out with the unbelievers. During lunch, I would read my Bible on a bench and talk to the

---

[1]Augustine, quoted by Richard Baxter, *The Reformed Preacher.* (Vancouver: Regent College Publishing, 2001.)

students about how much God loved them. My lunch times became my evangelism times (read Matthew 9:10-13).

I bet the Christians in that little circle probably thought that I was compromising, hanging out with the "sinners." However, I would hang out with the sinners to reach them, not to imitate them. God has called you to reach the lost, not to become like the lost.

Who Is in Your Circle of Friends?

Think about it. If the dictionary defines the word "friend" as an intimate companion or associate; one attached to another by affection or esteem, then this "friendship thing" should be very serious to you. My question to you is, whom are you attached to? Remember, whatever you are attached to, it is also attached to you. Have you ever heard people say, "Your friends are who you are"? Why? Because friendship is an attachment! Everything your friends believe or do, most likely you will also believe and do. Sometimes you see friends who are so attached to each other that they wear the same things and even start looking alike. They are sort of like twins who are attached at birth that never separate, whatever one of the twins does, the other one does.

A bad friend can cause you to sin against your God, compromise the call of God on your life, and corrupt your good character.

> *Do not be misled: Bad company corrupts good character.*
> *1 Corinthians 15:33*

> *Blessed is the man who does not walk in the counsel of the wicked or stand in the way of sinners or sit in the seat of mockers. But his delight is in the law of the Lord, and on his law he meditates day and night.*
> *Psalm 1:1-2*

We need to love sinners, but hate the sin. I am in no way telling you to cut off all of your non-Christian friendships. And I am not saying to ignore these friends, avoid them, or treat them in a rude way. But what I, and the Word of God, says is to avoid close friendships with the world. Your non-Christian friends should be your mission field. Your Christian friends should be your fellow missionaries who encourage you to live a life of character and Godliness, and help you fulfill the calling of God on your life, to reach this world for Jesus.

Pursue Christ-Centered Friendships!

"Once I told my old man, 'Nobody likes me.' He said, 'Don't say that—everybody hasn't met you yet.'"

Rodney Dangerfield

I want to start this section by talking to those of you who feel like you don't have any friends. I have been working in youth ministry for about fourteen years. One of the things that I have noticed is that in every youth group there is usually that one person who is always sitting alone. When seeing these people, I would go up to them and love on them, and so would some of the youth; however, they didn't respond and didn't seem to want to talk to or sit with us, so, it was kind of hard to reach out to them. If you are one of these people, I want to give you some advice; if you want friends, then you need to be a friend! If you are reading this and you are always saying to yourself, I have no friends, everybody hates me, nobody talks to me, etc., have you ever thought that maybe people are freaked out that you might reject them when they are reaching out to you? You see, friendship is a two-way thing. If you never open up to people by even saying a little, "Hi!" then why expect people to open up to you? Please pray for God to give you boldness to make friends and direct you to the right friends.

Remember, God is good and wants to bless you with great Christian friends, but it is time that you stop looking down on yourself and stop singing that 'loner song' in your head, all day long. Start reaching out to people. I dare you to say, "Hi!" and smile at five people in your youth group or at school, and just see how they respond. I am sure you will get a better response than just sitting there and saying nothing. Remember:

I can do all things through Christ who strengthens me.

Philippians 4:13

If you want friends, you must reach out and be a friend!

Take a Look in the Mirror!

Yes, it is your choice what kind of friends you will have or if you even want to reach out and make friends, but it is also your choice what kind of friend you will be! We have talked about what a bad and good friend is, but I want to ask you a question–What kind of friend are you? Earlier I asked–What is your definition of a friend? Whatever your definition is–that is what you should be! When I ask young girls what they want in a husband, they whip out their long lists and begin to describe their "prince charming": a man of character who loves them, adores them, reads his Bible every day, prays all the time, never cheats on them, etc. I could keep going on but it would take too long. I am sure that you have your long list as well. After an hour of hearing their lists, I love to look at them and say, "Keep that list because everything that you want him to be to you, is what you need to be to him! Every time I say that, my girls give me a look that says, *Oh, no! I have to read my Word, pray every day, and become a woman of character.* See! It is different when the roles change.

The same principle applies when you define what a friend is. I am sure you think of all the things that you desire for someone to be for you. So keep your definition of what a friend is and make it your goal to become that definition to someone else. The Bible says to treat others as you would want to be treated. Would you want your friends to gossip about you? Then don't gossip about them! Do you want someone to listen to you and stay loyal to you, no matter how "tuff" life gets? Become a good listener and be an encouragement in their lives. Pray that Jesus helps you to be a Godly friend! Just like Michael W. Smith's sang "Friends are friends forever, when the Lord is the Lord of them," remember to always find friends that love God and let that be the bond that connects you to your friends!

We know that God wired us to desire friendships. Not only are they important to us emotionally, but physically as well. It is your choice what kind of friendships you will have and whether or not you want to reach out and make friends. It is also your choice what kind of friend you will be. Always remember to put God in the center of your friendships, so that they will last. Whatever you do, don't let your name appear on someone's "bad friends list," in fact, let it be just the opposite; become one of the friends that can be counted on just one hand!

"My" Thoughts:

How do you define the word "friend"?_____
_____
_____
_____

The Bible is full of scriptures on friendships. Read these two scriptures and then write them down in your own words.

"Wounds from a friend can be trusted, but an enemy multiplies kisses." (Proverbs 27:6 ⋮⋮)_____
_____
_____
_____

"A perverse man stirs up dissension, and a gossip separates close friends. A violent man entices his neighbor and leads him down a path that is not good." (Proverbs 16:28-29 ⋮⋮)_____
_____
_____
_____

What type of friends do you have? Rate your friends with this simple "FRIEND TEST":

Do they influence you in a positive way?_____

Do they challenge you to be more like Jesus?_____

Do they support the vision and the calling God has on your life?_____

Do they listen to you and give you Godly advice?_____

Do they cause you to sin against your God?_____

Does their influence compromise your calling and purpose in life?
_____

Do they hinder you from living a Godly life? _____

Do they gossip, criticize, or make fun of you?_____

Do they focus more on themselves?_____

The first four answers should be "yes," and the last five should be "no." Take your time and answer these questions honestly, this will reveal a lot about your friendships!

Now, let's twist it around just a little. Take the test again, but this time rate yourself as a friend!

Personal Challenge:

Become the type of friend that someone can count on just one hand!

The Bigger Picture

When I was in high school, I loved God! I went to church and I was pretty involved in my youth group. There were times I was tempted to make bad choices - you know, hanging with the wrong crowd, watching bad movies, going to parties, or getting together with the wrong guy. One of the biggest things that kept me from it all was when I looked at the bigger picture.

You see, when I looked at the "bigger picture", my friends were there with me. Maybe I could handle one or two beers, but my friend might be introduced to a life-long addiction. If I brought a friend to a party, they could end up loving that whole partying scene, hooking up with the wrong guy, getting drunk or doing drugs. If I went to bad movies or listened to crude music, what kind of example would I be setting? I didn't want to be a stumbling block to my friends!

I remember one of my best friends showing up drunk (for the first time) to her sweet-sixteenth birthday party. Some kids in my youth group had gotten her drunk. I can't tell you how much it hurt me; it was as if someone stabbed me right in the heart. I loved her and cared about her so much! The saddest part of all was from then on, her life plunged downward!

At times, it was pretty overwhelming when I realized just how important my words and actions were. I was far from perfect but I made it a priority to make a difference and to influence my friends to love and serve Jesus Christ. There was sadness over the loss of some of my closest friends, lonely times, and a lot of rude remarks when I wouldn't go with the flow. But I had a 'blast' going on youth events, mission trips, and doing fun and crazy things that didn't involve bad choices. Whenever my friends needed someone they could trust; they always called me. Looking back, I am so thankful that God opened my eyes to the "bigger picture". I have to say, the biggest reward of all was knowing that in my heart of hearts, I was being an encouragement, making a difference in those around me, and really being a true, Godly friend!

Suzie

'forever friends', yeah right!

"Friends forever," that's what we were supposed to be. On November 12, 2006, I found out just how long forever would last. I won't exactly go into detail about what happened that day, but what I learned from it will forever change my outlook on friends.

I and my two best friends were like the "three musketeers." It had always been that way since freshman year. We did everything together. Each was a member of the other's family. If one of us got in trouble, we all got in trouble. We were more than friends, we were family. But like in any family, we had our own set of problems. One of us was an alcoholic and a prescription drug abuser, the other a constant target for stupid guys and all their drama, and the other, well, the other was too scared to speak up for herself and tiptoed around everyone else.

Our friendship had been through a lot of ups and downs. We'd been through boyfriends who didn't know how to treat us right, family issues that all of us had become involved in, and the constant fog of trash talking behind each others' backs. Our friendship was a ticking time-bomb that was well overdue for detonation. After some point, we all got fed up with what was going on and exploded. I guess after spending every day for 3 years with someone, tensions are bound to be built up.

In the weeks leading up to our explosion, my youth pastor had been talking about friendships. I had always listened to what he said, but only after our time bomb had run out of time did I *really* listen to what he had to say. I mean, it wasn't like I had never heard what he had to say before. I had heard the same message countless times from other youth pastors, head pastors, my teachers, my parents; I'd even heard the same message on TV. His words didn't mean much to me back then, but, looking back, I know God meant that series for me and my search for good friends.

The first time my pastor began talking about the meaning of friends, I knew that the friendships that I had with my two best friends weren't exactly the greatest, most positive relationships possible. I had been having some problems with one of my friends in the previous months and wanted to stop being her friend, but just couldn't bring myself to do it. I had slowly come to see that hanging around her didn't make me happy anymore; I always felt like I was being dragged

down every time she talked to me. But, because we had been through so much together, I thought that she'd take it the wrong way. I'd be made out to look like a horrible friend if I decided to break off our relationship.

As I continued to listen to my pastor's Wednesday night messages, I felt like something was tugging at my heart and my soul, but I refused to listen. I refused to listen to God when He was trying to talk to me, when I knew the situation was only getting worse between the two of us. One day, my problems all came to the surface and exploded.

Sunday, November 12, 2006, was the day I ran into that "brick wall." We all got into some trouble and decided to cover-up for ourselves; we'd lie about it, and nobody would find out. I went along with the lies for a while, but I knew what I was doing was wrong and that if we were found out, things would only get worse, so I "fessed up." I knew it was the right thing to do, and I thought that my friends would follow my example, but they didn't. Instead, they continued to lie about what had occurred. The next day, one of them told me that I had "dogged her out" and to her that wasn't a true friend. She told me to stay away from her and pretty much tried to have everyone that we knew disown me. I stuck by the truth, and when asked about what happened, I told the truth regardless of whether the person believed me or not. I soon came to realize that by my telling the truth and maintaining my dignity, people around me began to respect me more. Even those who didn't like me let go of their grudges against me and became closer to me.

Since then, I have found better, more uplifting friends to surround myself with. Friends that I once took advantage of, put on hold, or disliked because of my old friends' influence, have now become my best friends. Kids in my youth group who back then I would have never associated myself with, are now like family.

It took a lot for me to see what God wanted for me. I was headed down a path of destruction, but only by His grace was I saved. A lot happened over the past 3 years with my friends, the "three musketeers", but I learned an immense amount from the situation. I just wish I had listened to God way before I ran into that "brick wall!"

Section VI

"He's no Romeo!"

"…Is he my hottie or best bud?"

FROM boyz 2 MEN

"How FAR is too far?"

"Should I date him?"

Myspace Blog: Sex Talk
Current Mood: Contemplative;
as so very often it is.

This subject comes up like 22 million times a day at school, no lie! We've been having these amazing cheer devotions that are like completely eye opening, and sometimes I walk away from them completely blown away. There is just so much that I've never known.

So, the other day our coach was talking about what a virgin really is. A virgin is someone who is pure in every way. This meaning that they've never even come close to having sex. It's not just the physical act but all the thoughts, actions, etc., that go along with it. Hearing all of this made my head spin. I was so disappointed in myself because I had been completely oblivious to it all. My commitment to myself and God is to be a virgin when I get married, but it is so much more than just a commitment to not have actual intercourse.

Did you know that sex is anything that arouses a sexual desire? It could be even just as simple as trying to be sexy. But did you know that to be "sexy" is actually to be "sex-worthy". That is something that nearly every girl tries to be. Speaking from experience (being as how I am a girl), I've always wanted guys to think I'm beautiful, sexy, stunning, all the above. I'll just say it. I know that it's something every girl wants. It's a feeling of acceptance. It was just a shock to think that my actions, despite my belief in their innocence, really weren't so innocent after all.

I don't know, I guess this is just something I wanted to share because my eyes have been opened. Even though I have been raised in a Christian home and have been educated in a Christian school, some things have just been expected to be understood. I want to be able to speak to those of you who haven't heard. To be sexually pure is more than just not having intercourse. It is about carrying yourself in a way that is righteous and holy, in every aspect. My mother always says to set yourself up for success, not failure. The next time you have to make a decision that has a potential to turn into a compromising situation, do yourself a favor and bypass it altogether. The best way to keep from disaster is to avoid the situations to begin with.

Britni

chapter 8

ROMANCE

Heidi Bents

Everyone loves romance, especially us girls! Have you ever thought about why we do? For one thing, love truly does make the "world go round," right? Whether you have your heart set on some lucky guy right now or not, let's face it, someday soon there's going to be a certain someone who captures your heart. If you're a girl, living and breathing, which you are because you are reading this book, you have noticed a boy or two along the way, right? Guys kind of have a way of catching our attention and taking up some of our mental space. Isn't that what we girls are best at talking about? The minute someone pays special attention to you, says, or does something nice, maybe calls your cell or posts a comment on your blog, isn't that what makes front page news with your girlfriends? Usually the first thing you do is share what's going on with your best friend. However you get in touch with your friends, text, blog, email or actually have a conversation (imagine), boys are a hot topic!

There are those healthy crushes that we all go through, sometimes as quickly as football season is over. Or, what about the new and improved hottie who, before summer break, was just a pesky little dork or the cute guy whose locker is just down the hall - you make sure there are lots of reasons to stop by. Or, maybe you've noticed someone where you work and your brain moves to overdrive when he's on your shift. Then, there's that special someone who comes along and just makes life seem all good. Somehow, he lights up your world, makes your heart skip a beat, gives you butterflies, and, for once, you start to dream about a future with him in it. To us, guys are an inspiration to be infatuated with, to be admired by, adored, and above all, loved.

Why does this happen? What is it about guys and romance that makes our hearts tick? Volumes of books have been written—fairy tales, both fact and fiction, stacking as high as Heaven regarding the mysteries of love and romance. Every culture, every religion, from philosophers to scientists—since the beginning of time—reveals their thoughts, feelings and grand exposés about this complicated, mysterious condition.

The truth of the matter is, in the dreamiest dream of every girl, there is something deep within our souls, a secret longing, to experience a love beyond the extraordinary. When you think about it, isn't it the near tragic "hang-on-to-the-edge-of-your-seat" kind of fantastic love stories that inspire us the most? Doesn't your heart just melt when a hero comes on the scene, one who is courageous, valiant, and willing to risk everything, even death, to save the love of his life? We admire sweet acts of kindness, the thought of another giving up part of himself to save something precious to him. We are refreshed when we hear stories or witness events like this because we want our own lives to be meaningful and defined. We want to be worthy of such a love. Just a peek at recent box office ratings reveals what we as ladies are hungry for—chick flicks! And it's okay to admit it. We become captivated by movies on the big screen that tug at our deepest emotions. Some of the best in recent past are movies such as *A Walk to Remember, The Glass House, Diary of a Mad Black Woman,* and *Ever After* because here you see a glimpse of love that is larger than life. With all that wraps us up as "female," (and true to our heart of hearts), we desire, we seek, and even need to experience true love in our lives.

The Perfect Fairy Tale

The best of all love stories holds the common thread of suspense. Who are the players and whose story will captivate us? Is there a plot of good-versus-evil? Will the two characters we're cheering for discover each other and fall in love? One element of a fantastic love story that intrigues us the most includes someone's dream that is in danger of being dashed. Perhaps the heroine faces a dire and impossible circumstance, or holds a dark secret that could do her future great harm. Maybe there's a deceitful, cunning character whose interests are only for himself and who poses a great threat to the heroine's dreams. We're captivated by a story where love takes flight between the heroine and her lover; we reach for tissue when the relationship blossoms into a full-fledged romance. Our hopes are dashed when things turn sour and something causes the lovers to go their separate ways; our hope rises again when tragedy causes our damsel-in-distress to cry out for her lost love. In the end, no dynamic love story would be complete without the larger-than-life hero emerging: her tender-hearted lover who comes valiantly on the scene to rescue the one who holds his heart. A Prince taking charge, he conquers the Evil Villain by foiling his plans, and rescues his future Queen. Tragedy turns to triumph! Of course, they always live "happily-ever-after," right? Followed by "The End," and we see the happy couple riding off into the sunset, headed for their fabulously romantic future together. So, does the story really end there, or is it just the beginning?

We All Dream of a Fairy Tale Romance

Are our fantasies of great love a valid part of our truest desires? Why is it that every female dreams of this adventurous "fairy tale" romance? All of us have a dream for our own lives. As we become aware that there's a future yet to be lived, we are filled with suspense, wondering when things will happen, and how. Who will be the lucky guy? Will I be the lucky girl? Who will win my heart and loyalty, and have I met him yet? Will I meet him at school, work, or wherever my career takes me? How will he propose, and what will my engagement ring look like? Will we have a storybook wedding and will I make a beautiful bride? Will we go on the honeymoon of our dreams? Where will we live, and what jobs will we take? How many children will we have, and who will they look like? What will we make of our story, and will I be happy living in it? Most importantly, will I like the ending?

So often, we spend our childhood looking forward to being all grown-up, and we spend our teen years testing out our ability to take flight into an unknown future. We spend our adult life looking back at our childhood dreams, wondering if we've really achieved them. Do we measure up to our expectations or has life brought us unexpected blows?

There is great news to the answer of all these questions! God Himself is the maker and holder of ALL our dreams! He breathes into each of us the desires of our hearts, and He longs for us to trust Him to fulfill them in His good timing. We never really stop dreaming or hoping about our futures. Once God fulfills one dream, He allows us to have other dreams that He's planted in us to grow, and give birth to. He is the "Author of Love," He is Love, and most of all, He loves us! He creates each of us with a completely unique design, and your story, and my story, will amazingly be "one-of-a-kind!"

He crafted your life apart from any other, and He has perfectly crafted the life of another to complete your own some day. Part of recognizing our "perfect match" is in discovering more about what God planted within us from the beginning. And so, to find a love worth waiting for, we must seek out those hidden dreams and treasures within ourselves first.

Since we are the stars in our own "fairy tale" adventure, let's take a look at understanding ourselves, "The Princesses." As Princesses, it is true to say that our most defining moments are those in which we choose to give our love away. What does that mean? Whom we choose to love and build relationships with has a great deal to do with how we feel about and value ourselves. From choosing our closest friends to the guy we pick out of the crowd, it all says much about our self-reflection.

God has given us special abilities and insights that can be lost if we're unaware they exist. Whether we feel we play a great role as "Princesses" or not, does not change the fact that God has created us to wear a crown! Keep an open mind as we journey together through some of the greatest love story classics of times past.

Beauty and the Beast

Hopefully, you are one of our readers fortunate enough to have read these stories for yourself, but more likely, you may have grown up watching these via the fantastic imagination of Walt Disney.

Take a look at "Beauty and the Beast." Out of true love for her old, crazy father, Beauty goes to his rescue at the Beast's castle and takes her father's place as prisoner. In the course of her stay, she begins to see past the beastliness of her captor, and this gives the Beast hope that he can change. Beauty saw some "bit of goodness" that she fell in love with, her love broke the cursed spell, and a handsome Prince emerged!

Now, before you get your hopes too high, remember that this is a fairy tale! Let's focus in on Beauty. This tale reveals a Princess's ability to make tremendous personal sacrifice for those she loves, even if there's little in it for her. A true Princess is also able to look past the exteriors of others and see into the heart, sometimes only to hang-on to the one good thing they possess. This is truly a gift. A Princess will often place much higher value on the integrity and inner character of her Prince than what his appearance may afford. And, it is wise to remember as well, that "beauty is only skin deep!" The basic moral of the story here is, that in many ways, a Princess will truly give up her life for the sake of those she cherishes.

Cinderella

What about Cinderella's story? Cinderella maintained her integrity and character even after she lost all she loved to a wicked stepmother and two very mean, selfish stepsisters. She served them with a humble spirit and a kind heart. Keeping her own dreams close to her heart, she bade her time serving the undeserved dreams of others. Then, through miraculous circumstances, she was richly rewarded with the most outrageous dream of all: dancing the night away in the arms of the most eligible bachelor, the Prince, as jealous onlookers stood in awe of her beauty. She was uninhibited, and in-the-moment, in spite of being a no-name slave girl who was competing with every hottie Princess in the Kingdom. But there is something deeper to this story we may have missed at first glance. By losing her glass slipper, she created desire and suspense for the Prince, intriguing him so desperately, that he searched his entire Kingdom in relentless pursuit of the one who stole his heart. Cinderella represents the best of us, evoking beauty, pure-heartedness, and the mystique so necessary to win the loyalty of a Prince's affections.

Sleeping Beauty

The story of Sleeping Beauty is one worth giving a second look. Who wouldn't want a handsome hunk to slash through miles of thorns and bramble, fight the venomous dragon and defeat him, then bound up the castle steps to find true love and right all wrongs with a simple, luscious kiss? Remember, Sleeping Beauty was taken by the good fairies deep into the forest to be protected from every spinning wheel in the kingdom so she would not prick her finger, which was foretold to cause her death. But alas, she had her coming-out party at the castle, a "debutante ball" if you will. She was tricked by an Evil One to touch the spinning wheel and pricking her finger, she fell into a deep sleep. The whole kingdom celebrating her party fell into an enchanted slumber as well.

This story goes deeper than what it seems on the surface: Sleeping Beauty wears the "crowning glory" of innocence. She lies unawakened to passion until her valiant Prince comes to awaken her to be his true love. His first kiss breaks her unconscious daze, awakening her to love itself. A true Princess guards her gift of innocence until it is appropriate to be awakened to passion and desire by her Prince. The Prince has fought hell and high water to win her heart and trust, proving it is safe for her to give herself to him. The appropriate time of that awakening is granted by The King, and His mandate is that passion and physical intimacy be kept asleep until after The Royal Wedding!

The Frog Prince

Our final romantic story will be that of The Frog Prince. You may remember that in this story, the hopelessly romantic Princess wearily waits for "Prince Charming" to come on the scene. She often laments about so few courtiers coming her way. She finds comfort at the pond in the Royal Gardens by talking to her own reflection, and strikes up an unlikely conversation with a toad. The ugly, warty toad often croaks out his take on her plight with great intellect and reason. He hears her story with a sympathetic ear and encourages her to hope for true love. In one dramatic moment, he convinces her he's not really a toad at all, but is under an enchanted spell. If she would simply grant him a kiss on his slimy self, a handsome Prince would emerge. Figuring she has nothing to lose, she takes a chance, and in utter amazement, she finds herself in the presence of the dreamiest Prince of all. As unlikely as this love story is, it reveals a Princess's vulnerability in her desire to trust the love of another, even if the stakes are high. A true Princess desires to believe the very best in her purported Prince, often seeing past the façade of a toad, because by nature she is filled with the power of hope. In the end, a true Princess needs the security of knowing that her Prince really is who he says he is, and tests his actions to reveal the truth.

In the Court of the King

Perhaps through our fairy tale adventure, you've recognized some things about yourself that you haven't noticed before. We have several God-given attributes, hidden within us as young women. We are beautifully unique, and fearfully, wonderfully made! Father God intended us daughters to be very different from His sons. We are sensitive and vulnerable, and we often base our self-worth on the opinions of others. We have a tremendous ability to sacrifice our lives for the sake of those we love. This can sometimes mean even being willing to give up our own hopes and dreams for the benefit of those around us. We hold the power of innocence and beauty that a valiant Prince would be willing to risk his life for. We can often bear tremendously difficult circumstances while still maintaining our character and integrity. We possess the key to unlocking the lasting love and affections of another by maintaining an aura of mystery and intrigue. By nature, we are hopeful and trusting in our response to those whom we love and desire to believe in. This is just the beginning of what God has given us as women.

Consider these incredible elements of being a Princess while you are growing your way into "Queen-hood." As you can see, these virtuous, positive aspects can be very much at risk depending how we choose to use them. They can be the most fantastic building blocks to a happy, successful, and prosperous future, or, the most devastating elements of a tragic romance.

Though the lives we live are far from the fantasy of fairy tales, the story our lives tell will be no less fantastic. God did not create us to live dull, uninspired, hopeless, and troubled lives! He is preparing us today for a very real future with Him, one that will make whatever fairy tales we dream up look like cheap imitations.

We are, in fact, children of the Living God, Creator, Redeemer, and soon coming King - if we have chosen to ask Jesus Christ to be Lord of our lives. We are Royal Princesses even now! He has promised that we will rule and reign with Him in His Holy Kingdom. He sits on the throne, and we must see ourselves through God's Fatherly eyes; we are royalty—Princesses in training. He has already placed His crown upon us as members of His royal family! We have incredible rights to His Kingdom as His daughters. He sees us as His very own; He has adopted us through His Son, Jesus. We are marked by His blood and saved from eternal death! If God thinks we are worthy of the greatest treasures in His Kingdom, don't you think you should? He delights in our understanding of Him as our Father!

How does a true Princess, who possesses all these fantastic attributes, behave? We must humbly bow our lives to the mandates of our Father God, and serve our relationships with the utmost of care. We must keep ourselves in balance, respecting our crowns with every step we take. When we wear our crowns high on our heads, we are acknowledging that a high price was paid for us; therefore, a high price will be demanded from one who wants to seek us out as his potential Queen. As God's own daughters, He will allow our lives, character, and integrity to be challenged and changed, to be molded and shaped in preparation for the future that He holds for us. To sum it up: life is a crash-course journey on the road to a fantastic, present and eternal future with God.

"My" Thoughts:

In all of the fairy tales that were mentioned, there were hidden messages that we can actually learn from. Fill in the blanks (you may have to go back a few pages).

Beauty and the Beast

This tale reveals a Princess's ability to make tremendous personal _____ for those she loves, even if there's little in it for her. A true Princess is also able to see past the exteriors of others and look into their _____ , sometimes only to hang on to the one good thing they possess. This is truly a gift. A Princess will often place much higher value on the integrity and inner character of her Prince than what his appearance may afford. And, it is wise too, to remember that "beauty is only _____ deep!"

Cinderella

There is something deeper to this story; by losing her glass slipper, she created _____ and _____ for the Prince, intriguing him so desperately, that he searched his entire kingdom in relentless pursuit of the one who _____ his heart. Cinderella represents the best of us, evoking beauty, pure-heartedness, and the mystique so necessary to win the loyalty of a Prince's affections.

Sleeping Beauty

A true Princess guards her gift of innocence until it is appropriate to be _____ to passion and desire by her Prince. The Prince has fought hell and high water to win her heart and trust, proving it is safe for her to give herself to him. The appropriate time of that awakening is granted by the King, and His mandate is that passion and intimacy be kept asleep until after The Royal _____!

Frog Prince

As unlikely as this love story is, it reveals a Princess's vulnerability in her desire to trust the love of another, even if the stakes are high.

A true Princess desires to believe the very best in her purported Prince, often seeing past the façade of a toad, because by nature she is filled with the power of hope. In the end, a true Princess needs the _____ of knowing that her Prince really is who he says he is, and tests his _____ to reveal the truth.

Did you learn anything new about yourself?_____

_____

_____

_____

What do the relationships you've had so far say about you?_____

_____

_____

_____

_____

Personal Challenge:

God cherishes you more than you realize. You really are His Princess! Read these verses in Psalms 139 and ask God to seal them over your heart and mind:

Psalm 139:1-10; 13-17; 23-24

"O LORD, you have searched me and you know me.

You know when I sit and when I rise; you perceive my thoughts from afar.

You discern my going out and my lying down; you are familiar with all my ways.

Before a word is on my tongue you know it completely, O LORD.

You hem me in—behind and before; you have laid your hand upon me.

Such knowledge is too wonderful for me, too lofty for me to attain.

Where can I go from your Spirit? Where can I flee from your presence?

If I go up to the heavens, you are there; if I make my bed in the depths, you are there.

If I rise on the wings of the dawn, if I settle on the far side of the sea, even there your hand will guide me, your right hand will hold me fast.

For you created my inmost being; you knit me together in my mother's womb.

I praise you because I am fearfully and wonderfully made; your works are wonderful, I know that full well.

My frame was not hidden from you when I was made in the secret place. When I was woven together in the depths of the earth, your eyes saw my unformed body. All the days ordained for me were written in your book before one of them came to be.

How precious to me are your thoughts, O God! How vast is the sum of them!

Search me, O God, and know my heart; test me and know my anxious thoughts.

See if there is any offensive way in me, and lead me in the way everlasting."

The Big Break up

June 2, 2006, my boyfriend had come over to spend some time with me in celebration of seven good months together. We could have gone out to dinner or a movie, but my stomach had felt funny all day, so he came over to my house instead.

What started out as a few good card games, a water bottle "fight," and a brief walk in my neighborhood ended up being a conversation about breaking up. Yup, on our seven months anniversary! Well, to be perfectly honest, I'd seen it coming and had spent about a week preparing myself for it. Our hearts were beginning to go in two different directions: mine with God and the things of God, and his back to his unsaved friends and parts of his old lifestyle. That's how I knew we'd have to break up.

So, after listening to him tell me that I was lucky to have him, and that, with my boundaries, any other guy would've been gone a long time ago, and all these months he really was coming to church just to see me; he was trying to decide whether or not he should break up with me right then and there. I went out to eat with my family and our guest ministers, not really in a mood to be going anywhere!!

At the restaurant, my dad mentioned that I'd just had a conversation with a friend about boundaries. He was gracious enough not to mention that it was my boyfriend and that he wanted to break up with me. Then, our guest looked at me and she smiled and said some of the truest and most encouraging words I've ever heard, "Boundaries create opportunities." I wrote those words down, and they stick with me every day.

However, I was doing my best to choke back the tears and put on a happy face as we ate dinner with our guests. I figured if I didn't talk much, then I wouldn't get choked up, and then I wouldn't have to cry. So, during dinner, I mostly just listened to the conversation that took place between my parents and our guests.

I so wanted all of this to just be over!

Next day, I get a phone call from my boyfriend. I could tell by the tone in his voice that this was it. He was breaking up with me. And, indeed, I was right!

Well, for a day or so, I was a real trooper. I went about my chores and other things I do during the day. Then, it hit me, "He's gone…for good!" That's when I started hurting. The breakup was necessary, but after seven months of really, really liking the person that you're dating, breaking up is an awkward and painful change. So, for five days, I walked around depressed. I felt like an utter mess. But, for once in my life, I decided to handle it differently than I had before. I decided to take the opportunity to draw closer to God because I knew that only He could give me the comfort and strength and love that I needed. I started by reading the *Daughters of Heaven* devotional. I didn't feel anything, I didn't get all tingly, and I certainly wasn't crying tears of joy. But, I stayed devoted. I knew God was trying to get through to me to help me out!

Finally, in the afternoon of the fifth day, when I had absolutely no idea what I was going to do with myself if I didn't get over it soon, my daddy walked out on the back porch where I was sitting just trying to get ahold of myself. He started talking to me, not sure of what to say at first. Then he said something I've heard all my life, but it never really clicked till then: "God loves you. He created this whole earth just for you to enjoy." It was as if God himself was standing right in front of me, smiling so warmly at me, and telling me that He loved me and created the earth just for me to enjoy! Suddenly I wasn't crying over the boyfriend I'd lost, but over the revelation of God's love that I'd just gained.

Since that day, as I have chosen to put God first almost every morning, things have begun to fall into place. Questions and thoughts that I've had for years have been answered. Healing has taken place in deep places where I didn't know I'd even been wounded. I have daily been aware of God in my life. Reading the Bible has been a "want to" instead of a "have to," which makes all the difference in the world.

When you realize—I mean truly know—God's love for you, you'll become aware of His grace, and then of your worthiness. By God's grace you are worthy, and that's why you deserve all that God has for you! When you know you're worthy, you'll live in such freedom and rest, trusting in the Lord. It's an awesome place to be! You won't want your life to be the way it was before. You won't want to be the way you were before, because life in God is so much better.

God gave me a gift right on time. He knew I would need it. He was looking out for me when my mom handed me the *Daughters of Heaven* devotional that our guest had brought with her. Through this book, God comforted me in a time when I felt quite destitute. Oh, how I love my Daddy God! He is so good to me!

I thank my God for the women who contributed to the *Daughters of Heaven* devotional. They truly allowed themselves to be vessels used by God so that, through a book, their lives could touch my life, and any girl's life who reads this book. I really believe that I am where I am, at this season in my life, because of the influence and encouragement beginning with a devotional called *Daughters of Heaven.*

Emily

chapter 9

TRUE LOVE
Heidi Bents

A Princess's greatest need is for true love; this is at the heart of all she says and does. When you read the words "true love," what emotions do you feel? Stop for a moment and ask yourself, "What is true love? Can I recognize it when I see it?" For some, you may be feeling discouraged by this question, or this may set off emotional alarms within you in a negative way. You may be thinking you don't have a clue because you feel you've never experienced true love yourself. Don't be discouraged; I have great news for you. True love is real! It exists at this very moment! If you haven't experienced it yet, please keep reading.

Our deepest dream is to have the "ultimate romance" become a reality in our lives. It is innate to us as young women to have this desire. God planted it there, for He is the ultimate Lover. Love was His idea in the first place. He created the desire; He is Love!

We have an incredible, God-given need to be loved and cherished. Our desire to have this need met is often what motivates us to enter relationships with others. We may have already experienced true love within our own families or with our best friends, but most importantly to us girls, we need true love from our relationships with the men in our lives, fathers included; it captures the essential need of our soul. True love quenches our craving for security, and tells us that "all is well" in our world. Without it, we can be left feeling isolated, unsure, and afraid that we aren't valued in the eyes of others. The eyes of true love tell us that we are worthy, lovely, and highly esteemed.

The Ultimate Love Story

If we really understand God's love for us, we will desire to have our first ultimate romance with Jesus himself. God created our heart with a desire for relationship that only He can fill! He desires to satisfy our needs as the perfect Lover of our souls. When we allow God to meet our need for true love, it becomes more natural for us to turn to Him instead of relying on others like friends or boyfriends, and expecting them to satisfy our deepest hunger. His love is more than enough for us! He can fill us with His presence, nourish our broken spirits, heal wounds, and bind together our broken hearts. Knowing God's love will reveal the truth regarding lies about unworthiness, guilt, shame, and hopelessness. His Spirit lifts ours, and His tender words are more precious than any other! This is why it is so important that we accept the love of Jesus first. Otherwise, our search for true love will never make sense, and our pursuit of it will never end.

The Search Is On!

Do you find yourself hungry for this kind of love? Have you bounced from one broken relationship to another, wondering if you'll ever find the "right guy"? You may even have friends whom you've noticed just can't seem to work things out, or maybe jump from one bad relationship to another, thinking things may be different this time. What are you searching for? What do we need the most? Fun? A good time? Romance? Intimacy? None of these will last!

Our search for true love will end in the arms of Jesus! The love of Jesus esteems us; we are important enough to Him that He died on the cross to save us. He knew all about us before He laid the foundations of the earth, and He determined then, our lives are worthy. God's Word says that perfect love casts out fear. Only the Love of Jesus is perfect!

Do you feel insecure at times or sense your friends are motivated by their own insecurities? Fear can become what drives us to seek out security through relationships; it breeds insecurities, like low self-esteem, low self-worth, and condemning thoughts. When we see our true reflection in the face of perfect love, this bondage of fear is broken, then we are able to see how precious we are in our Heavenly Father's sight. What are we afraid of? That we aren't lovely? That we aren't worthy? That we are undeserving?

Truth is, we are all these things in and of ourselves. With an honest look inward, we can all find fault and a bit of ugliness there. We can wear no masks with God. He knows every aspect and dimension of our hearts, minds, and lives, but we are His favorite anyway! He desires to satisfy our longing for love with a love that has no limits, knows no bounds, and one that will never fail!

If you read through these verses from First John, you will learn more about God's love and how to recognize it in action:

Dear friends, let us love one another, for LOVE comes from God. Everyone who loves has been born of God and knows God.

Whoever does not love does not know God, because God is love.

This is how God showed his love among us: He sent his one and only Son into the world that we might live through him.

This is love: not that we loved God, but that he loved us and sent His Son as an atoning sacrifice for our sins.

1 John 4:7-10

True Love Is About Sacrifice

God, the Creator of the Universe, demonstrated His perfect "true love" for us through the sacrifice of his Son (John 3:16). Jesus was brutally beaten, mocked, and executed as a common criminal, so that we might have eternal salvation and wear the crown of Life, being made perfect by His shed blood. His innocent blood covers and washes away all guilt, shame, and stain of condemnation in us, and we are made righteous in Him. This is the most powerful example of sacrificial love. No other love compares! In John 15:13, the Bible tells us that there is no greater love, than one who is willing to lay down his life for a friend. Jesus died as the ultimate sacrifice of love, that we would not die in our sins, but be delivered by the power of His love and forgiveness.

Jesus died to set us free, and freely gave Himself for us. Why? Because He has set His love and favor upon us, counted the cost of you and me, and decided we were worth it! He gave everything to be reunited with us. He came to earth to redeem us, and make a way for us to return to Him. How vast the heart of God must be!

The greatness of Jesus' love goes beyond His personal sacrifice. He demonstrated true love actively by serving the lives and needs of others. We can choose Him to be our role model and inspiration in how to love and demonstrate sacrificial love towards others, to change our behavior and character, and to renew our minds through His Word, the Bible. We can give back to Christ our very best, serving Him with our whole hearts and lives. The power of the Holy Spirit will help us, strengthen us, and guide us as we make this commitment to be like Him.

The choice is ours! We become one of His royal Princesses by accepting Jesus as our Lord and asking Him to forgive us for our sins. Through this decision, we open our lives to the power of a living, life changing, miraculous Savior!

"My" Thoughts:

1. What are some of the ways you have searched for "true love" that have left you empty handed?_____
_____
_____
_____
_____

2. Have you ever considered that your relationship with God is like a love affair? Write some thoughts about what this means to you.
_____
_____
_____
_____

3. What is it about Jesus' "sacrificial love" that speaks to you the most?_____
_____
_____
_____

Personal Challenge:

What is holding you back? Receive your crown of everlasting life! If you haven't asked Jesus to be the Lord of your life and the King of your heart, you can right now!

God's Word says:

...whoever comes to me I will never drive away (John 6:37).

That if you confess with your mouth, 'Jesus is Lord,' and believe in your heart that God raised him from the dead, you will be saved. For it is with your heart that you believe and are justified, and it is with your mouth that you confess and are saved (Romans 10:9-10).

Pray the following prayer aloud:

"Jesus, I come before you, just as I am. You say in Your Word that You won't turn me away, but will accept me. Jesus, I believe in my heart that You are God's Son and that You died for me and that God raised You from the dead. I ask You to forgive me of all my sins, wrong attitudes, thoughts, words, and actions that have not pleased You. I confess all my guilt, shame and failures and place them at Your feet. Thank You for dying for me and paying the price for my freedom. Jesus, I confess You as my Lord and Savior and give You permission to work in my life. Help me to understand Your heart and learn to love Your ways. Teach me how to purify my heart and my desires. Fill me with Your Holy Spirit. Thank you that I am now saved and that You are my Lord. In the precious name of Jesus I pray, Amen."

Welcome to God's family! You are now saved and you have entered into a "true love" relationship with God himself! The Bible says that all of Heaven rejoices when anyone comes to know Jesus! You just had your own cheering section going with the angels, saints and hosts of Heaven praising God for you! Isn't that awesome? Congratulations! Write your name here and post today's date and time:

All of Heaven stands to witness that:

_____

is saved and is part of God's Kingdom, on this day,

_____

Facing Pregnancy Alone

Growing up, I always knew I would someday marry a Christian man, but I hadn't maintained this boundary enough. Dating Christian guys had not been a priority…I thought they probably wouldn't be able to relate to me, anyhow, and would, no doubt, be too boring and "straight."

Several years later, after dating a few guys, I started falling for one in particular. We dated for quite some time before I finally decided to ask him, "Do you believe in God?"

His response, "I believe in myself."

I knew at that moment there would be no future and that I needed to end things. How could I be in this relationship and be "taking risks?" I cried when I found out that I was pregnant. Eight-and-a-half months later, my son was born.

My pregnancy was very lonely; I had turned to God in my time of desperation. I had made some new friends at church who were in a similar circumstance as single moms. I grew and became stronger as a result. Also, my friends from before were still there for me; they were like family now. Once I was back on my feet, the "old familiar comfort zone" I had once known was welcoming me as an outsider, beckoning to me….

Life was a bit more challenging to me now, raising a child on my own. I knew in my heart how important it would be to guide my child's steps toward a relationship with God. I had him dedicated as a baby; we rarely missed a Sunday service. I prayed with him every night before bed. My son and I had each done some growing up over the course of two-and-a-half years.

Now I was a little more mature and the perfect age to get married. I had idealized age twenty-five as being just right to find that "Christian man/husband." Also, I had learned that knowing his faith ahead of time was the key to having any sort of future relationship. I ventured out one spring day to play on the church softball team; surely; there would be a good looking, Christian man on it who would be fun and athletic. *Jackpot*, I began dating someone who I actually went to church with and was, also, a single parent. He was fun and outgoing, a great dad, and we could talk about God and our experiences.

A few months passed and summer was coming to an end; a good relationship had begun to form. I no longer felt alone as a single mom. I caught a glimpse of how he could be a good dad to my boy; I saw how nice he treated his own children. Maybe we should talk about a future? As a Christian woman, I just want to reiterate that I was now "saving" myself for marriage. Unfortunately, he did not share my belief and stated that, he's never had to wait before and didn't plan to now. I was crushed; how could this "Christian guy" be sitting in the same church services as me and not be hearing the same message? I didn't get it! But the subject of marriage came up a few times and then I found myself compromising. I felt somewhat locked in; I couldn't just walk away from this relationship, my son and I were vested in it and I had a relationship with his children as well.

However, knowing he was selfish and manipulative did not make me fall more in love with him. How could God's blessing exist in this kind of relationship? I had to be stronger than this! I had started seeing a Christian counselor; I needed someone to be accountable to. Maybe, after the holidays, I could risk ending things and turning everyone's lives upside down.

Instead, after the holidays, I took a pregnancy test; the results were positive! It was too late! I figured I had better make the best of this situation; maybe, my family could handle the news if I were engaged? I certainly didn't want to spend another pregnancy alone! How could I have done things in backwards order, AGAIN? Where was my resolve? God had been there for me; I had let Him down, again! What were my priorities, really?

After going through the motions, now in a miserable relationship, I had received a quasi-engagement proposal—with no ring! I sloughed it off.

Two days later (halfway through the pregnancy), I received a phone call. The voice on the other line was him and he began to say, "I don't really know how to tell you this, but this relationship is over."

I was flooded with anger and sadness. Abandonment had filled my being and the moment felt surreal. I couldn't be hopeful or look to the future now, there wasn't one. I languished in my own pain for quite some time. Even though I knew I really didn't want to marry the guy, how could he just up and leave me like this? And what would I tell my family now?

At this point, I didn't expect anyone to understand or accept me. Certainly God would be disappointed! Somehow, I still felt I needed to go to church and seek His Word. I remember sitting in church and hearing the pastor say, "Bitterness is like serving up a cocktail of poison for your enemy, then slowly sipping it yourself." No

one except me was to blame for my situation. Now, I was really desperate for God and Him only. He would now be "my everything." There would be no more putting Him on a shelf and picking Him up as needed. When we need air to breathe, we will choose it every minute of every day.

My daughter was born. I relied on God's strength and His direction and He gave us His peace. In trusting Him, I would learn the true desires of my heart. And in developing a lifestyle and relationship with Christ, I would learn the difference between what it meant to be religious and what it meant to be "Godly." I recommitted my life and my future to Jesus; I asked the Lord to restore me. For a season, I avoided dating altogether. I trusted God and relied on Him to shape my life and build my future. I didn't want to put myself in a compromising position again. I prayed for God to show me what He would have for me and allowed Him to work in my heart.

When my son was almost five and my daughter was 18 months, God brought a "special someone" into my life. A prayer had been answered. I had prayed about meeting a "Godly man" (and not just a church go-er) who had potential to be a strong spiritual leader. (As it turns out, three years ago, my fiancé had prayed that same prayer around the same time.) So finally, after eight years of being a single mom, which certainly wasn't easy, God has blessed me with a wonderful man who will be a Godly influence and a wonderful dad to my son and daughter. God gave me His grace and I allowed Him to turn my life into something beautiful.

Nicky

chapter 10

THE DAMSEL AND THE DUDES

Heidi Bents

Do you desire to raise the bar of expectation for your own life? If so, how does this expectation and proving process take place? What does it really look like in action? Let's take a look at some critical dynamics to a healthy dating relationship.

It All Begins with RESPECT!

We may have a great idea of what we want in a guy, but most of us struggle with knowing how to get what we want. Everyone desires to be respected by others, but what does genuine respect feel like? How is it demonstrated and who starts the process? Is respect in our relationships to be given, or to be earned? Or is it both?

As a virtuous Princess, you can effectively influence a valiant Prince to demonstrate his character in several ways. We let those around us know what our expectations of them are by our reactions toward the way they treat us. Our expectations first begin from within ourselves. If a Princess respects herself first, a Prince will realize she is a worthy Princess who deserves and commands the same level of respect from him. If a relationship has a chance at being healthy, the first building block must be based upon the self-respect of each person.

The idea of respect is not in a lording-over manner, as if you're "all that" and he needs to know it. It revolves around the fact that you are a young woman who has taken stock of herself; you know who you are as a person, and you realize the great value your life has. God has placed within you unique gifts, passions, dreams, and desires that belong only to you. His purpose for your life is given for only you to fulfill. You are aware that your life, body, and future are wrapped up in the will of God, and so you choose to seek Him in every decision you make. You view your life with a "handle with care" mentality, treat yourself with great esteem, and love yourself because of it.

On the flip-side, the Prince who sees that his Princess respects herself, will be able to trust her to meet one of his greatest needs, which is to be respected. She is actually doing herself a favor by being respectable, because the guy she's interested in will be drawn to her by what he sees in her! A guy won't allow himself to fully give his heart to anyone without respect. He knows that he can't risk being vulnerable to the one he admires, unless she is genuinely capable of meeting his need to be respected. He won't learn how to truly love her; therefore, it will be impossible for her to be satisfied in this relationship. Furthermore, if the barriers of respect are willingly broken down between the two of them, she has given this dude permission to dishonor her, and the next girl, and the next. She has just lowered the bar of his expectation! She plays an important role in either crippling or aiding her young man in the ways of love.

From whom do guys learn the most about ladies and romantic relationships? Us! We have the privilege of being our guy's "in" to understanding us and how we function. Isn't that humbling? This is how our Creator intended it to be. It's fascinating, powerful, and a huge responsibility!

We women set examples of love and express our expectations toward men our entire lives: while we date and after we're married. We show those around us how to value us by what we deem to be acceptable or unacceptable behaviors. We can also show men how to be great fathers to our kids, and especially how to relate with our daughters. As mothers, dads may need us to step in from time to time to explain our girl's needs and emotions. Then, we train our sons how to love us as their moms, and how to appropriately love and treat their brothers and sisters. Later on, our example will impact their behaviors towards their girlfriends and future wives.

This is why it is necessary that a Princess allow time in her life to be equipped as a Princess. As you mature in your character and spiritual fiber, striving to be at your best, you will be ready to show a Prince how to genuinely love you with his very best. In the end, where you are in your own personal journey will determine how many of your expectations you will achieve.

Honor and Trust

Honoring each other also opens the door for trust to be developed between a Princess and her Prince. Trust is the glue that binds any relationship at its core. Without it, a relationship will surely crumble! Respect and trust are two vital aspects that work together in any healthy, loving relationship. Here's a premium example: if a Princess has observed that her Prince is trustworthy, she will have the highest degree of respect for him and her deep admiration will soon follow. Because she is meeting her Prince's need for admiration and honor, he is even more motivated and determined to prove his trustworthiness, and daily demonstrates he is a man of high moral character. He proves that he has learned to treasure her heart instead of her body. As proof of his integrity grows, her faith in him and her desire to love him only grows deeper. Because he believes that his Princess will handle his heart with care, the Prince opens up to his deepest emotions, thoughts, and fears -- being vulnerable for the first time to truly trust another. She has earned the "right" to know him better than anyone else in his life! By their actions and attitudes, a worthwhile, healthy, loving relationship is being built.

Though God made a man and woman to become one by completing each other in marriage, they still have to begin with two whole, healthy halves! Both people are responsible to remain "whole" as individuals in the process, so that if the relationship does not succeed, the two can leave the relationship without compromising the integrity of the other. After all, two broken halves will only amount to a broken whole! Marriage won't provide the stability necessary to mend two broken people, especially if the disappointments stem from the relationship itself. It simply won't solve the bigger problem that neither party is healthy.

When we honor and respect one another, it means we place a high value, a high priority, in esteeming that person above ourselves. It goes back to the meaning of sacrificial love, which proves to a Princess her worthiness and value through the Prince's considerate behavior. Simply said, when a guy puts the needs of the Princess first, his own desires, needs and wants will take a back seat!

Biggest Battle Rages

As a Princess, we've talked about her greatest need being that of "true love." And at the core of this need is for someone to recognize that she is worthy, of great value, and deserving of high honor. A virtuous Princess is honorable by guarding her virtue as a virgin; she expects her potential Prince to show her the respect she deserves because of her example. In this way, a Princess shows a Prince how to earn her trust and tests his ability to remain trustworthy. There is no greater proving ground in the relationship to a Princess than regarding the subject of her honor, protecting her virginity, and sexuality. This is where the biggest battle, within ourselves and the one we love, is played out. It is where a Princess will learn from her Prince whether he thinks she is worth waiting for. It is here where both should recognize that, outside of marriage, neither party has earned the right to each other's most intimate gifts.

Outside of marriage, each person belongs to God alone, and anything less than honoring the other is robbing the most precious gift God has given us. God gave us the gift of sexuality for our enjoyment and pleasure—only in marriage. It's all good! The bond that sexual intimacy provides was intended to cement the very foundation of the marriage covenant. The covenant of marriage is a parallel to God's relationship to us, of His covenant with mankind and the redeeming love it provides. God meant it to mirror His deep passion, pursuit, and desire for intimacy with us. Sexual intimacy in marriage is the purest "face to face" encounter we can possibly have with another human being; in its purest sense, it is the redeeming love that binds the relationship. God intended it to be the most vulnerable, tender, healing, and loving act that humans can experience.

Future Husband's Prize

God gave your sexuality to you as a pure, precious gift to keep until marriage and with which to bless your Prince. Your virginity is your future husband's prize! He's the only one who should "unwrap" your gift; it belongs to him. "Saving yourself" for only him will prove to him that you cared so very much about his thoughts and feelings; it is his final reward for proving himself to be a valiant Prince. He demonstrated sacrificial love to you by restraining himself, treasuring your heart instead of your body, protecting, guarding, and honoring your virginity, proving you were worth the wait. He has truly esteemed you and proven his true love! You, in turn, feel valued, treasured, honored, and yes, truly loved.

And if he had failed to behave in this manner, he would have proven that he was not a valiant Price after all.

The process of respecting, honoring, and trusting each other is pivotal for building healthy, lasting relationships in our lives. The wise couple realizes there is a future to be built, and it must have these elements set in place in order to build a firm, unshakable foundation. By focusing on each other's uniqueness as individuals, taking interest in each other's qualities, interests, and character attributes, a Prince and Princess can fulfill the emotional, spiritual, and intellectual needs of each other. By loving each other in Godly, unselfish ways, they set themselves up for great future success in their relationship and potential marriage. Their commitment to respect and honor each other opens the possibility of enjoying incredible freedom within the relationship. They forego the pain of disappointment and the pressures of deep emotional attachments complicating their lives. Instead, they can be enthusiastic and confident about creating a meaningful, loving, and safe environment for their love to grow!

Let Your Prince Prove Himself

A valiant Prince also learns from a virtuous Princess how to actively demonstrate sacrificial love towards her. A valiant Prince proves to his lady that she is worthy of being truly cherished, and strives to love her selflessly. The greatest of Kings learns to be a servant of all! This is the message of sacrificial love; one who lays down his life, his needs, his desires, his dreams, his agenda, and his ego for the needs of others. Does your Prince have what it takes to be King? This is how Christ demonstrated His love for us. By laying down His life for us, He sacrificed Himself to cover and redeem our sins. In this way, He showed us the ultimate example of Kingship.

By this uncommon act of sacrificial love for His people, Jesus modeled how men are to treat us as women. Christ's example is one of being a servant. Are you being treated like this from the guy in your life? Are you determined to receive and give sacrificial love in your relationships? Even our simple friendships with guys show them what we need from them and how we deserve to be treated. Think about it. You could be a guy's only positive representation of what this looks like.

Seduce or Reduce

God has told us in His Word to stand firm in our convictions and to maintain His honorable standards regarding love and sex. He has given every one of His Princes an innate desire to be King. Men are born to be leaders! Whether a man becomes a good or bad King will be determined by how he handles his life as a Prince. What he learns or ignores during the younger years of his life impacts his future abilities. If a Princess becomes his stumbling block, she can permanently cripple his ability to rule through the power of her seduction. We can choose to help equip the Prince to be ruler as King, or make him a peasant: poor in spirit, character, and crippled in his manhood. In essence, we have the power to seduce our future Kings and reduce them to someone expecting nothing more than the next free handout of meaningless, casual sex.

God's plan is to equip his tender Princes to be capable leaders, and part of this process is through the courtship with the Princess. His self-reflection comes first from understanding his value in the eyes of God, and secondly, from the respect and admiration of his Princess. When he lets his guard down by becoming sexually active, he is diminished as a man because instead of maturing and developing the more important aspects of his life as God intended, his focus shifts off-track to his sex drive. This, in every way, short-circuits the growth and development necessary to mature him into a well-rounded, vibrant, stable and confident adult.

Demonstrating Sacrificial Love

We've discovered the proof of our worth by looking at ourselves through the eyes of our loving Father God. Now that we have a sense of our great value, what should our expectations be of those we have relationships with? What should our behavior be as a virtuous Princess? What does God expect of us and our influence on the opposite sex? We have a very special, unique purpose in the lives of His sons.

We naturally want and need sacrificial love to not only be demonstrated, but to be proven to us by the men in our lives. But do you know that a valiant Prince learns from a virtuous Princess how to truly love? Before you meet, your guy will have experienced various relationships including those with his father and mother, brother/sister, or other role models which impacted his life. This may have well-equipped him for stable, loving relationships, or maybe not. He could be very mature and capable, already in a great position to take on romantic love. Assuming he's at his best, when it comes to his ability to have a deep female friendship, you will play an important role! It's not that you are out to "change" him (by the way, that does not work), but to open his understanding as to what your needs are as a young woman.

You may have discovered this already for yourself, but in case you haven't, your guy will probably be at a loss as to how to meet your emotional needs in the friendship you share. You see, we girls are so good at this with each other, that sometimes we think our man should be our best girlfriend. Wrong! We girls have our own language and most of the time, we really understand each other. Guys on the other hand, may nod and grunt in our direction as if totally getting what we're saying and feeling. But chances are, we will have to have this conversation a few more times before it will sink in and actually mean something to them. With our emotions, passions, and desires, we will find that as girls we are far more complicated than our counterparts! And, though for centuries, women have been asking God, "WHY?" the simplest answer is that He obviously thought the partnership works best this way!

The "X" Factor

Part of our unique ability as females is that we are equipped with a "knowing" of how to build healthy relationships. This is mostly because, as an "X Chromosomer," our brains connect well between our logic and reasoning (left brain), and our thoughts, feelings and emotions (right brain).

Our wonderful counterparts, the guys, are generally "left brain" thinkers, attending to details of logic, analysis and reasoning. They have to work harder at developing a connection between facts and the emotional aspects of an issue. So, a guy will tend to be oriented towards projects and task-mastering, which can leave his lovely lady feeling a bit lonely or isolated at times. He's more set towards each new agenda or challenge and focuses on conquering it, while relational items can be unintentionally left off his list. This isn't because guys are completely insensitive, it is simply because they are wired more on a one-track, problem solving mindset, and we pretty much have a maze of zigzags that we're dealing with! There are many differences we will discuss, but the point is that because God has given us this "womanly intuition," we are in a nurturing position to lead our significant "other" into a deep, fulfilling relationship with us. Our job starts with friendship with our man, and may end at "'til death do us part!"

If we choose to lead out of love, we possess the key to unlock emotional doors into the very heart of a Prince. Through tender nudging and intimate conversation as to the needs of her heart, a virtuous Princess helps her Prince to emotionally grow and mature in the relationship up to and beyond marriage. This is true especially since males tend to mature much slower than females in communicating and processing their emotional needs. She is, in effect, grooming her future King in how to love, cherish, and nurture her deepest needs. If handled appropriately, this will bless the marriage for her entire future with the King. This process also blesses the King, as he confidently takes the lead role in the home as a provider, and also helps him to be a loving, nurturing father. A Prince will be properly equipped to lead and rule as a mature King, after he has developed his ability to respect, honor, serve, and love sacrificially. What are you doing to encourage the guys you know in their pursuit of Godliness? Reflect on this for a moment.

The Makings of a Prince

A valiant Prince is "fearfully and wonderfully made" by the King of kings, Father God...

… He is created by God to be physically and sexually attracted to females. His greatest relational need and desire is to display his affections through physical contact with his Princess. It is vital that he gain healthy esteem through the honor and acceptance he receives from others through admiration, appreciation, and devotion.

… He needs to be honorable in his behavior, and feel respected to have a healthy self-reflection.

… He needs to restrain from pursuing his sexual desires and, instead, turn his energy towards developing, nurturing and maturing his relational and emotional skills.

… He learns a lot about his emotional and affectionate self through the gentle prodding of the Princess. She allows him to develop, grow and prove his love and devotion to her through serving her need for sacrificial love. If he maintains self-discipline and self-control, she will be convinced of his true love and his ability to remain faithful to her.

… After marriage, sexual intimacy with his bride will complete the Prince as a King.

…His whole "kingdom" will benefit as he matures into the lead role with the authority that God has placed within him, as he learns to serve his Queen, his children and those closest to him.

… He loves Jesus and his heart is sold out to our Savior. A life marked by the Love of God is hard to miss!

... He stands apart from the crowd, does not bend to social pressure, and is not ashamed of his commitment to stand with God. His manner should be impressive: considering the needs of others first, and being quick to repent and humble himself in any wrongdoing.

... His character, though not perfect, should mirror that of Christ, and his intentions should be toward pleasing God. This will become more obvious as he grows even closer to Jesus. As life moves on, his resolve to let nothing stand between him and God is priority, and he pursues this with diligence.

The Makings of a Princess

A virtuous Princess is also "fearfully and wonderfully made" by the King of kings, Father God...

... She is created by God to be relationally and emotionally attracted to males. Her greatest need is to feel secure through sacrificial love and devotion from her Prince.

... She gains healthy esteem through the Prince's proof of true love and devotion by his honoring, respecting, acceptance, and appreciation for her uniqueness.

... She must be convinced that she is loved for her pure heart and inner self in order to maintain a healthy self-reflection.

... She receives high value and worth on her life when she is honored by those who love her. If she allows a Prince to prove his sacrificial love to her through honoring her virginity, she will naturally be drawn to give herself freely to her Prince; her King after marriage, and will be the crowning glory of her King.

... She will trust, respect, and honor her King, for after all, he has won her heart. The covenant of commitment with her King will complete her as Queen, just as God intended. Their whole "Kingdom" will benefit as she matures into her vital role of Queen, wife, mother, and castle builder.

"My" Thoughts:

1. Circle the critical building blocks to a healthy dating relationship:

a. Respect   b. Money   c. Great car

d. Honor & Trust   e. Good looks   f. Sacrificial Love

2. Do you respect yourself? Why or why not?_____
_____
_____
_____

3. What message are you sending? Do you show respect towards the men in your life? How? Why or why not?_____
_____
_____
_____

If you have lost any respect for yourself because of past failures, the incredible news is that God is a God of second chances! There is always hope, always forgiveness, and always restoration for children of the King. Jesus sees you perfected by His own cleansing blood. His perfect will and plan are for you, His precious daughter. If you humbly bow your will, ask for His forgiveness and repent, your heart will be changed and He will give you new desires and new dreams. He is a faithful, loving Father who cherishes you enough to lay down Himself for your faults and failings.

Take a moment, even now, and ask Him to speak to areas in your life that He desires for you to change. You are not alone in your thoughts and prayers. God sees your pain, your suffering, your guilt, and He desires to remove it from your life. Will you ask Him to speak to your heart, to help you purify your mind, and to forgive you from past inappropriate actions and behaviors? He holds the strength you need to make a change in your life, and He will give it to you. It is in our weaknesses that He is made strong!

Personal Challenge:

Read through and reflect on the thoughts in these verses as you bring your heart before God. Spend some time in prayer, then journal what God is speaking to you:

Psalm 51:1-17

(For the choir director: A psalm of David, regarding the time Nathan the prophet came to him after David had committed adultery with Bathsheba.)

Have mercy on me, O God, because of your unfailing love. Because of your great compassion, blot out the stain of my sins.

Wash me clean from my guilt. Purify me from my sin.

For I recognize my rebellion; it haunts me day and night.

Against you, and you alone, have I sinned; I have done what is evil in your sight. You will be proved right in what you say, and your judgment against me is just.

For I was born a sinner—yes, from the moment my mother conceived me.

But you desire honesty from the womb, teaching me wisdom even there.

Purify me from my sins, and I will be clean; wash me, and I will be whiter than snow.

Oh, give me back my joy again; you have broken me—now let me rejoice.

Don't keep looking at my sins. Remove the stain of my guilt.

Create in me a clean heart, O God. Renew a loyal spirit within me.

Do not banish me from your presence, and don't take your Holy Spirit from me.

Restore to me the joy of your salvation, and make me willing to obey you.

Then I will teach your ways to rebels, and they will return to you.

Forgive me for shedding blood, O God who saves; then I will joyfully sing of your forgiveness.

Unseal my lips, O Lord, that my mouth may praise you.

You do not desire a sacrifice, or I would offer one. You do not want a burnt offering.

The sacrifice you desire is a broken spirit.

You will not reject a broken and repentant heart, O God."

Getting out of a destructive relationship!

I accepted Jesus Christ as my personal Savior, when I was in junior high school at a weekend youth group. I was so excited and wanted to pursue this newfound relationship, but most of my friends were not at that same place in their lives. Many of us who were there, found Him that weekend, but when we returned home, the common challenges of the teenage years overcame us. Satan knows when and where to hit; he knows our weaknesses, and attacks with the most force when he feels our souls are in jeopardy. It is no mistake that he strikes where we are weak, for his greatest fear is that he will no longer be in control. Peer pressure, puberty, and bad choices slowly consumed many of us during our teen years.

I found myself pregnant at nineteen; my boyfriend was only eighteen; both of us, barely adults. Because I had been raised a Christian and he had been raised morally; we felt the only "right" thing to do was to get married. From the beginning of our relationship (at age fifteen), we had several issues to deal with; it seemed as though we would break up, just to make up. We believed we could overcome our differences. We had a child we wanted to bring into this world knowing he had two parents who loved and wanted him, and, so, we did what we felt was the "right" thing. He was the first of the two most precious gifts I have ever been blessed with. Several years later, we had another son whom we loved and wanted just as much. God blessed us with two of the most wonderful sons and our love for each of them will forever remain faithful.

We were two insecure people who looked in all the wrong places to find comfort, peace, and self-worth. Drugs and drinking became the medication for the pain, only to deepen the wounds and allow Satan a larger playground. Guilt and blame became a weapon. Mistrust became the sword. Anger and bitterness struck with vengeance and fury. The tongue became a dagger, ripping and shredding away already wounded flesh. Words, mightier than the fist, left wounds bleeding so deeply in the depths of my soul, where no one else could see. All that could be seen on the outside was a struggling woman, confused and unsure of herself and weakening more every day. Those years of all the bitter words spoken—how unworthy I was, how bad I was, how it was all my fault—still echo in the night and in the shadows of my soul. It has taken years, a lifetime of prayers, and God's healing love for me to see the good in myself and to learn that there was never anything I could do to "change" the man in my life. He did not want to change. God can only help those who ask Him into their lives. God can only help those who want His help. I wanted His help, yet, I was not allowing Him to be the answer.

I would do my best to hide what I could from my kids, my family, and friends. One night, God opened my eyes to the real truth. It was because of what I saw in my dream that I finally began to understand that I could never hold this burden by myself.

My husband's tongue had become more bitter, and, each time, he became a little more physical. A push, a shove, a hole in the wall, maybe a bottle of beer hurled at me or poured over me. It wasn't until the very end that he actually hit me. The day I left for the last time, he said, "You had better leave before I kill you," as his hands were around my neck.

For many years, I struggled to overcome the low self esteem and shameful person I had become. I spent hours, days, months, and years drowning in guilt over those words, "I had failed my family." Night after night, voices echoed in the dark telling me I was bad and not worth loving. Though I had always loved God and knew He was waiting for me to listen to His voice, I knew that I had to completely surrender my own will and ask God to take control of my life. Even though I was looking for Him to "fix" my life during those desperate years, I had never completely given my life to Him. I was looking and expecting unconditional love to come from a man, but what I failed to see was that during my whole life, God's unconditional love was always there. Night after night, the Lord held me, sharing my tears, waiting for me to want that love from Him. I slept every night with my Bible on my chest, but during the day walked the streets of men. God could not change my husband, nor the men I met after, but He helped me find the strength to change myself. All of those nights, when I lay crying, thinking I was alone and that He wasn't listening, His tears were falling for me and He was hoping I would call out to Him. He was waiting and watching, hurting for me, feeling my same pain, His own tears falling. He had to wait until I came back to Him before He could help me, but I had been running in every other direction.

No man on this earth could ever love me as unconditionally as Jesus, my Lord. This I know because He has never left my side. When I stumbled, He was always there ready to help me up. When I was fighting, He was fighting for me. When I was turning in every wrong direction, His light was there to show me the way.

He never gave up on me! Despite my despair, at that time in my life, He never allowed me more pain than I could handle. Even though I felt alone, I could now hear His voice. When I was too weary to face another day, He walked beside me and showed me how to find something good in each one. When I had no money, He found me a job. When there was not enough money, He found me another job. At one point, He found me three jobs. In all that was bad, He taught me to search for goodness and to this day, I can look at the worst of situations and believe that, though I may not see it today, somewhere in all things, there is or will be something good.

I started over, hand in hand with my Lord, baby steps - one at a time. Though the cuts were deep, and the memories will always remain shadows, they have healed and the scars are finally fading. When I am on my knees now, I feel His gentle hand as it reaches for mine as He helps me rise to my feet.

That child within me that has always been so precious to God, now has inner peace and strength. To please Him, I only need to love Him. To find peace, I simply need to rest in Him. To find forgiveness, I need only to ask for it. To find strength to overcome any weaknesses, I must seek His wisdom. I have found nothing stronger in myself, than the faith that God's plan for this moment will result in a better place, a better time, and a plan far greater than my own. I have learned the hard way, through the "self guided chapters in my life." When I felt like I had to control or "fix" the moment or a relationship, in reality, I was taking away the power of the Lord and creating a detour from His plan with my life. I have spent the better part of my life making things harder, my pain last longer, and suffering needlessly because of my desire to please myself and others, rather than listening and following Him. I have found my strength to come from God. I could never meet the expectations of anyone else, especially myself, until I allowed God control of my life, my heart, and my footsteps. Too many times, I gave it to God but took it back in the same breath, because I felt like if I tried one more time, I could make it better.

These new chapters in my life still present many challenges, but my life has been blessed by many new gifts. I am now married to a wonderful man who loves each and every part of me. He loves and accepts my weaknesses and helps me turn them into strengths. We love and respect each other because our relationship is guided by God. We have both traveled down long dusty roads to get here, but we both love and trust God to guide us through the challenging moments that lie ahead

Dianne

chapter 11

TOAD OR PRINCE VALIANT?

Heidi Bents

In a perfect "fairy tale" setting -- how would you sum up your life story? Would you rate your life as a "two thumbs up," success story? How have your past relationships with guys turned out? Are you a hopeless romantic, lady-in-waiting, or a damsel in distress? Or have you been through one tragic romance after another?

To Be? Or Not to Be?

Let's go back to the good 'ole days of kings and kingdoms when arranged marriages were the topic of the day. When a prince wanted to wed, the royal family would seek out other royalty to help find the perfect princess. Oftentimes, marriages were used for creating alliances which were utilized to build strong political ties for entire kingdoms. Royal marriages often bound countries together, including their cultures, commerce and even their armies sometimes joined forces for conquest. An entire kingdom would be built on the strength of the throne. In fact, a marriage gone bad could lead to treaties and alliances being broken, a revolt, or the outbreak of war. Much could be gained or lost for the sake of the throne!

The royal family would seek out a potential princess for their son, and the prince would begin to "court" her. The prince and his princess began a simple relationship to learn more about each other. They became familiar with the other's family, their interests, and the role they would play as potential king and queen. The couple would attend social events like palace balls and fine dinners with the royal family who would then observe the behavior, manner, character, and wit of the princess. They would often test the princess on her knowledge of the political state of the country, and her likes and dislikes regarding social matters, to determine whether she was a candidate for such a role as future queen. The king and queen wanted a perfect match; after all, the stability of the throne and the entire kingdom would someday be under the couple's power.

The royal family considered marriage to be serious business! It could impact their economy and perhaps endanger the future status of the monarchy. Would this future king and queen be fit for the makings of a royal family and would their marriage survive the duties of the throne? Would they breed responsible successors who could manage the monarchy with integrity? The very fiber of the kingdom relied upon the stability of the king and queen!

Is Today so Different?

Much like this, the success of dating, love, and marriage today is the same. Your life and your future partner's will be "tested" as well. Remember, as a Princess, your most defining moment will be whom you choose to love and build a life with. Why is this? Because your choice of a mate will greatly impact your future! Are you both mature, and capable of making a commitment to love each other sacrificially? Do your strengths and weaknesses complement each other in a healthy way? In no way is this suggesting that either person is perfect; no one is! But, there has to be serious lines drawn that you refuse to cross! As you spend time getting to know your Prince, beware that if you begin to notice or feel uncomfortable about chinks in his armor, it may be time to put him back on the saddle and give his steed a swift kick on its way. You do not want to be held captive in your own castle by a toad wearing King's clothing. You need to make sure that this guy really has potential to be your "knight in shining armor"; otherwise, what's the point? It should be fairly obvious from first impressions, or even on your first date, whether your guy has the "makings" of a Prince. God gave us fantastic instincts, so use them!

Let's take a moment to think this through. The bare minimum should be that he is kind, courteous, respectful, and considerate. Since he will be a product of how he is raised, you will be able to tell a great deal based on his home life and the type of family relationships he has. Does he act lovingly towards his parents, especially his mother, and his siblings? What are his feelings about his friends, professors, his employer, and fellow employees? Watch his attitude when he is challenged or hurt; how he acts or reacts are cues to his level of maturity, ability to communicate, and whether he is willing to be held accountable for his behavior. Is he patient or hot-headed? Is he quick to resolve conflict or is he demanding that he must have things his way because he thinks everyone else is wrong?

Regrets

There are so many stories that end in disaster. Often, you will hear people say with regret, "When I look back, I realize the warning signs were there, I just didn't want to see them." Thus the expression, "love is blind!" It is even more painful when a person has compromised so much, she is at a loss as to how she even got there. She becomes so blinded by her emotions and feelings, that she can no longer see the truth. She may be totally bewildered and confused, wondering how things got so out of control. There are many such sad, tragic stories of girls having sex with their boyfriends and getting pregnant; girls finding out their "lover" has given them a sexually transmitted disease; and girls who panic and run to cover their "mistakes" by choosing to end the life of their babies through abortion. None of these stories began with this tragic end in mind! Nor did these girls stop to think that they might have to suffer through the brunt of their choices. Nevertheless, the consequences are real. The devastation and scars left from their decisions create life-shattering affects.

One such tragedy has left such a horrific mark on a friend that it has taken her over thirty years to come to grips with her actions. She chose long ago to terminate a few of her "unwanted" pregnancies when she was in college. Now, she would give anything to go back and have those babies, no matter what the cost. The embarrassment and guilt over getting pregnant led her to make a panicked decision that has nearly cost her, her own life. Even as an adult, her shame and remorse has led her to the brink of suicide, though she has a beautiful family filled with the joy of life and the love of God. She has suffered through deep depression, anxiety attacks, thoughts of unworthiness and mental anguish, eventually becoming dependent on medication—just to survive! Her healing has been a very long time in coming; it has required time on her face before God, routine counseling, and fervent pursuit of truth in God's Word. She is now free from this bondage, but the cost to get there has been excruciating. She was finally able to forgive herself, and to accept God's forgiveness for her sin.

How do we let ourselves become so deceived that we make such costly mistakes? It's those little compromises that we make along the way that open the door to the possibility of these tragedies becoming our own. The difference between success and failure in any relationship is whether we set ourselves up for success or failure! We should decide ahead of time how we will handle each situation. It is possible to avoid all of these tragedies! We don't usually enter relationships to fail at them; we expect them to succeed and we hope for the best. Often, though, our actions do not run parallel with our intentions. We must choose to behave in a way that sets us up to succeed. We need to make good choices. It is important to pay close attention to the "warning signs" and "red flags" in our relationships. It is crucial to recognize what kind of guy is worthy of our time and energy and what kind is not!

Red Flags

Here's a "red flag" example: your guy asks you to go to a dance. Let's say you really don't feel comfortable at a dance because you don't like the environment, loud music or obnoxious, intoxicated people who will be there, and/or maybe your parents won't allow you to go. Your guy really wants to go out and doesn't feel there's anything wrong with it. He can't understand why you don't want to go. Even though he knows this, he keeps asking, even begging, you to go. Then, he starts to also make fun of you and makes sarcastic remarks that you're too uptight and need to relax. He may criticize you or your parents for being too "straight" or boring. If that doesn't work, he may argue that your thoughts or beliefs don't really hold water, and continue to pressure you until you give in.

Or, maybe you don't like to go to certain movies because you feel they are too graphic and vulgar. If you do go, it really bothers you and you have a hard time getting certain scenes out of your mind. But your guy really likes to go and complains that you're no fun. He pressures you to go, or decides if you're not going, he's going without you with his friends. Or, he may even taunt you by saying he's going to take another chick.

There are two words to solve this problem "buh-bye!" These types of pressures or compromises are just the beginning of a guy attempting to break you down; you'd better believe the control and manipulation will only worsen. Tie your emotions into the deal, and before you know it, he'll be saying things like, "If you really love me, you would," or "You're so hot, come on, I just want you so bad," just to get you in bed. This relationship, you can be assured, is doomed! The saddest part, for you, is that if you stay in that relationship, you will become more insecure, more fearful, and more degraded. You may even become consumed by the relationship; slowly losing sight of the person you used to be inside. You cannot afford to take the risk! If you are in this situation, God gave you two legs - RUN!

It's Over When....

The telltale signs that a relationship needs to be ended are usually more obvious to those on the outside looking in. To be sure you will have no doubt, run through this short checklist to see how your story is stacking up:

- Is your guy trying to control you?
- Have you compromised anything about yourself, such as your relationship with God and others, or your commitment to your beliefs and convictions?
- Are you afraid?
- Does he hold threats against you or manipulate you through other tactics?
- Does he tempt you with things like alcohol, drugs, money or sex?
- Are his promises empty?
- Have you lost trust in his words and actions?
- Have the two of you become sexually active, or has he already had many other lovers?

- Have you been physically assaulted in any way, or threatened to be?

- Have you broken it off many times but he keeps "winning" you back?

If you or he, is actively involved in any of the behaviors just mentioned, you are not capable of managing your life well or making clear-minded decisions. You must break this relationship off, and ask for accountability from an outside source, like a parent or counselor, as to how to handle things.

Put It to the Test

Testing your guy and making a wise selection will ensure that your future is a place of love, security, protection, and peace. The kind of guy you need and desire is out there! If you ask God, He will be faithful to reveal these things to you. Ask your King for His opinion. He knows whether this guy is "the one." He desires nothing less than His best for you! We often are misled by our own feelings and perceptions, but God is the perfect judge of character for the Princes that come your way. You have the "home court" advantage when he comes to your door. Now, you are equipped to know what you are looking for. You can challenge, test, and determine whether he is a "Prince Valiant" or just a toad. Let's take a look at the differences between the two.

Is He a Prince?

A real Prince Valiant will pursue your heart, mind, and spirit. This is God's plan for initiating a potential relationship. This guy will prove he is worthy of your love because he lays down his own needs and desires in order to win your devotion. He wins your trust because he has the heart of a servant. He demonstrates sacrificial love towards you by meeting your greatest need--security. He asks for nothing in return for himself. It is by his actions that he wins your respect, honor, and adoration. He is aware that you are giving him the ultimate prize, your heart, which is your most precious possession. He values and cherishes you above himself; his love is Godly and pure. His gentle manner and humble spirit esteem you and lift you up. You see character and integrity in all he does. He honors your sexuality by maintaining self-control and abstains from all types of intimate, sexual behavior.

This Prince knows that the stability of the royal family lies on his shoulders, and he sets his sights on the fulfillment of ruling his Kingdom with his Queen, above selfish desires of the moment. He is diligent in the building of your relationship and demonstrates he is respectable, honorable, and trustworthy. His focus is to prepare for a prosperous future with you, his true love. He works hard to secure an immovable foundation for your castle to be built upon. His heart belongs first to God, and then it is yours. He is your biggest fan! His actions raise no doubts as to his integrity because he proves himself time and again that he can be trusted and that he is worthy of your love and affections.

Or Is He a Toad?

What if you discover your Prince is really just a toad after all? This may be confusing at first until you read on about our own evil villain, The Prince of Toads, and his plan to foil your future! The Frog Prince says all the words you so desire to hear, but his behavior does not line up with the things he says. This becomes confusing and causes you to question whether or not you can trust him. It seems his excuses are unending, and he can't seem to imagine why you have a hard time believing him. Somehow, he begins to blame you for the choices he makes and the things that he does. He blames you for how he treats you. His bad behavior demeans you, and you begin to lose sense of who you are and what you thought life should be. You become confused and less confident, which increases your dependency on the Toad. You want to believe in him and see the best, but, somehow, this causes a great struggle within your thoughts and emotions; you feel things aren't quite right. He abuses his power over you; after all, he is a thief in disguise. He often hides behind his success or good looks or the admiration of others. But in your heart, you know he is demanding, prideful, arrogant, and often, unapologetic.

He begins to take over more control of your life; he may even exhibit fits of jealousy and rage, or demand that you change something about yourself to make him happy. His behavior turns threatening and more hostile when he doesn't get his way. He treats you with little consideration, and behaves more like a dictator than one with whom you want to share a life. You may find that there truly is little room for you in his heart, and observe he is often disrespectful to the God-given needs of you and others. He often lies to manipulate those around him to get what he wants.

In the end, he has a heart of a traitor and cheater. His selfish desires steal away your values and moral sense, ending in your broken self-reflection. At his worst, he is cunning and full of deceit; his desires can't be satisfied. He has given himself over to the control of God's enemy, the Prince of Toads, who comes to steal, kill, and destroy all the perfect gifts given to you by God. He desires to rack your life with confusion, remind you of your faults and failings, and prevent you from seeing that Royal Blood flows through your veins! Your evil villain's plan is at work in your life; you become hopeless, helpless and deceived.

Send Him Back to His Pond!

So, what should you do if you realize your "Prince Valiant" is really just an ugly, slimy, warty toad? Send him back to his pond! You are a Princess destined for the palace, not his murky pit! Get yourself back on track to maintain God's plan and purpose for your future! You are a Princess in the court of the King! Royal blood flows through your veins! Let that toad go! God's dream is still within you! You cannot magically change the toad into a Prince, no matter how many times you kiss him. He is an imposter. You have been held captive by his slimy grip long enough. The only hope for him is that one day he will have an encounter with God—you cannot make that happen.

ESCAPING the Swamp

Run back into the court of the King where there is safety, security, and fresh rain to wash off every last drop of mud on your royal robe. Bathe yourself in the love, light, and truth of the King of kings. Your Father's arms are open wide and He has fresh clothes waiting for you! He desires to crown you once again as a Daughter of Heaven.

God himself will help you defeat the evil villain's plan to rob, steal, kill and destroy your life. Come back under the protection of your loving Father. He will guide you in the ways of righteousness and the paths of truth. He knows everything you've done, everywhere your heart has been, and He, alone, can heal your brokenness.

Won't you ask Him now to help you see yourself through His eyes? There is hope in forgiveness, and hope in second chances. Every sunrise, you have a new day to begin fresh and new with God. It's a day worth living when He is in it. Next time, trust God for your special Prince, He knows exactly who the right one is for you. In fact, He knows all the details about your fabulous royal wedding! But for now, let Him be the true love of your life. He is faithful and will never leave or forsake you!

"My" Thoughts:

There is so much that goes into building your future. You can't afford to ignore the truth. You must be able to see yourself clearly; your relationship with your Heavenly Father must be established and strong before a third party can come on the scene. Your health and your royal bloodline's future are at stake. The stability of your kingdom is at stake. Your relationship must have a firm foundation to stand the test of ruling over your castle because when the wars come, and they will, that is when the strength or weakness of the palace is revealed. Take a long look at the following questions. Stack them up against where you are right now in the relationships you have or have had. Be honest with yourself, and if necessary, ask your parent or best friend for insight.

Am I Ready to Start Dating?

1. Am I a whole person? Have I taken a healthy look at my present state, and have I dealt appropriately with all the issues in my past?

_____

_____

2. Do I have a good understanding of my strengths and my weaknesses?_____

_____

_____

3. Have I discovered my dreams, goals, and desires -- do I have a plan in place to achieve them? _____

_____

_____

4. Is God in control of my life? Am I mature enough to handle the pressures and responsibilities of dating?_____

_____

_____

Personal Challenge:

Can you honestly answer all these dating questions for yourself in a way that puts your spirit at peace? Can your aspiring Prince answer all of these same questions for himself? Do your answers compliment or disagree with each other? If they disagree, please consider breaking off this relationship and take some time alone with God.

Prince Valiant (P) or Toad (T) Quiz:

1. Even if you tell him he doesn't have to, your guy asks your father or mother for permission to date you.   P or T

2. He attends church with you and your family, but later on, he's planning to get wasted at the next keg event with his friends.
P or T

3. Your best friend tells you that "your guy" told her she's "hot" and that he wishes he was going out with her instead.   P or T

4. You find out that your guy is planning a special date for you and has even asked your sister what activities you enjoy the most.
P or T

5. You and your guy are shopping at the mall and he tells you he wants to buy you something special, so he takes you in to Victoria's Secret to shop.   P or T

6. Your guy over reacts and accuses you of liking one of your guy friends when he sees the two of you talking. His jealousy starts to control your relationship. He gets angry and threatens that he's going to take him down. He tells you that you need to stop your friendships with other guys.   P or T

7. You think your man is taking you out to dinner at your favorite restaurant. He surprises you by taking you to a beautiful spot on the beach, instead. In his trunk, he brought a picnic blanket, candles, and take-out of your favorite meal. He knows you love to watch the sunset, and he wants to share it with you. He ends your

date by thanking God for you and for the fun times you have had together. P or T

8. Your guy uses his cell to snap a quick, unexpected picture of you when you leaned over. He thinks you're hot. He posts it on his blog to show you off to all his friends. P or T

9. Your guy is late getting you home on time for curfew. He asks you to call your parents and make up some bogus excuse why you're running late. P or T

10. You perform at a concert that means a great deal to you. Your guy cancels his own plans and shows up to greet you with a bouquet of fresh flowers and a sweet card. He's your number-one fan. P or T

11. While digging through his car for something you lost, you find a package of condoms hidden under the seat. When you question your guy about it, he laughs and responds, "Well, I want to be prepared, you know, 'just in case.'" P or T

12. You and your guy get into a heavy make-out session. Things are getting a little too tempting. He breaks away and says, "I'm sorry, I need to get you home! I'm thankful for you in my life. I want to handle our relationship right, and really treat you with the respect you deserve." He keeps his word, walks you to your door, and says he'll call you tomorrow. P or T

Can you see through these few examples, how a guy either behaves respectably or disrespectfully in the situation?

So, let me ask you -- are you dating a Prince or a Toad?

Answers: 1. Prince, 2. Toad, 3. Toad, 4. Prince, 5. Toad, 6. Toad, 7. Prince, 8. Toad, 9. Toad, 10. Prince, 11. Toad, 12. Prince

(Suggested reading, *Datable* by Justin Lookadoo & Hayley DiMarco.)

I never thought I would have had an abortion

It happened when I was 19 years old. My 2 year-old daughter and I had just left an abusive relationship that I had been in, living with this guy for over a year. He even wanted to marry me. I didn't know I was pregnant until we left him. I had heard "I love you and I'll never hit you again" for the last time!

With my first child, by a different father, there was never a doubt in my mind that I wanted her. I loved her from the minute that I found out I was pregnant at 16 years old. But this was different; I had made a clean break! The only thing I could think of was that I would never get this abusive man out of my life if I had his child. I thought the only solution was an abortion.

I asked someone in leadership at a church for advice. He said that in this case it would be alright. I now know he was wrong! But at the time I was very vulnerable. My dad wanted me to get an abortion and my mom did not want this guy in my life either. She was scared for my safety. Somewhere, deep inside, I knew it was wrong to have an abortion, but I was looking at my circumstances instead of what I knew "deep down in my heart."

The abortion took place in a cold, impersonal, and sterile environment. I felt a chill in my heart and just wanted to get it over with so I wouldn't have to deal with the issue of what I was doing. I didn't even want to think about it. After all, I thought I did it for a good reason. After having the abortion, I felt a deep loss and I knew I would never be the same. Later, when I learned how much my baby was formed, I was horrified at what I had done. I was filled with shame and guilt. No amount of justification could convince me that what I had done was right. I was wrong!

I believe that going against what I knew somehow to be true, along with trying to cover up pain from my past, contributed to my falling deeper into drugs and alcohol for several years. Before, I had been more of a "social user," but after the abortion, I plunged deeper and deeper into a world that few can understand. Once I got caught in this web, it was extremely hard to get out. What much of the world considered normal was foreign to me; the abnormal became the normal.

The times I did try to stay clean and sober, I fell prey to Satan's deception, every time. The old saying is true—Sin will keep you longer than you ever wanted to stay, make you pay more than you ever wanted to pay. Yet, I knew all along that I didn't want to spend the rest of my life like this. I knew there was hope for me if I could just find it. I knew there was a God and that I couldn't run from Him forever, that He had a better plan than this for my life. God's grace was there with me while He was calling me, pulling on my heart. I finally made the decision that I had to come out of this lifestyle, even though I didn't know how I was going to stay clean and sober.

I then made the decision to turn my life completely over to God and really started seeking the Lord with all my heart. God showed me that I would need to rely on His strength instead of my own. He showed me that I needed to stand on His Word, get to know Him better, and deal with the pain from my past, the pain that put me there in the first place.

You see, if I had only known that it would've been this easy, that this was all I had to do to get unstuck from sin's web, then I'd have done it a lot sooner. After all, who would want to stay there that long, if they knew of a way to get out? I had wasted so many years. I think a lot of people in similar situations don't want to be there, but they don't know how to get out. They wonder, "If I quit, how am I going to stay sober and clean?" They don't even realize that things from their past or bad choices or bad things that have happened to them put them there, or even why they are there, they are just there! They are in such deception; they can't see much beyond the drugs or alcohol addiction.

As I look back, even though as a young child I went to Sunday school and church, I didn't know Jesus personally. I remember when I was in high school, try-ing to stay clean and sober on my own strength, trying to have a relationship with God and live a Christian life. When I was witnessing and talking about the Lord to my friends, Satan would lie and say, "See no one is turning to the Lord, you're not affecting anybody's life, you're not doing any good." I didn't know the Bible well enough; I didn't know about planting seed and that maybe someone else would come along and water or harvest the seed. This was one of the first times I believed Satan's lies so I went back to socially using alcohol and drugs again, not realizing I was heading for more trouble.

Later, after I completely surrendered my life to Jesus, I knew I had to trust, that since God wanted me and had a plan for my life, He would have to give me the

strength that I didn't have to stay sober and face the pain from my past. Day by day, whenever I got weak or tempted, I called on the Lord to give me His strength! One of the scriptures that helped me the most was "…My (His) strength is made perfect in (our) weakness" (2 Corinthians 9:12 NLT), and I saw that I had to believe that—when we are weak, He is strong. As I read and applied God's Word to my life, I found it to be true. I also developed a personal relationship with Jesus and I began to realize God really loves me. He helped me to deal with the pain from the past, the abortion, the abuse, and everything else that had happened to me; those things that were covered up and buried that had contributed to my downfall. I was later thankful that my mom had walked the floor, late at night, many, many years, pleading the "blood of Jesus" over me and praying for me. She had never given up on me, but stood on God's Word, knowing that He is faithful to perform His Word.

At the time of the abortion, I thought I would be married someday and that I would have more children. Now, I know that I will never have another child. I often wonder what my second child would have been like. It has left a void in my life that will never be filled, even if I had had other children. I now have a strong relationship with the Lord and I know that I am forgiven and healed. I look forward to meeting my child in heaven someday. What would have been my child's purpose in this life? What was God's plan for this child? How would my life have been different?

I know now that God would have worked everything out in my life in regards to this child. But I can never go back to change what I have done. I should not have let other people influence my decision. In my heart of hearts, I knew it was wrong. If I had known the Bible or been closer to God, I believe regardless of the people or circumstances around me, I would have done the right thing. If you have already had an abortion, know that God will forgive you. First John 1:9 says, "If we confess our sins, he is faithful and just and will forgive us our sins and purify us from all unrighteousness." (NIV). If you are pregnant and not ready for the responsibility of a child; God still has a purpose and plan for your child; adoption could be a good solution. You may be holding the "miracle" a couple is desperately praying for! No matter what, God wants you to be healed and whole. God will make a way!

Lisa

chapter 12

DIAMOND IN THE ROUGH

Heidi Bents

How much value do you place on your life? If you haven't received an expensive piece of jewelry yet, maybe your first experience will be looking for your engagement ring with your fiancé. The diamond is one of the most beautiful stones our world has to offer. Deep in the earth, veins of diamond ore were created by thousands of years of pressure from rock, sediment, and other stone crushing together microscopic atoms of carbon. It's amazing that what begins virtually as ugly black dust, compresses into the clearest diamond crystals, refracting the most beautiful, brilliant light.

The Perfect Diamond

When shopping for a diamond, you will see how quickly the cost rises based on the color, clarity, cut, and karat weight of the stone. Premium diamonds, those which are virtually flawless, will cost tens of thousands of dollars per karat. A perfect diamond will be clear in color, will have no cracks, fractures, or mineral deposits, and the cut will maximize a variety of facets shaped to set off the ultimate brilliance of the stone. If you ever have the chance to diamond shop, be sure to look at the gem under a high powered jeweler's scope. What is invisible to the naked eye becomes very apparent through the lens of the microscope.

What is interesting about diamonds, even though they are mined only on certain continents so as to seem rare, there is virtually an endless supply of diamond ore. A little lesson in economics here: what drives up the price is the value that people and culture place on this stone. It is highly desirable, and usually, the more or bigger, the better! The other factor contributing to a diamond's expense is that the diamond companies restrict the supply of cut diamonds. If you could afford the most expensive gem, your local jeweler would probably not have this stone on hand. He would probably need to contact a diamond trader in New York, who may possibly have to make a call to his connection in Africa to purchase this rare jewel.

Supply and Demand

The demand for these gorgeous stones is very high, but the restricted supply of them causes the price to skyrocket. Manufacturers keep them "rare" to maintain the high prices. Diamonds are very beautiful, but much of a diamond's value is in the eye of the beholder. It is the mindset of the people and culture that create much of the worth or value of the stone. This same idea can be applied to our value as women. On this planet, there is virtually an endless supply of us, right? Well, we can definitely do something very culture-altering about our value as women!

The way our culture stands now, this vast supply of women also brings a potentially vast supply of sexual availability. Sex itself is not valued as precious or rare because it has become so readily available in our society. You cannot live a day without sexual bombardment from the T.V. shows and news media we watch, the music we listen to, and more than all of these, the Internet. The women perpetuating this decline, have sold themselves out dirt cheap for a few sweaty dollars, believing the lie that if she bares all, it will increase her desirability and value as a woman. This works completely against the laws of economics, common sense, and most importantly, the preciousness of womanhood that God created in us.

What is Wrong with This Picture?

Our society is perilously sick. We are suffering from a complete meltdown of the sanctity of life, from our unborn, to the sanctity of marriage, to our aged. People are sick in their hearts, minds, and souls because they have forgotten God and the preciousness of their existence. There is no greater realm affected than that revolving around our sexuality.

The most criminally minded of all can become totally controlled by sexual or emotional addictions that lead them to the farthest corners of despair and bondage. All the ugliest of sexual predators (the molester, the rapist, the pedophile, the abductor, and the killer) begin their abusive relationships somewhere earlier in their lives. A person does not just wake up one morning and decide to commit a heinous crime. Instead, the whole of their deviant experience, so contrary to God's intentions, is acted out in violent behavior against the innocent, one by one. This should send a very obvious message: how we handle our sexuality, with the uttermost respect or abuse, is incredibly impacting upon our futures, and the success or failure of our future relationships.

A Little Secret

I'll let you in on a secret: every guy, and I mean every guy, wants to be the "first" for his girl. Regardless of his personal behavior or experience, deep in his heart, he is created to desire, even need, a virgin. Part of a guy's uniqueness as a male involves his ego. His ego is affected by how he feels about himself, and his perception of his girl's esteem towards him. The competitive, introspective nature of a man boils down to this question: "Do I have what it takes to be a man?" Sexuality is a tender, vulnerable spot for guys. Now, guys who aren't healthy and mature in their self-reflection may take what they can get, play the field, sow their wild oats, and mess around. But, when it comes to the serious business of making a lifelong commitment to a relationship, every guy truly wants a virgin.

We've talked a lot about our differences so far, but let's talk about a few basic differences between guys and girls regarding our sexuality. Males and females come toward sexual interaction from different aspects. A guy is often motivated by simple sexual urges and physical attraction towards a female. He is primarily driven sexually by the need for physical satisfaction. God created his sex drive mainly to procreate, as He commanded Adam and Eve in the Garden of Eden, and God also made it a pleasurable experience to bless the intimacy of a married couple. But because guys generally tend to develop their emotional side more slowly than the ladies, it is possible for them to somewhat detach themselves from their emotional state. A guy is capable of having a sexual experience that may or may not be as meaningful to him as it is to his partner. Because men are generally "left brain" natured, they have to learn how to connect the need for sex with their emotional, "right brained" thinking. Part of the maturing process necessary to create sexual health and true intimacy in a man's life, is in learning how to connect these emotions and feelings with his sexual desires.

A female, on the other hand, tends to respond out of "right brained" thinking, and will enter into a sexual relationship for emotional satisfaction. Her desire is often based on her need for security: to feel loved and needed. For her to feel validated, she needs to know her man's desire for her is because she holds the key to his heart. A woman will be sexually motivated when she trusts the integrity of a man's heart and emotions. The two enter a sexual relationship for opposite reasons, and as we know, opposites attract! Whether married or not, a man's greatest challenge in life will be in controlling himself in the sexual arena: his thoughts, his fantasies, his tendencies, and mastering his sex drive. A woman's greatest challenge in life, will be in controlling her emotional and mental state which revolves around the relationships she has.

Both guys and gals participating in promiscuous sexual interaction take a huge risk spiritually, mentally, emotionally, and physically. For a female, she risks the most precious things she has when she gives in to sex: her heart and her virginity. For a guy, he risks the most precious thing about himself when he gives in to sex: his manhood. We humans are simply not equipped to deal with the consequences of sex outside of marriage because it's not in our "makeup" to do so! We cannot handle the backlash we experience when we go against the grain of how we are created.

Not only this, but the couple can be catapulted forward into a decision-making process they are not capable of dealing with, concerning issues such as pregnancy, sexually transmitted diseases, or pressure from the situation to quickly get married. Lack of control in these areas is where we see unhealthy, co-dependent type behaviors and relationships that are destructive, often leading to irreparable damage. These people become broken down in their neediness and insecurities, and are lost in the disasters they face every day.

Often, couples will think the solution to their issues is to get married, so, they rush to the altar imagining this action will "fix" it or make it right. But getting married does not solve these problems. It will not provide the comfort or security necessary to keep the relationship together; it truly can become the "beginning of the end." The instability and habits created earlier in life will seep out in other ways from within the marriage. There will be trust and respect issues. The instability of the individuals will potentially escalate towards each other through bitter fights, rage, and casting blame. The marriage will be unstable, and will not provide an environment of safety, security, and love that the couple had expected. The innocent baby or child will become the newest victim of the chaos, learning many of the worst behaviors from his immature parents. Other problems that can arise may be difficulty overcoming such issues as: addictions to alcohol and drugs, pornography, extra-marital affairs, visits to inappropriate "sex" clubs, hiring prostitutes, and worse. The abuses in the marriage hinder the ability for it to succeed, and more than likely, the marriage will end in divorce. This is not the path for blessing our lives as God has intended!

The Ultimate Trophy

Healthy sex is created by two healthy people, who commit to marriage for all the right reasons. The marital act of lovemaking is an ongoing process; it requires commitment, trust, love, respect, honor, and kindness to thrive. The need to be sexually fulfilled continues throughout our lifetime. It still has to be held in check by both partners "as long as we both shall live." Whether we will be satisfied someday in marriage depends on how we've trained ourselves in the process.

Just like your Prince, you must learn the self-discipline necessary to control your decisions, thoughts and emotions. Have you learned to depend on God? Have you allowed Him to rule your needs, wants, and desires? Do you know Him as the lover of your heart?

Even within marriage, you will have to trust and depend on God to fulfill you. He is the only perfect husband. He will have to fill up the balance of what your relationship lacks. There is no perfect marriage, even if your match is "made in Heaven!"

The life we lead in our youth directly challenges and affects our future. We are creatures of habit. If we allow ourselves to cross the boundary and have sex before marriage, it can lead to great harm, heartache, and dysfunction. Let's get over the question of "how far is too far?" All premarital sexual behavior, of any kind, whether you go "all the way" or not, is inappropriate and is a sin against ourselves, each other, and most of all, God. God's love is pure; He is holy. If we truly are sons and daughters of God, we too will strive towards His holiness and purity. Our bodies belong to Him. We are His temple. He hates sin because it destroys our lives in its perversion. He hates sin because it separates us from Him. He hates sin, because it will send us to its master, Satan himself. True purity and virginity begins in our hearts: the outcome is validated by our actions, choices and lifestyle.

Real sexual intimacy can only be found and satisfied in a wholesome way, and that is through marriage. God has wrapped in each woman the power to complete the man He has chosen for her. Isn't that amazing? Part of completing him as a man is to "get lucky" with you as his Bride! When he knows he's your only lover, it's like he ran this incredibly exhausting and grueling marathon, and he persevered, crossed the finish line, and won the ultimate trophy—YOU! For a guy, if he doesn't get to be "the one" to be blessed with your virginity, to unwrap your precious gift to him, it feels to him like being awarded "runner up" or "second place." He gets a "trophy," but it's more like an honorable mention instead of capturing the grand prize.

Ugh… It's a Fake!

Imagine how you would feel if your man proposed and gave you this amazing engagement ring with a gorgeous, huge diamond in the middle. You're so excited you can't wait to shout the news! Later, after you show it off to all your family and friends, he admits,

"I'm sorry I could only afford this stone in a cubic zirconium, but it looks real, huh? I wish I would have saved up more money along the way to give you what you really deserve. I'm sorry I can't give you what I know you're worth." All kinds of thoughts and emotions would be triggered within you, right?

It would kind of hang in the air like his stale cologne. It would feel as if you were suckered into a counterfeit deal; "It's a fake!" The point isn't that you expected an impressive, expensive ring, but that you've received a treasured gift that's real and from the heart. It's exactly the same way for a guy too, from his perspective. He's first attracted to the "package" of you; everything looks beautiful and dreamy to him, but he wonders, what's on the inside? Is this girl for real? He too would struggle with thoughts like, *Did she not think that I should deserve her best? She's my girl, I feel cheated like someone else got the best of her!* Or, *Did she not give a thought to how this could hurt me and our future together?*

When your husband is your only lover, it makes him feel fantastic about himself. You are his amazing trophy, his "crowning glory!" It boosts his ego; he doesn't have to struggle with the fear of competition or rejection because of your other "lovers." His ability to believe in you and your commitment to him are secure in his mind. He is more likely to remain faithful to your marriage by restraining himself from other women because of the special bond you share.

Our young men are often cut short of expecting virgin brides in their futures because so many young women have already been spent. We are partly responsible for lowering their expectations, and for devaluing ourselves by how we've degraded our most precious Godly gift. We've lost the uniqueness of mystery, intrigue, and suspense that physical attraction and satisfaction requires. Let's make a change and set a higher standard of appreciation for our own sexuality as females. Men, young and old, need our help to protect them from their sexual vulnerabilities by not tempting them with how we dress, behave, act, and what we say. Let's help regain the sanctity of our most treasured promise in life, the covenant of marriage: "Forsaking ALL others; to have and to hold;

to love, honor, and cherish; for better or for worse; for richer or for poorer; in sickness and in health, and 'til death do us part!" Isn't it refreshing just to imagine this is how it could be? Let's send the message that everyone needs to hear, that we need our guys to be real men: respectable, pure-hearted, and wholesome, Godly men!

It's Worth the Sacrifice

Making a marked change for the better takes courage, self-discipline, and action. You may feel stretched when you think of a commitment like this, but God is ever so proud of you! Let His strength shine through your weakness; that's where you will experience the incredible power of God breathing through your life. God's power is real. God's healing touch is miraculous. Your obedience is a pleasure to Him, worth more than any sacrifice you could make. He delights in the treasure of your pure heart. When you present yourself to Jesus, faults and all, His love and forgiveness overshadows your guilt and sin. He blots them out with His blood. Your determination and commitment to please God by living according to His standards will abundantly bless your life! Live each day by laying your life down at the feet of Jesus. Choose to die to yourself each day as a "living sacrifice," letting Christ be alive within you instead. This is your lifestyle of worship: yielding to Him daily, letting Him truly be your Lord and King. You will not be disappointed!

A Living Sacrifice to God

And so, dear brothers and sisters, I plead with you to give your bodies to God because of all he has done for you. Let them be a living and holy sacrifice—the kind he will find acceptable. This is truly the way to worship him. Don't copy the behavior and customs of this world, but let God transform you into a new person by changing the way you think. Then you will learn to know God's will for you, which is good and pleasing and perfect.

Romans 12:1-2

"My" Thoughts:

1. In what ways do you see our society influencing how you think about sex? What actions can you take to change your own environment?_____

_____

_____

2. Have you been impacted by, or been a victim of, sexual abuse? If so, have you gotten help?_____

_____

_____

You need help! It is crucial that you find an adult or Godly counselor that you can confide in. You cannot go it alone on this one. Being a victim of any type of abuse can cause deep wounds, and leave you crippled as a person. It is also critical for you to understand that it is not your fault. Get rid of the guilt: don't hold this dark secret inside anymore, go get help!

2. What "actions" do you permit in your guy relationships that you know deep-down should not happen? Before you try to deny it, let me ask you if you have ever gone just a little "too far" and felt shame for what you did?_____

_____

_____

"Shame" is an interesting word. Do you know the definition of shame means to dishonor or disrespect? If you feel any shame when it comes to a physical relationship, you can rest assured that you are being disrespected and dishonored. Going back to the very basic building blocks that make a relationship solid, you need to be respected and honored. Ask God to forgive you and put a stop to it once and for all!

3. God desires to restore you. Whether you had a choice or no choice in the matter, let God restore the broken pieces of your heart. God promises in His Word that He will make all things new. No

matter where you've been or what you have done, God desires to cleanse you and give you a fresh start!

Isaiah 1:18-20

"Come now, let us reason together," says the LORD.
"Though your sins are like scarlet, they shall be as white as snow; though they are red as crimson, they shall be like wool. If you are willing and obedient, you will eat the best from the land; but if you resist and rebel, you will be devoured by the sword." For the mouth of the LORD has spoken.

4. What do you want for your future?_____
_____
_____

5. Wouldn't you like to present your future husband with the "ultimate trophy?" What steps can you take to be sure you're giving him the real thing?_____
_____
_____

Personal Challenge:

To change our culture, it takes one precious lady at a time. Sex outside of marriage is a fake! It's just a cheap counterfeit to what God's plan provides.

How do you increase your value in our society? You are the real thing! You are a precious jewel, a prized possession. The Master Jeweler, King Jesus, has hand picked you. Under His all-seeing eyes, He has hand crafted and formed you with so many amazing, unique facets as a woman. With tender care, He has carved you out of the ordinary: His "diamond in the rough!" You are a rare find, a priceless treasure, a beauty who reflects the Light and Love of our Creator God.

I urge you to commit to abstinence until after marriage. Restrict the supply of sex that is now so readily available to any guy. Increase the desirability of the one-of-a-kind jewel that you are. Demand a high price for your life! Don't throw yourself away to every love that comes to your door. You set your own price tag: marriage. You are worth a bidding war. Sell out only to the highest bidder, the one who is willing to pay with the commitment of his life through marriage. He will be the worthy owner, the one who beholds you as the most priceless, rare, uniquely beautiful treasure of all. You tell your Prince, "I am worth waiting for!"

(Suggested reading, *The Truth About Sex* by Kay Arthur.)

chapter 13

HAPPILY EVER AFTER?
Heidi Bents

Truth or Fiction?

Fact or fable? Can "happily ever after" be a reality in your life? As you have been reading so far, you may have thought that I am crazy for telling such stories about love and life. Maybe it seems that all this talk about God's love is more like fictitious imagination than what real life offers?

I have been involved in church ministry for years and it has afforded me many wonderful opportunities to listen to the stories of young women all across the country. I've personally witnessed many success stories of love and marriage along the way. On the other hand, many have opened up and expressed some of their deepest hurts, disappointments, and struggles about their relationships with guys. Often, they have fallen victim to hopelessness, and are not able to comprehend that their lives could be better than what they've known. Many have let their guard down and given their heart or body away more times than they can count. They feel trapped in their mistakes, overcome by shame and guilt, and feel powerless to change the behavior that takes them to this place of despair. If you are one who understands what I am saying, please stay with me through the rest of our story!

God Gave Me a Second Chance!

I would like to offer some personal insight and share what I have experienced with God because my own life is a product of being given a second chance. First, I need to establish that it is only by God's love that He graces us to understand and learn from the lessons we experience in life. What He has brought me through and delivered me from is truly amazing. But I am no more special or sought after by God than you are. I was simply willing to open my heart to hear and follow His voice. I have found that how quickly I learn to obey what God instructs me to do, can determine whether or not I have to face the same lessons again and again. I came to a place where I decided I'd had enough of doing life my way!

Each one of us is on a different path with God. We share a broad variety of backgrounds, circumstances, and childhood experiences; each is unique from the other. Your story and the life you lead is no less important than any other person on the planet. God wants to work in your life, even if you don't see it or haven't yet found the solution to the problems you face. Somehow, God wants to reach you right where you are and work through your life in a way that will always lead you back to Him.

God's Unconditional Love Changes Me!

There is one very good reason that our talk so far has revolved around the subject of being a virtuous Princess: because the world has lied to us by telling us "it is not possible!" My hope is that you are now inspired with the Truth about yourself, coming straight from the heart of God, your adoring Father. You truly are the apple of His eye. You are His favorite! If you can let this truth soak into your spirit, everything about your life and world will change. Why? Because unconditional love changes us. It changes our hearts, heals our emotions, and gives us a true perspective about ourselves. It changes everything about how we make decisions for our lives and futures; our sense of value and self-worth rises. And, above all, our love for God grows. We learn we don't have to make crucial decisions based on how we feel about ourselves, but instead, based on the truth of Godly love and principles. More than anything else, unconditional love provides the meaning of God's grace in our lives; when we understand it, it is the beginning of desiring to please and honor God. If you have been discouraged by how others have treated you or made you feel, you need to know that this doesn't change God's heart towards you. You are His prize possession, a Daughter of Heaven, deserving of His best!

As a Teenager...

When I was young and dreamed about my future, the sky was the limit! I felt perfectly capable of living my dreams and was very inspired and passionate about many wonderful things. But as I began to throw myself into the lives of the guys I dated, those initial dreams God gave me began to dim. The dreams that were once vivid and crisp in my heart slowly began to fade into something that felt more like a wish or imagination, or, like a fairy tale. I began to search for a guy who might share the same dream as mine, but I didn't notice how my own insecurities were affecting the way I viewed others, and even myself.

Hopefully, by now you have a good grasp on identifying the differences between a valiant Prince and a toad, and you realize your life is worthy of God's very best! For me, despite my very conservative family-life and background, I got the Prince and toad a little mixed up. Unfortunately, the impact of making the choice to involve myself with others who were not "sold-out" to God, brought consequences in my life reaching farther than I could have imagined.

Everything I initially dreamt about ended up being wrapped around the guy I chose to give my life away to. I didn't realize I was beginning to give up parts of "my dream." I seemed to be a magnet for the "bad-boy" type of guys, even though I was very innocent and naïve. Remember, opposites attract! This did nothing for my esteem or self-reflection. I wasn't a mature Princess and I didn't fully listen to the voice of God, until it was too late to reverse some of the choices I'd made. Instead, I began to place my confidence in the flattering words of one whose heart wasn't pure. I thought that if I really wanted to prove myself to this person, I should be fun to be with, adventurous and show him a good time. Though this started out in innocence, my daring spirit and need for attention, at times, led to game-playing and manipulating my boyfriend's emotions and feelings. I sometimes took advantage of the control I held over my guy's heart, but more often, I was the one being taken advantage of.

I began to follow through with "heat of the moment" decisions by letting down my standards, fooling around and eventually having sex. I thought this might convince my boyfriend that I was worth his love and help me keep him as my "own." I might become that extra-special "someone" to him, above the other girls he knew. I naively believed the words he said, rather than his actions or how they made me feel. My insecurities caused me to second-guess my own God-given instincts. I became frustrated with my failure to stack up with God's thoughts and standards. Discouraged, I thought I was beyond living them, so it was easier on my conscience to just cross them off my list. After all, a guy's attention was real and tangible; visible. God sometimes seemed to be more abstract and obscure; invisible.

Our Needs As Young Women...

I'm sharing with you honestly because I desire to shed light on our uniqueness as women. What does our behavior say about us? I later recognized that my behavior was based out of my own deep need to feel loved, valued, and secure. These are needs we all share. They are not to ruin or destroy our lives, but to be guarded, protected, and given over for God to take control of and satisfy. Our needs are valid, God-given, and meant to bind together our relationships, yet, created to be met and completed in marriage-- not a moment before!

The lie is that we can get these needs satisfied from our relationships with guys, but the truth is - there is a timing issue here. Your needs can only be met by one guy, your husband! It's only after the commitment has been made to be with you forever that any of these needs make sense or are satisfied because God created you that way as "woman!"

I Can't Emphasize Enough...

A Princess innately must have a commitment for love and sex to make sense, to be satisfied, and feel truly loved. Anything less is simply fantasy. "Safe sex" only occurs in a healthy marriage. Without the long-term commitment that marriage provides, fear and insecurity become what drives a couple. From my own experience, I have seen how the relationship will take on a somewhat desperate tone as each tries to hang on to what little safety and satisfaction the relationship can provide. Inappropriate sexual activity cuts to our very souls!

By abstaining from sexual behavior, a woman has nothing to lose when "testing out" her potential Prince. The relationship stays fresh, new, and alive. The dream stays within reach. There is mystery and intrigue about the other partner and suspense plays a big part leading up to the commitment of marriage. The relationship is safe, the Princess feels secure, and her Prince continues to earn her love with acts of kindness and devotion. Time is truly invested in placing invaluable building blocks towards their future.

The couple is free to hear from God because they aren't living opposed to God's commands. They aren't strapped down by sin and guilt. If the romance ends, each can walk away with their emotions, personality, dreams, and integrity intact. They remain whole individuals through the process, and can learn valuable relational tools, taking with them the best of memories. If the romance succeeds to the altar, the relationship is blessed by God for the couple's obedience, and good seed is set in motion for a fruitful, wholesome marriage.

God's Design

We, especially as Princesses, are not designed to give away our hearts, time and again. We are not created to have multiple relationships or lovers. Each woman was designed to truly love only one man, her Prince, with whom she should spend her entire life and future, loving him deeply, intimately, and freely.

Here's an amazing fact that proves how fantastic God created both sexes. God wired us so that our first sexual experience is so powerful, it engrains certain impulses, chemicals, and attractions into the brain so as to cement that bond between a couple. God designed our "chemistry" this way so that we would be completely satisfied and fulfilled with only one true love. If we go God's way on this, the marriage relationship will be bound with an unbreakable bond through sexual intimacy. The marriage will be a sanctuary, a safe place - a haven of love not to be shared with anyone else. How precious is this gift that God has given us!

On the Outside Looking In

I experienced some devastating blows to my dreams in my early twenties. I had been given so much in my life to that point; I had one of the greatest childhoods that I know of. My family never missed going to church, I was surrounded by Godly relatives, and our home was peaceful, loving, and full of celebrating life. On top of all that, my parents were financially successful and took full advantage of the opportunities life afforded. You would imagine that I wouldn't have settled for anything less for myself.

On the outside, everything looked perfect, magical! I was living the dream! Yet, an emptiness ached on the inside - I still hadn't found what I was looking for. I knew the truth in my mind, but hadn't yet experienced it fully in my heart. I began to part with the truth that I knew, and sold myself out to some believable lies. I allowed God's vision for my life to be corrupted by my own self-centeredness and need to be in control. I began to think I knew what was best for me and what would make me happy. I traded God's "true love" in for worldly passion, thinking I could set my sail on the winds of wild romance, only to find I was adrift and alone after the storm died down. Honestly, the wild boys may have been more exciting to date, but I've noticed they make really lousy husbands and are beyond poor examples as fathers. Looking back, I was really too young to throw myself into a world that even adults seem barely capable to survive in. Knowing what I do now, I personally think it's wise to put off adult decisions (engagement, marriage, having children, etc.), until at least the mid-twenties because we change so much in these critical years.

When it really mattered most, my choices led me down a path that I never imagined I'd be on. When I was young, it was hard to believe that one day I'd come face-to-face with the consequences of my foolish decisions. But believe me, the choices made in your teens and twenties will be the blessings or consequences for the rest of your life! It's hard to imagine the decisions you are making right now can have such an impact on your future, marriage, family, and career, but that truly is what happens! Poor judgment, made in innocence or not, still pays a heavy price.

It took me many years, and lots of tears, to understand that the real needs of my heart could only be met by a deep, satisfying relationship with Jesus. I had looked to be affirmed and valued through my relationships, when in fact, the very thing those types of inappropriate relationships produced was lack of self-esteem, a dimming of the truth, and a loss of the beautiful dreams God had given me.

A Real Evil Villain

Contrary to God's plan, Satan wanted my life to be weakened by my choices, lost to the circumstances I'd created, and bound to my sin and selfish ways. Stuck in this trap, I became ineffective to the dreams, visions, and spiritual fiber God's way would have provided for me. I forgot about the needs of others: to represent the truth about Jesus, and impact their lives and the world around me in a positive light. Instead, Satan tried to keep me selfishly focused on "me," becoming obsessed with problems of my own making, so that chaos became a normal, routine way of life. The lack of living out the standard that God has set for living a blessed life is what crushed me as a person. This is a tale I know very well, because it was torn from the pages of my own life story. I began to settle for a second best, second-rate experience. The expectations for myself and my future failed because of my own poor decisions. The door to temptation I had unlocked, forcefully blew wide open and I found myself powerless to change the outcome. The beautiful story my life had begun to pen, took an ugly twist, where Satan, the enemy of my soul, sought to steal, kill, and destroy everything noble, honorable, and worthy about me.

Addicted to Our Own Vices

It's quite ironic, but through his deception, Satan attempts to lure each of us into his counterfeit traps by putting a pretty face on sin. The lies of Satan are what we must conquer in our minds, every day. With his prideful spirit, he will try to whisper to our self-centered nature, encouraging indulgences and personal liberties we're not created to take. Pride has always been at the base of failure, and it always will be. It was through the consequences of my prideful decisions that I learned first-hand the tactics of my enemy. I realized I was no match for his power on my own. I needed God's help through His Spirit to break the bondage of my sinful behaviors.

The Long Way Home

As God began to pick up the fragments of my shattered, broken life, He was so faithful, gentle, yet firm, in showing me the truth. As I allowed Him to truly be in control and refashion my future, He let me take a long look back down the bumpy, uneven path I'd chosen. Actually, it looked more like a path that had been cut narrowly along sheer mountainous drop-offs, and steep cliff faces marked with intimidating boulders! He began to point out the many times that He'd provided an exit off this trail, which would have taken me down the road He had planned. Not looking for the warning signs, I had blindly plowed on past the "Bridge Out," "Dead End," and "No Outlet" signs that beckoned me to turn around! What God showed me, humbled me so deeply that all I wanted to do was listen, and learn. I had made such a mess out of my life; I couldn't imagine that even God himself, could make anything good come of it!

What Do You See?

Once I understood my own behaviors, the lives of those around me began to take on new meaning. I ran for cover to Godly mentors who could offer me sound Biblical advice. I ran to God's Word to have my mind set straight. I noticed how far from truth the ones I loved had gone. I saw the morale and integrity of my family begin to crumble. I was appalled at the actions of others, continuing in their chaos and self-deceit. It seemed they would make the same foolish choices over and over again, unable to stop their destructive tendencies. I saw the brunt of their mistakes: broken people, marriages torn apart, relationships destroyed, and devastated God-given dreams. I saw them defeated, faithless, hopeless. These destructive behaviors led to deeper bondage - worsening addictions to alcohol, drugs, money, affairs of the heart, sex and pornography. These are the tools wielded by the Prince of Toads, Satan himself. He seeks to defeat us through his deception and chain us to these vices. It is here where hope dies, the light dims, and truth fades.

But God made a way out for me! Though it broke my heart to watch tragedy in motion around me, God did come to my rescue at last! He preserved my life and delivered me out of the trap I was in and I never want to go back.

Sometimes, we have to be broken to the point that we are willing to let God take control. And, sometimes, we have bound up our lives in so many tangled webs that we simply have no choice but to give in. The easiest way to live is to give our life over to God up front and let Him handle the details of our future. Create a daily habit of consulting our Loving Father, and let Him guide our decisions and rule our hearts. Only He can bring things miraculously together on our behalf. And, only when He is truly in control, can we be at peace with ourselves.

Casualties of War

So, God turned time back for me and lovingly showed me how to do life His way. He pointed to some of my past failures, those times I had injured others, and let me pick through those events to learn why and to seek out the lessons in them. I wounded a few pure hearts along the way and I, too, was deeply wounded - a true casualty of war!

I took some time in my life to simply lay it all down. I made the choice to let God open up all my wounds: spiritual, emotional, relational, and even sexual. One by one, I asked God to reveal to me my sin, and He did. I realized my own actions and hardened heart had created many of the consequences I faced. I had to "own" my mistakes, face the results, and accept that I had created a lot of life's challenges for myself. I had often blamed God for not rescuing me, but now I realize, it was through those very things that He built His character in me.

I asked Him to forgive me for all my wrong behaviors, actions, words, and thoughts, and to cleanse my heart of everything impure and ungodly. And He did! What an amazing load was lifted off of me! Years of pain, regret, unforgiveness, bitterness, and anger slowly began to melt out of my heart. God's love and compassion began to fill it back up. His healing power and anointing began to restore and rejuvenate my soul and spirit. There were times of instant personal healing and a change of heart in me, and times where I had to make a choice to fight for it. It was a time of putting areas of my past to death for good, and a time to receive fresh vision and direction from Jesus—a grueling, but rewarding process! God was at work performing deep surgery to recreate and renew me as His Princess. I had come to a place of reliance on God, where the details really didn't matter; I just was happy to be in His presence. His power is real, His Spirit is comfort, and His forgiveness is like fresh Spring rain!

Becoming a True Friend of God

I desired more than anything to be a true friend of God: to love what He loves, and hate what He hates. I desired for Him to remake and refashion me to be more like His Son, Jesus. It requires daily personal dedication, diligence, and obedience. A relationship with God is an active thing. How great it is or is not, depends on how much I invest my life and energy in the relationship. If I had only checked in from time to time, my love for God would not have grown much deeper. I have to pursue God's heart just as He pursues mine—with my entire life! He desires all of me, not just a slice or my leftovers. He wants my love for Him to shine through every dimension and aspect of my life with unashamed, vibrant passion. It's this lifestyle of pure-hearted worship that brings a smile to God's face. That's when I truly become filled with the mind of Christ. I want to learn what He likes, what makes Him smile, what makes Him laugh, and what brings Him joy and pleasure in me as His child, and He is still showing me these things!

God Gave Me a Vision

God gave me a picture of one thing that really humbled me and helped me understand how to value His sons as God desires they should be valued. God gave me a vision of a Prince: he stood tall, with broad, strong shoulders and was very handsome. There were rays of light coming down over him, like it was shining down from Heaven, washing over him from the top of his head to his feet. It looked as if the light passed through him, filling him up and giving him strength, and his face was turned upward as if to absorb God's presence. The vision of this Prince was actually of a real man: my own tall, strong, handsome "Prince Valiant," whom God had miraculously brought into my life. God showed me that He had placed a crown on my Prince's head, like an aura of anointing that he wore to be a Godly man. This anointed crown was his Godly protection to keep him from sin and error. The crown represented God's authority in his life and the anointing of the Holy Spirit to walk out God's plan and purpose for his future.

God showed me that I would be usurping the authority of God and the conviction of the Holy Spirit in his life if I were to become a stumbling block for him. Basically, I, myself, could play the role of "Evil Villain" in the life of one that I loved so deeply! My actions towards him could cause his very dependence on God to fail. I could be the blame for removing God's voice and wisdom that shielded his heart. This was a real wake-up call for me! God showed me it was my responsibility to be a Godly Princess and to not tempt my future King into sin because I could cause him to lose his anointed crown. Everything about his character, integrity and reputation could be altered if I interfered! God warned me that I would be held accountable for my behavior if I caused my Prince to lose this Godly covering.

Was I Willing to Change?

But God also wanted to give me a new, fresh look at His amazing grace. The pattern of behavior in my past relationships could be broken now, if I was willing to change. God challenged me by showing that He was giving me another chance to prove I truly desired to be His precious daughter. He wanted me to put into practice everything I had learned - all those hard, devastating lessons that had brought me to this place. He showed me that I had the makings of a true Princess, and that by His strength, I was equipped to bestow the appropriate respect and honor that His Prince deserved. This was so completely powerful and humbling! I realized that now, more than ever, I needed to be close to the heart of my Father God. In no way did I want to compromise the second chance God was giving me. I learned to place a higher priority on doing the right thing and making good decisions, and saying "no" to selfish desires. I learned to trust God's heart over my own thinking. The exciting part is that God totally delivered me through this process! He powerfully restored me, and watching my life change was so rewarding! I could see a new confidence building in my faith and trust in God. I felt God's strength, heard His voice, and sought after His Word, like never before. Little by little, I was becoming teachable; I saw His goodness rebuilding and reshaping my life.

With God, All Things Are Possible!

You may be wondering now if it is truly possible to have a relationship that is blessed by God. If there is no one you personally know who can say this, let me say it to you now: Absolutely! Everything I have shared with you is what I have witnessed in my own life, and in watching the lives of others who have needed healing and redemption. Though my own actions brought tremendous, life-long consequences, God still had a redeeming plan for His love to meet my life in powerful, miraculous ways! In every way He has blessed my obedience, the obedience of my valiant Prince, and the marriage that God gave us. I've experience God's mercy in ways that I didn't even have the hope to pray for!

My Knight in Shining Armor

God graced my life with a whole, capable man who proved and taught me many of the things I have shared with you on these pages. He saved his virginity for me because he knew that I'd be worth it. He esteemed the principles of God above himself, and made decisions knowing that it's simply the right thing to do. The sacrificial love he shows me absolutely cements my trust in him regarding his integrity, character, loyalty, and faith. I can tell you first-hand, that I do not doubt the love of my husband. I never doubted him once while we dated for over two and a half years.

I am completely humbled by God's grace, because I have seen it in action in my own life. I am grateful because I know I did nothing to deserve or earn it. Over the years, God's strength and Spirit helped me make the changes in my heart; His wise counsel gave me the guidance and courage to live obediently according to His truth. And, as if that weren't enough, He blessed me abundantly beyond my dreams with my own real, larger than life, "Knight in Shining Armor!"

Our marriage resembles nothing of my past relationships. I truly have been given a fresh beginning. I've been given another chance to live life God's way. There is no price tag to pin on the freedom from guilt and self-demeaning behavior that I have found. It is priceless! It is possible, not by my own strength, but by both of us depending on God, to learn how to live to please Him. I know this lesson from experience; that sin takes you farther than you want to go, keeps you longer than you want to stay, and has a high price that you won't be very willing to pay. Having a clean slate on my life now is worth everything I suffered, just to watch God take a disaster and re-make something fresh and new out of the ashes. God is so good. His compassion goes beyond my understanding!

After all that I had done in my past to sabotage the plan of God for my life, my valiant Prince proved that I was worth waiting for. How amazing is that? Out of a pure heart, actions speak. He did nothing less than esteem me completely, and he continues to esteem me every day. It is an amazing thing to be chosen by a Prince. Out of all the choice Princesses along life's way, he has chosen to be devoted to only me! It is with me he will build his castle, create heirs to his throne, and rule our entire kingdom. I decided early on, I didn't ever want to make him sorry for his decision. I cannot tell you how greatly I respect this man, how high he stands in my heart, and how humbling it is to realize that Father God knows best. In a degraded world where everything pure, noble, and lovely seemed to have vanished, God chose to shine His truth on my experience through the life of one of His Princes: My husband, my hero!

Even more miraculous, is to watch first hand the amazing heart of my Father God, whose mercy knows no end, whose love reaches beyond every fault and failure, and whose power mended my broken heart, my broken dream, and restored me, the broken Princess, to become the Queen of my King's dream!

Ever After

As we end this dating and relationship section, would you ask God to cement in your heart all that He has spoken to you during your time with Him? Ask Him to bring to your mind the sins that need to be settled and dealt with in your life. God's Word is powerful enough to change your heart. The truth of His Word is a lamp to guide your feet and a light for your path. It will cut to your soul, weeding out the deception and lies of your enemy, Satan, the Deceiver. Learn to love and treasure God's love letters to you. He has written you so many. Ask Him to give you Godly wisdom and knowledge. Ask Him for the strength and faith to make the changes in your life that are pleasing, holy, and acceptable to Him. He will revive your soul and soothe the disappointments of your past. You can trust Him; He is faithful, and will never leave you or forsake you! You are His priceless treasure, His Daughter of Heaven!

"My" Thoughts:

1. Can you relate to my story? If so, how?_____
_____
_____

2. What personal weaknesses and insecurities could cloud your judgment in a relationship? Are you paying attention to them?____
_____
_____

3. Are you willing to commit your life into God's control and allow Him to manage your decisions, actions, and choices according to His Will, not your own?_____
_____
_____

4. What daily actions will you take to set aside whatever stands in the way to keep this from happening?_____
_____
_____

I am giving you a chance to put your words into action. If you are willing to commit to the following challenges, insert your initial next to each one.

I Am Committed To ...

I commit to spend time on my face before God daily through prayer, reading His Word, and in learning a lifestyle of worship that is pleasing to Him. _____

I commit to ask God for insight and guidance as to which guys I should have as my friends and develop relationships with. _____

I commit to abstain from any and all sexual behavior from this day forward—until I marry the man God has chosen for me. _____

I commit myself to be held accountable by a Godly mentor, parent, or youth leader, that I can trust -- who will speak encouragement and correction into my life. _____

I commit, if needed, to go to Godly counseling on a regular basis to assist me in discovering and breaking free from any past destructive tendencies. _____

I WILL NOT make relational choices based on my emotions or feelings, but upon the expectations of God and His Word. _____

I WILL NOT entertain a relationship with someone who does not serve Jesus with all his mind, heart, and strength. _____

I WILL NOT tempt a guy into sexual sin by what I wear, what I say, or what I do, no matter how I may feel at the moment.   _____

I WILL NOT provide an opportunity for fooling around or having any sexual activity in any premarital relationship.   _____

I WILL NOT be alone with a guy where temptation will be at its peak: not at home, not in the car, not on a trip, and not any place where we are isolated from the presence of others. We will keep our physical relationship accountable. _____

Feel free to add any other thoughts to this list as God directs you!

_____
_____
_____
_____
_____
_____
_____
_____
_____
_____

Personal Challenge:

Covenant of Commitment

I, _____ , commit my
life on this day, _____ ,20____ to serve You,
my Lord, Jesus Christ, in every aspect of my life, with all my heart,
mind, strength, emotions, spirit and body. I choose on this day to
lay my life down to do Your will and serve You as a living sacrifice,
one pleasing, holy and acceptable to You. I ask You, God, to fill me
up with Your goodness and grace, and to anoint me to make the
changes in my life that your Word directs. I submit my heart to be
shaped by Your loving hand. I truly desire to demonstrate by my
Godly lifestyle how much I love You, Jesus, my Savior and King!
Amen!

(Suggested reading, *Redeeming Love*, by Francine Rivers, a romantic,
fictional story based on the redemptive love found in the book of
Hosea.)

Section VII

"What gives me butterflies?"

TREASURES WITHIN

"What is

God's plan

for my LIFE?"

"I don't have any special TALENT…"

Treasure Sports

It was the summer before my sophomore year of high school. I was practicing with my new team. With our red and black basketball jerseys on, we ran drill after drill. Basketball was my life! Everything I did was basketball. I played and trained at least eight and a half hours a day. All my friends, thoughts, and dreams centered around basketball.

I remember my best friend that year, Linda Maria Cuartez Fuentez. I called her Linda. She and I hung out all the time. We played ball together, we walked the halls of school together, and we hung out at each other's houses. Often, we even did our hair the same and wore matching outfits to school. She and I had the same outgoing personality. We had so much fun together. Linda and I were inseparable. We even thought almost the same. Except for one thought, *Who is Jesus?* Linda did not share my faith in Jesus.

I remember praying and praying that I would have the guts to tell Linda about Jesus. I prayed I would somehow, one day, be brave enough to invite her to church. I remember a lot of times feeling like a failure because I was so nervous that I never said anything. I often felt like a failure because I didn't know if Linda even knew I was a Christian.

It was November and pre-season games started. Our team had a seven-day San Diego tournament over Christmas break. While we were gone, our coach thought it would be fun to have "Secret Santas," so everyone drew a name from a hat and got that person little surprise gifts throughout the week. A while into the tournament, we came back from a game into our hotel room and there on my bed was a little box. From far away, I couldn't see what it was but as I got closer the wrapping became clearer to me. My "Secret Santa" gift was wrapped with pictures of naked women. A nauseous pit began to form in my stomach. I couldn't unwrap the gift, much less even look at it. Tears welled in my eyes. Why would someone do this? Linda and another friend of mine, Sarah, were in the room. They were shocked at my hurt because to them, and to everyone else, it was just a joke. A bunch of the team had gone to a grocery store and stole condoms and wrapped them in pornography as a surprise, just for me. They told me it was a joke because I was the Christian.

That evening, all three of us girls sat on the stiff hotel beds and talked until the early hours of the next morning. They were curious why such a silly gift would bring tears to my eyes. I began to tell them my story; my story of living in a home with verbal abuse, where violence lived everyday, and the police regularly visited my home. A story where I remembered being a little girl and accidentally finding, in my drawers, videos with degrading pornographic images on the cover. Those images were branded into my mind and tormented my heart as a tiny girl. I told the girls my story about how I didn't know where I would be if I hadn't known Jesus. Jesus filled my heart when nothing else could comfort my pain. I told them my story! My story wasn't about a "goody-two-shoes" Christian who didn't know real life, but a story about a girl who knew the depths of pain, and, out of that, was given life. The air was intense, deep, and thick that night. The conversation was one that I couldn't have planned and I would never have been brave enough to speak if it wasn't for the condoms wrapped in pornography.

The only person who went home from that tournament a Christian was me. No one was saved and there was no big revival.

That week, Sarah went to church with her grandmother.

Weeks later, I was driving home from school and my cell phone rang. I remember the conversation so vividly that it feels like yesterday. It went something like this.

"Hello?"

"Hey Shi! It's Linda."

"Hey."

"Hey, you go to church right?"

"Yeah."

"What time does it start this Sunday?"

"9."

"I am going to meet you there. OK?"

"OK."

"Bye."

"Bye."

I clicked the red "End" button on my phone, and as I finished driving home in my empty car, the only words that I could speak, I repeated over and over, "THANK YOU JESUS! THANK YOU JESUS! THANK YOU JESUS...."

I wept in my car.

Linda came to church on Sunday. She accepted Jesus. She brought her boy-friend to our youth outreach event. He went down to the altar and asked Jesus to be his Savior! Linda and John were two of the most popular people in our high school, and were now filled with the joy of Jesus! And, it all started with some condoms wrapped in pornography.

I had felt like a failure so many times for not being brave enough to share about the love of my life, Jesus. But, the reality was, I could not have planned anything better. Linda did not get saved because of me trying to add Jesus into every conversation. It was by prayer, loving her as she was, and my least expect-ed moment of brokenness, that my basketball friends saw who Jesus really was.

Colossians 4:2-4 says, "Pray diligently. Stay alert...Pray that every time I open my mouth I'll be able to make Christ plain as day to them" (MSG).

Christina

Treasure Writing

I was seventeen when I had my first piece of writing published. It was only a small part of a larger work, a devotional study for a young women's conference, but it was something. While having something published provided me with a small sense of accomplishment, I had long been reaping the benefits of expressing myself through writing. Writing enabled me to articulate thoughts and express emotions that otherwise would have remained hidden — elusive even to myself.

Do you remember the diaries we kept at 10, 11, 12-years old? Mine read something like this . . .

Dear Diary,

Jamie got mad at me because I played with Rachel during recess. She said I wasn't her friend anymore. I like Jamie, but I didn't want to sit and talk on the bench. I wanted to play tetherball . . .

Silly? Yes, but I didn't think so at the time! Writing was the way I processed my thoughts. It was a tool I learned to use at a very young age. Teachers soon realized that I had a knack for writing. My dad attributed it to the countless hours I spent pouring through mystery books. The Mandie and Nancy Drew series were my favorites.

I think my "way with words" was the inevitable outcome of my dad consistently correcting me every time I attempted to say something in a way that was grammatically incorrect. In order to say anything at the dinner table, and be heard, I knew I had to use correct grammar. The alternative was an abrupt re-phrasing of the statement by my dad, which I was then expected to repeat.

You may think this would take all the fun out of writing, or even speaking. Yet, quite the contrary, it ingrained in me a love for words that I have never abandoned. I revel in the ability to express my thoughts precisely. Since my tongue is much quicker than my mind, writing slows me down, allowing me to articulate my thoughts clearly, without coming across bewildered or speechless. Yes, I have been the greatest beneficiary of my writing endeavors.

Although I initially began writing for my own benefit, I quickly learned that my gift could also be a blessing to others. Scripture says that "Reckless words pierce like a sword, but the tongue of the wise brings healing" (Proverbs 12:18 NIV).

This is just as true of our written words as it is of what we say. I discovered that what I communicated in writing, through a card, a letter, or even a short story, was highly effective in encouraging others. One very close friend, my mentor, even kept what she called a "Rebecca file." There, she stored the countless cards, notes, and letters I wrote to her to express just how much I admired and appreciated her. I felt good knowing that my words put a smile on her face.

When I was fourteen, I embarked on my first, major adventure in writing. I decided to write a novel. It began as a short story assignment in my 9th grade English class. I received a 98% on the assignment, from a teacher who graded rather harshly, and I immediately knew it was confirmation that I was born to write. It was my gift to the world! (Do you detect my sarcastic tone?) Over the next year/year and a half, I added another nine chapters to *War on the Homefront*. The main characters were all close friends of mine, set in a 1940's backdrop. They enjoyed reading each new chapter and always asked me what would happen in their characters' lives next. I never knew, but I continued writing until I finally lost interest in my novel. While nothing ever came of *War on the Homefront*, the hundreds of hours I spent with a dictionary in one hand and a thesaurus in the other have served me well. You wouldn't believe the number of adverbs and adjectives I discovered through that process! And, what ever happened with my novel? Well, I still have it. It's great for a laugh when I start to take myself too seriously. The author, who, at fourteen, expressed such whimsical longings and ideals just dripping with romanticism, has not changed much over the past decade.

Writing is fun and it serves so many purposes. While the process itself benefits the author, the finished product has the potential to touch others. Has God ever dropped a word, a story, or a picture in your heart? Put it in writing. I did. During high school, I composed many short stories. Each one depicted some spiritual truth — a lesson God was teaching me. I began to communicate these valuable lessons in word pictures and soon discovered that my creative stories touched people in a way that mere facts could not. After all, why did John, the author of Revelation, create such powerful and vivid imagery? He aimed to reach the reader on a level other types of literature bypassed. His goal was to evoke an emotional response, not merely impart information.

Your words, your thoughts, have great potential. Is it time to pick up your pen and write? Maybe you need to start journaling and allow God to speak to you

as you sort through your own personal thoughts and ideas, or maybe there is something in your heart that needs to be shared with others. Whatever it is, write it out! Who knows . . . you may end up with your very own version of *War on the Homefront*, which you can enjoy for years to come, or you just may come up with the next "best seller."

Rebecca

chapter 14

FINDING THE TREASURE WITHIN

Suzanne Rentz

Do you know where the richest place in the world is?

a. Buckingham Palace   b. The Taj Mahal

c. Monte Carlo   d. Other

The answer to this question is very different than you would expect. The richest place in the world is actually the cemetery! Buried in the cemetery are treasures of immeasurable value; books never written, songs never sung, dreams never realized, business ventures never embarked upon, and ideas and concepts that could have revolutionized the world.

Isn't that tragic? It is inevitable that one day you will leave this earth. Will you take your treasures with you? Or, will you live a life where you took chances, a life that made a difference, a life with no regrets?

Recently, I was visiting Eureka, a historical city along the coast in Northern California. I went there to help my sister pack up all of our belongings in the house that I grew up in. We had lived there for over 30 years and now it was going to be sold. Needless to say, we had a lot to pack up! With my three boys in tow, I arrived ready to roll up my sleeves, pitch in and help.

To keep my boys entertained, I decided to send them on a "story book" adventure. You see, as a little girl, I had taken some of my treasures, locked them in a jewelry box, and buried them under some trees in my back yard. I drew a treasure map ... my boys dug, climbed, hammered, and traced their steps thoroughly. They desperately searched for hours on end to find the buried treasure. At the end of the day, my boys were covered with dirt from head to toe, exhausted and frustrated. One was hanging from a tree, the other was knee deep in the pond, and the third was playing fetch with the dog. I tried to draw their attention back to looking for the treasure, buried in the dirt, hidden somewhere, just waiting to be found. Day two of the treasure hunt proved to be as unproductive as well. By the third day, they had lost all hope of finding the buried treasure. They were discouraged and thought all their efforts had been for nothing. They gave up!

Girl ... It's Time to Go on a Treasure Hunt!

God has buried treasures deep inside of you. Sometimes they are easy to discover and other times you have to dig deep, long and hard to find them. Regardless, they are there! You have valuable treasures in your possession!

You might not see yourself that way.... Maybe you feel that you have nothing, but you do! God created you with awesome treasures! You were made by the magnificent hand of God. You are His workmanship, or should I say art project. You have special value to Him.

> *For we are God's workmanship, created in Christ Jesus to do good works, which God prepared in advance for us to do*
> *Ephesians 2:10* ⠿⠿⠿

When God formed you, He tucked treasures inside of you. Those treasures come in the form of your personality, your talents, your gifts, desires, and your dreams.

God has given you these treasures for a purpose - more importantly for HIS purpose. You might feel as though God could never use your life. You might feel like you are not good enough and you have nothing to offer. It is so easy to compare yourself, your experiences, and your abilities with others. But God doesn't play the "comparison" game. He desires to use your life! He has an amazing plan and purpose that is perfectly tailored for you and only you. As you read the next three chapters, I challenge you to see yourself through God's eyes – full of value and full of treasures!

What is Ministry Anyway?

Sometimes, in our minds, we have these silly misconceptions about what ministry really is. Is it being a pastor or an evangelist? Is it being a missionary in a foreign land, or having a magnetic T.V. personality? Is it about hype, big time personalities, success, or popularity? No, none of these roles define ministry. It's really about serving. Serving God with the treasures he has entrusted to you.

The Bible was originally written in Hebrew, Aramaic, and Greek. If you are ever confused or want to do a little research in the New Testament, a Greek dictionary will give you the clearest, most definitive meanings. When I looked up "a minister" in Greek, it meant a servant! What is a servant? A servant is someone who serves. You are a servant of God, called to use and take good care of the gifts and the treasures He has entrusted to you. They are in your possession, but yet they are not your own. God has called you to serve Him and that means that you have a ministry! Not when you are older, not just when you graduate, but, right where you are now - while you are young - you have a ministry!

I was eighteen when I enrolled in Bible college. I was so excited to learn more about God. I loved my youth group, but I had a lot of personal questions that needed answers. The Bible college I choose to attend was a two-year course. The first year was devoted to building a foundation to grow in the Lord, and the second year was to equip students to go into full-time ministry. After the first year, I was in turmoil. Part of me wanted to go back for the second year but I wasn't sure that God had "called" me into ministry. I remember that year, waiting on tables in order to pay for tuition; I would watch the pastors, evangelists, Bible teachers and their families, as they came into the restaurant. I had this longing to be like them. I desired to be in full-time ministry. The problem was that God had never spoken to me from a burning bush nor did He speak in a resounding, loud voice; I was never prophesied over in front of hundreds of people. The bottom line was that I questioned whether or not I was called. I felt like God's calling was for the "elect" and I ignored the desires of my own heart. I felt as though God had favorites! The crazy part is that my thinking was the farthest thing from the truth. Sure, God does use very talented and gifted people, but He also uses "simple" ordinary and very imperfect people.

I now realize how true it is that God does not show favoritism but accepts men from every nation who fear him and do what is right.

Acts 10:34-35

Does God have favorites? Absolutely, but we are all His favorites. He desires to use each and every one of us! The world looks at the outside but God looks at the inside.

Look around you. Right now - you can serve God in so many ways. Maybe you are a good athlete or maybe you are passionate about music. Do you love working with little children? Do you love to go on mission trips? Do you write for hours on end? Are you artistic? Do you want to help the homeless? Can you dance or act? Do you love to share about Jesus? God desires to use your life! You have a ministry right where God has placed you. You can have a big influence in your school, your work, your family, and with your friends.

IMPACTING .... Your World!

The following words were written on the tomb of an Anglican Bishop in the Crypts of Westminster Abbey:

When I was young and free and my imagination had no limits, I dreamed of changing the world. As I grew older and wiser, I discovered the world would not change, so I shortened my sights somewhat and decided to change only my country.

But it, too, seemed immovable.

As I grew into my twilight years, in one last desperate attempt, I settled for changing only my family, those closest to me, but alas, they would have none of it.

And now as I lie on my death bed, I suddenly realize: If I had only changed myself first, then by example I would have changed my family.

From their inspiration and encouragement, I would have been able to better my country and, who knows, I may have even changed the world.

Changing Yourself and Becoming Like Jesus.

The most important step that you can take to develop your God-given treasures is to pursue God. As you seek Jesus, everything else falls into place.

> *But seek ye first the kingdom of God, and his righteousness; and all these things shall be added unto you.*
>
> *Matthew 6:33*

A very cool thing happens as we pursue God; we become more like Him. His character becomes our character. Our thoughts, choices, and motives can begin to mirror Jesus. You have the perfect opportunity while you are young to mold yourself and shape yourself with the Word of God. The Bible can transform your character.

For one minute, think of play dough. When it's fresh, right out of the container, it is easy to form, but once it sits out for a while, it becomes hard, dry and cracked. While you are young, you are much more moldable than when you are old. Allow God's Word to shape you and mold you into someone He can use in awesome ways!

God has chosen you to be His minister, His servant! Do you have a heart after the Lord and a desire to serve Him?

> *For the eyes of the LORD run to and fro throughout the whole earth, to show Himself strong on behalf of those whose heart is loyal to Him.*
>
> *2 Chronicles 16:9*

Wow! God is looking for someone to reveal Himself to. The most important thing to God is something that you and I can't see – He looks at the heart.

God wants to use you now; don't wait! While you are young, God desires to use your life and, at the same time, God is encouraging you to pursue Him. As you begin to change, you will start changing your world!

Don't let anyone look down on you because you are young, but set an example for the believers in speech, in life, in love, in faith and in purity.

1 Timothy 4:12 ::::

The Treasure of Your Personality

Developing your character is a challenge that can be very hard at times. Have you ever asked God, "Why did You make me this way?"

Our personalities are given to us by God and yet, with every positive strength, there is a negative giant just lurking in the darkness. For example, maybe you are outgoing, fun, and tend to be the life of the party. At the same time, you may have been labeled superficial or phony; if you are loyal, kind, and quiet, maybe you feel boring, shy, etc. You could be a deep, artistic perfectionist and yet struggle with depression and isolation. Or maybe you are a natural born leader who gets things done, but your friends call you bossy and opinionated. It is a double edged sword! The key is knowing and using your strengths, and, at the same time, overcoming your weaknesses.

The more you read and study the Bible, the more you realize that many of the Godly kings, prophets, and disciples struggled to overcome the negative sides of their personalities. That should be a huge encouragement to you! God does not require perfection in order to use our lives. While some of our negative personality traits may fall by the wayside, some will be a challenge to us, but we can overcome! Pray about these areas in your life and learn to be on guard. The bad and the good go hand in hand, so remember, you can't have one without the other. Accept yourself the way God made you. Run with your strengths and let them shine the brightest.

The Treasure of Your Talents

Another set of valuable treasures that you possess are your talents. It is very important that you use talents and gifts in a careful way. Balance them out with wisdom, Christian-like character, and humility. Time and time again, you see incredibly talented people exchange true fulfillment and happiness for temporary success and popularity. Eventually, they become slaves to drugs, fame, and money. I was recently looking at a magazine, and I saw a very famous young woman. Her photo has appeared on several magazine covers. She has performed on T.V. shows. She has performed for numerous concerts. She has known fame like very few will ever experience. As I looked at her picture, my heart was grieved as I saw an empty, plastic, lost expression in her eyes. Her body was exposed for the world to see. She had known God as a young person, she had attended a youth group, and her dad was in leadership at the church. She had exceptional talent, but she exchanged the truth for a lie. Use your talents wisely! You must know that the devil would love nothing more than to exploit you, use you, and then dispose of you. Beware of the major pitfalls: seduction, greed, money, and fame.

It may not have been quite as extreme, but you might know someone who has sold out for all of the wrong reasons. It might be you, but don't worry; it is a challenge we all face. Doesn't everyone want to become successful, popular, rich and famous? What the world tries to hide is that "me" centered success is shallow and empty, always demanding more, and yet never quite satisfying. Remember, the devil wants to take from you, but God desires to give you life and life more abundantly.

The thief comes only to steal and kill and destroy; I have come that they may have life, and have it to the full.

John 10:10

Success that is centered on God is exactly the opposite of what the world offers. It is exciting, encouraging, humbling and most of all fulfilling!

The Treasures of Your Dreams and Desires ...

Are you ready to go to the next level? Phrases like, "It is such an adrenaline rush," "I am so amazed," and "This is totally awesome!" are all expressions that have been used by young women like you that have followed after their God-given, Holy Spirit-inspired dreams and desires. When God uses your life and you are living out the desires that He has placed in your heart, your life will take on a new level of contentment. There is really nothing more fulfilling! But the rewards of the pursuit, though they may be incredible, do not come without the sacrifice.

It is easy for us to observe the finished product without seeing the persistence, hard work, discipline, and sacrifice it took to get there. Giants of apathy, laziness, and selfishness have to be slain to achieve greatness and excellence. In my family, there are four girls. One of my older sisters, Julie, is strong, an excellent athlete, and she was oblivious to people's opinions. I, on the other hand, wanted everyone and their extended family to love me. I never was very competitive, and athletics didn't come so easily to me. I remember complaining to my dad, that I wasn't strong or "tuff" like Julie was, and he told me something that made an impact on my life: To be strong and to be tough didn't just mean to be physically strong or resilient, but that another form of strength and toughness meant to go after your dreams, never giving up! I could be strong and "tuff" in my own way. And that type of strength and resolve can be pursued by anyone who has a strong desire to do so.

During this pursuit, you will constantly be refined, sharpened and polished by your Creator, Father God. And the more you work on you, the more God will be glorified, and the more He will shine through you! Shine, not by the world's definition, but God's. Mother Teresa is a perfect example. She started countless orphanages and hospices, as well as the Missionaries of Charity, which is now active in over 133 countries. God was glorified and reflected in and through her life. She was one of the most beautiful, gifted women in the world. What a great role model for us. She followed after her dreams and desires, and God has used her in amazing ways!

Commit your way to the LORD; trust in him and he will do this: He
will make your righteousness shine like the dawn, the justice of your
cause like the noonday sun.

Psalm 37:5-6

Do you want to shine for Jesus? The good news is that during the
refining process, through your imperfections, God is made perfect.
In ministry and in my daily life, I pray constantly for God to use
my life. I ask God to pour himself through me and, where there
are chips and cracks, I have become completely dependent on Him.
God has been so faithful and He has given my life purpose. He has
shown me my strengths and gently revealed to me my weaknesses.
For any God-given dreams or desires that He has given me, He has
always been faithful to give them wings.

My grace is sufficient for you, for my power is made perfect in weak-
ness." Therefore I will boast all the more gladly about my weaknesses,
so that Christ's power may rest on me.

2 Corinthians 12:9

Life Is One Big Treasure Hunt

The Bible is the treasure map and in it are the keys to your
treasures. There is not just one, but many treasures that you will
discover along the way. God is faithful. His Word promises that He
will finish what He started in your life.

being confident of this, that he who began a good work in you will
carry it on to completion until the day of Christ Jesus.

Philippians 1:6

I was a little girl when I buried that worn, tattered jewelry
box. Had my boys kept looking for the treasure, they would have
found it. They could have been basking in piles and piles of plastic
pearls and bright colored beads, old coins, and maybe even a few
historical artifacts! The sad part is, they will never know what lay
just beneath the earth's surface. Just like my boys had given up in
their quest for the treasure, many give up their pursuit of finding
their own personal treasures that lie within, treasures tucked within

us by God's very own hand. Somewhere along life's way, they have just given up.

Can you identify with my boys? Like them, have you given up? You might feel as though God would never use your life. You think your personality isn't good enough, you have no talent and you really have no purpose. God has given you treasures for a purpose —more importantly for HIS purpose. Don't miss out on discovering and utilizing your treasures that lie within—the treasures that God himself created in you! He buried them in the very core of who you are: your personality, talents, desires, and a dream that only you are destined to fulfill. While pursuing excellence, live your life to the fullest, not with regrets. Make your life count. Use your God given treasures for His purpose and His glory. God is calling you now to begin digging beneath the surface, and He will help you discover your treasure that lies within!

"My" Thoughts:

Breaking it down, what "treasures" do you possess?

Personality:

Talents:

Dreams:

Desires:

Things to guard against:

Do you see any weaknesses in your personality? How can you change them? (Hint... being aware of your weaknesses is half the battle.)_____
_____
_____

As far as talents, if the devil was going to distract you from using your talents and gifts for Him, what would your biggest temptation be?_____
_____
_____

How can you avoid this?_____
_____
_____

What insecurities are holding you back from using your treasures for His purpose?_____
_____
_____

Personal Challenge:

Take your time and really think about your answers to the questions in the previous section. If you are drawing a blank, maybe you could ask a close friend or someone in your family. Definitely pray and ask God to start showing you your treasures—I promise you, He will!

Running for Student Government

One of my biggest fears is public speaking. I'm so afraid that if I speak what's in my heart, that I will fail to touch people the way I want to. Junior year was the year that I decided I didn't care. I had so much in my heart that I wanted to share with my class. I decided to run for Class President. It was very intimidating and I didn't think I could do it, but I had felt in my heart since that summer that this was the year I could make a difference. So, I practiced my speech, I said many prayers and I trusted God that this was something that He wanted me to do.

Sometimes in life, God asks us to do things that we are uncertain of, and we can ask questions, maybe pitch a few fits, but in the end we have to realize that God has a plan for everything and He most definitely knows what He is doing. News spread through school pretty fast and I ended up running against two other girls who, in my mind, were way more qualified for the job than I was, but I still trusted that it was a God thing.

So I ran, and in the end I won. I was ecstatic. But being Class President was so much more than just a popularity contest. I made a decision to be an example for Christ. I knew that there would be a lot of eyes on my behavior, not just from my peers, but from teachers and administration as well. It's a lot of pressure sometimes but it keeps me in check. It makes me realize that no matter where you go, when you are a Christian and you make yourself known, you're going to be watched. People are going to wonder what it's like. You have to make sure that you're being an example and being someone who represents Christ. It's a day to day decision. It's not perfection, it's effort. You pray, commit and decide that you're going to be the best Christlike example you can be.

Britni

Treasure Leading Worship

I have been playing the piano since I was 5 years old. My mother had my older sister take piano lessons, and after each one of her lessons, I would sit at the piano, and play what she had just played. My mom recognized I had a gift, so she started giving me piano lessons. You see, a gift doesn't necessarily mean that you are an expert at what you do, or even that you're great at it. Being gifted by God in a certain area can mean that you have a special ability to learn about and understand that area. Mozart wasn't born with the skills and abilities that he had when he was 20 years old. It took some time to develop those skills and abilities. Just because you are not at a certain level yet does not mean that you don't have the gift. Gifts take time to develop, and if you have the ability to learn and understand, then I encourage you to develop that gift further, and see where the Lord will take it.

I had been taking lessons for about seven years, off and on from various teachers, when my middle school youth pastor asked me to play back-up keyboard for our Wednesday youth service. I was so excited, and yet a little scared at the same time. There were two other older accomplished pianists who I ended up playing with, and that was a little intimidating. But as I started to show up for practice, and do my best to follow along, I learned more and more. A few years went by, and those two pianists were called somewhere else to lead; and so I was asked to take their place. It was my turn to be the "lead" pianist on the worship team and I believe God prepared me for it. You see, not only do you need to be gifted in your particular area; you, also, need to have the right heart. Through my youth pastor, I had learned that worship leading is really only about one thing: to usher people into the presence of God. It is not about us, or our abilities, but about pointing others to Him through music.

Since that time, I have had so many wonderful experiences leading and partici- pating in worship music. I believe it is important to have confidence, confidence in the Lord that He put you where you are and that you are capable of doing what He has called you to do. Let me be honest with you, though, confidence can take some time. Like I said earlier, when I was first asked to play on the worship team,

I was intimidated. It took some time for me to settle in and realize this is where God wanted me. He wanted me to give back to Him the ability He had given me to play the piano.

So I encourage you to pray about these three things if you are considering joining a worship team. Pray about the gift God has given you. When you are following the passion that God has given you for a particular thing, opportunities will then come your way. Secondly, I encourage you to evaluate your heart and your motives. Make sure you understand that worship is about God, and how we let God use us to help others connect with Him. And then, if you are scared or nervous, pray for confidence. Pray that the Lord will confirm where He wants you to be. If at all possible, a good practical way to develop your gifts and discover your leadership abilities is to position yourself under an existing leader that you admire and trust. Learn everything you can from them, and allow them to participate in your growth. Not only will you gain valuable experience and knowledge, but when the need arises to fill a vacant position, you will be ready and available to step up and answer the call.

One other very important thing that God has just recently shown me is that it is impossible to into enter into His presence and leave unchanged. I encourage you to use the gifts God has given you, and allow Him to develop them and grow you to be more like Him. Revelation 4 gives us a small glimpse into heaven, allowing us to see what our worship should be modeled after. Verses 8-11 say; "...And they do not rest day or night, saying: 'Holy, holy, holy, Lord God Almighty, Who was and is and is to come!' Whenever the living creatures give glory and honor and thanks to Him who sits on the throne, who lives forever and ever, the twenty-four elders fall down before Him who sits on the throne and worship Him who lives forever and ever, and cast their crowns before the throne, saying: 'You are worthy, O Lord, To receive glory and honor and power, For You created all things, and by Your will they exist and were created'" (NKJV).

Sheena

chapter 15

DEVELOPING THE TREASURE WITHIN

Suzanne Rentz

The other day, I was sitting at the kitchen table helping my son Andrew fill out a questionnaire for his teacher. She wanted him to describe himself using four positive adjectives. Munching on a bag of Doritos, it took a lot of explaining to convince Drew that "making awesome forts" was not an adjective and that "crazy" was not necessarily a positive. We had to go a little deeper! We spent what seemed like eternity trying to think of the words that most summed him up. The four words we finally came up with were: creative, persistent, smart, and energetic. As I looked at his description, it hit me. I said "Drew, do you realize what type of person these words describe? They have just described a world changer! Drew, with your innovative thinking, creativity and brains, not only do you think outside the box, but you are persistent enough to not give up and still have the energy to press on. You won't settle for the status quo! You are the very type of person that will leave your mark on this world!" Four simple adjectives, and what a tremendous value that lies behind each word when they are combined; these are attributes of a world changer!

Later on that day, I started thinking about my other two boys. Our oldest son Luke, with his love for learning and truth, his Christ-like character, and his tender heart towards the Lord, is also a perfect candidate for God to use in amazing ways. And then there is Elijah! He has the confidence and determination that few can match. He loves to worship God, and it doesn't matter who is listening or watching. When he is shooting hoops in our cul-de-sac, all of our neighbors get the privilege of a full blown concert. He will fulfill the awesome call God has placed on him! If someone tries to get in his way, they had better watch out because he will just simply run over them! I am eagerly waiting for our little Gabriella's personality and gifts to unfold. We already know her little puffy, pink lips always seem to curve into a smile and she is quick to share it with any stranger coming her way. She is very loving and kind. She has a gentle and sweet spirit, and cuddling is her favorite pasttime.

Did you know that you have the potential to leave a mark on this world? Your specific, unique personality combined with your God-given talents, are priceless. You are designed with a winning combination! Your value is sky high! Your treasures are limitless! In fact, your value literally reaches all the way to Heaven!

How would you define the word treasure? In the last chapter, I wrote about my boys going on a treasure hunt in northern California. Like most of us, when you think of the word "treasure," you think of "hitting the jackpot," or "inheriting a fortune." Or maybe when you think of "treasures," you think of simple joys like a steamy, hot cappuccino on a cold, rainy day, or "a stolen moment" laughing with your best friend, or maybe even an outfit with all the accessories for under fifty-five dollars. Treasures can be all around us. But no matter how you define treasures, one common denominator is this--they all have special value!

God has entrusted you with treasures that can really make a difference in other people's lives. It would be crazy to think that simply possessing them was enough. Absolutely not! There is no easy way around it; you need to develop these treasures. This takes work and lots of it, in the natural and in the supernatural. But with God's help and effort on your part, you can develop the treasures God has given you and see them multiply. Get out of your comfort zone, take your potential, and run with it – excitement and fulfillment like you've never experienced is within your reach.

First and Foremost ... Become Teachable!

How do you develop your God-given treasures? One of the best ways is to become teachable. The most amazing teacher of all is God and He uses life as His chalkboard. Life, in general, is full of lessons. Ask, learn, and listen. Your boss, your parents, close adult friends, teachers, youth pastor, and Sunday School teacher – they can teach you by example. As you watch them and listen to them, you can learn what to do, and, unfortunately, sometimes what not to do! If you can find mentors that you admire, spend time with them and serve them anyway you can. Some of the most Christ-like, successful people I know are that way, not because they were born with perfect genes, but because they were teachable. When they were starting out in ministry and life, they became like sponges and they absorbed as much wisdom and knowledge as they could. Even as they matured, that same hunger to learn was still present. It is a lifelong quest. And on the flip side, some of the most miserable people I know are the ones who will not receive instruction. They refuse to be teachable!

In the book of Psalms, David prays a similar prayer over and over again. David was someone who was very close to God and I believe this prayer was truly the cry of his heart. If we could adopt David's prayer as our own, God would teach us some amazing things. David's simple prayer was this:

Teach me your way, O LORD, and I will walk in your truth; give me an undivided heart, that I may fear your name.

Psalm 86:11 ▓

Stop, for just one minute, and think about it. When was the last time you prayed to God and asked Him to teach you HIS way? God longs to teach you HIS way but it is important that you ask, and ask on a regular basis.

Like David's prayer, if you desire for God to teach you His way, fasten your seatbelt and get ready for the ride of your life! God wants to teach you through HIS Word, through prayer, through past failures, and through the craziest leaps of faith you will ever experience.

God's WORD

The first way to make the most of your God-given treasures and fulfill the ministry He has called you to, is to know what God's

Word says. By reading, meditating on, hearing, and speaking God's Word, it will change you and impact your dreams, your prayers, and your ministry.

You should be plugged into an ongoing Bible study (if the church you are attending does not have a Bible study, maybe you could approach your youth leader or pastor. You just might be the catalyst to get one started.) As you study God's Word, you will discover layers and layers of truth. A simple verse that you were taught in Sunday School will take on a whole new meaning as you discover the setting or the context in which it is found. Your faith in God will increase by the boatloads! The more you study the Bible, the more you will realize just how perfect, awesome, and precise God has orchestrated it. There is so much to learn about God's commitment and covenant with you. You will learn about the most amazing and, yet, fallible, Godly men ever created. You will see God's powerful and awesome truth like you have never seen it before. It will revolutionize your ministry and change your life.

Not only is an ongoing Bible Study a good idea, but you should also take the time to memorize and meditate on scripture. Make it a part of your daily life. Take a scripture, write it on a note card, and stick it on your mirror so you can see it as you put on your makeup. Find a beautiful setting, like the mountains or the beach, and as you take in the beautiful surroundings, meditate on God's Word. God's Word may just take on a whole new dimension as you overlook God's awesome creation. Be creative; maybe you could even watch the sunset or sunrise while meditating on God's Word!

The world in which we live is full of discouragement, pain, and broken hearts. If there was ever a time to incorporate God's Word in your life and ministry, now is the time! You desperately need it! Without it, you are just going through the motions. God's Word never comes back void. His Word is full of promises to us. He will do what He says He will do. God will demonstrate His glory and His power in amazing ways, and they will cut through the darkness. God's Word will heal the broken hearted; it will set the captives free. You have been called! Called to preach all of the exciting, powerful, life-changing truths that are in His Word!

For the word of God is living and active. Sharper than any double-edged sword, it penetrates even to dividing soul and spirit, joints and marrow; it judges the thoughts and attitudes of the heart.

Hebrews 4:12

When you include God's Word into your life, you will multiply the effectiveness of the talents and gifts you have. If you are a writer, adding God's Word will make your message come alive. If you have an opportunity to speak, God's Word will take an ordinary message or sermon and transform it with life. God's Word is a sword that will penetrate the hearts of those who hear it. If you like to sing, were born to lead, etc., God's Word will make all the difference!

PRAYER Life...

The second way to develop your treasures and enhance the ministry that God has given you, is to pursue a powerful prayer life. Don't settle for a mundane, blah, boring time of prayer with God. Talk to Him; share your thoughts and feelings. Pray over yourself, your family, your ministry, your church, and your country. Your prayers make a difference!

You need to commit anything you do to the Lord. Ask God for help with every step you take. Be sensitive to the Holy Spirit's leading and direction. Become dependent on God for every move you make.

The Bible says to pray without ceasing, but if you tried to pray in a prayer closet 24/7, you would not accomplish anything else in life. That is what you call being heavenly minded but doing no earthly good. But God does want you to be in constant communication with Him, and it is very important that you stay in tune with the Holy Spirit. In a nutshell, praying without ceasing means to stay in constant communion with God.

Text messaging, Myspace, chat rooms, and phone calls are all ways you communicate with your friends. Isn't it an awesome thought, that you don't need a computer or a cell phone to communicate with God? You can pray throughout the day, anytime and anywhere. He can hear you wherever you are. One very effective way that I find to pray is to pray and walk at the same time. I find I am not so easily distracted then. I have also called out to God in my bed at different times during the night. At times, I will be driving my car or walking in a shopping mall, communicating with God. And then there are the times when I am on my knees seeking God intensely, with tears flowing freely. Whenever I go to speak at camps or conferences, staying connected to God is crucial! I need His anointing and power to be effective as a minister, to reach the hearts and spirits of those listening.

There may be times when God asks you to fast, and there may be times that you need to spend time simply waiting in God's presence at the altar. Prayer is also about thanking God for big and little blessings, or asking Him for forgiveness when we say or do the wrong things. It is about asking God for help throughout the day. Again, it is about constant communication.

> *Trust in the LORD with all your heart and lean not on your own understanding; in all your ways acknowledge him, and he will make your paths straight.*
>
> *Proverbs 3:5-6*

Did you know that God wants to give you constant direction? He wants to order your steps and direct your paths. He doesn't want you wandering around aimlessly. The more you pray, the more you will learn to hear God's voice. God wants to lead and direct every decision you make, the small ones and the big ones!

Also, knowing that you are on the right path and in the center of His will, will help you through tough times. There will be incredible highs and painful lows in the process of developing your ministry. Prayer will sustain you. Pray God's promises. In other words, when you pray, speak the Bible verses you are learning. Remind yourself of what His Word says. Remember, you have a covenant with our Father God!

> *"For I know the plans I have for you," declares the "plans to prosper you and not to harm you, plans to give you hope and a future. Then you will call upon me and come and pray to me, and*

I will listen to you. You will seek me and find me when you seek me with all your heart."

Jeremiah 29:11-13

God wants you to stay connected to Him and travel on the right path; God wants you to seek after Him! There is a whole lot He wants to reveal to you. When you seek Him, you will find Him. Go for it! It is never too late to develop a strong, powerful, and intimate prayer life with God.

Ouch ... FAILURE Hurts-- Or Does It?

The third way to develop your treasure is to see failure, believe it or not, as an excellent teacher. So often, we run from our mistakes or try and hide them, yet, we end up doing the same thing over and over again. You need to look at your failures and learn from them. How can you avoid making the same mistakes again? By examining your mistakes, you will see where and why you failed. You will begin to see patterns, pitfalls, and choices that resulted in disappointment. The key is learning to work smarter and not harder. You can work very hard to the point of burn out, but that does not guarantee success. By putting a little thought or brain power and even planning into the equation, you may come up with better results. Do you know someone who is sincerely dedicated and devoted to their dreams or ministry, but, yet, they are always disappointed with the outcome? It happens all the time. Don't fall into that trap! Working smarter could mean seeking advice, setting goals, believing God for more, changing your methods, or changing just a few things around to achieve better results. I have heard some speakers actually say to "embrace failure." What a great perspective! Girls, let's learn from our mistakes!

While God wants us to learn through our failures, He also wants to see us succeed. He wants to use our lives to touch others and He desires that we bear much fruit. How about a little lesson in gardening? I do not have a green thumb, but I am desperately trying to learn how to garden. I dream of the day when I can look out my picture window and see a beautiful, luscious, colorful, park-like setting. In my pursuit of becoming Joe Gardner, I have discovered the three most important rules to gardening. It all starts with sowing seeds (without the seeds you have nothing), then comes watering (if you ignore this part – your plants will dry up and wither), and, last but not least, you have to prune the plants (cutting off the dead flowers, leaves, and branches). If you skip this part, then all the plant's energy goes to the dead parts and it can't grow or produce fruit. By cutting off all that dead stuff, the energy in the plants can cause the plants to grow big and healthy, and they will in turn produce a lot of fruit.

> *You did not choose me, but I chose you and appointed you to go and bear fruit-fruit that will last. Then the Father will give you whatever you ask in my name.*
>
> *John 15:16*

God chose you, appointed you, and He desires for you to bear lasting fruit. That is HIS plan for your life. God will allow you to go through personal seasons where you are planting, sowing, and, yes, even pruning so that you can see amazing fruit grow in and through your life. All of this is necessary and the rewards are worth it. Failure can be a positive in that it will reveal to you where you need to focus your energy. Maybe you have not sewn enough seeds, or maybe you have not "watered" (taken care of) your spirit and the gifts God has entrusted to you. Have you cut away any dead habits or relationships lately? Maybe it is time to do a little pruning so you can spend your energy producing fruit.

There is definitely a downside to failure. Sometimes you can get so overwhelmed by it that you think of nothing else. If you let failure dominate your thinking, it can lead to depression and discouragement. Don't allow that to happen. Don't let failure stop you in your tracks.

> *No, in all these things we are more than conquerors through him who loved us.*
>
> *Romans 8:37*

In other words, you are not a loser. And if you stay in the race, no matter how bad it looks, you will win. It doesn't matter if you doubt yourself; God is quick to remind you – you are a champion! God did not place something in your heart to let it wither and dry up, quite the opposite, He wants the dream in your heart to take on wings and fly. You are a winner in His eyes. Don't give up!

Step Out in Faith...

The fourth way to develop your treasures, your talents, and your ministry, is by learning to take risks. You have to be willing to lose in order to win. You have to risk failure in order to succeed. You have heard the expression, "sink or swim." Maybe you are a perfectionist, and you just don't have everything in your life completely together. Maybe the opinions of others seem to keep you from moving forward. Maybe the fear of failure has held you back, but now is the time to start moving, to take chances! The best part of all is you are holding the awesome, powerful, and strong hand of your Father God while you're doing it.

In my own life, I have done things that some might say were crazy. I have said "yes" to God when every emotion inside of me was screaming "no!" I have taken chances where, if I had fallen, it would have impacted me and others in the process. Yet, I can say that God has never, ever let me down. The scarier the situation the more I marvel at God and Him alone. I have learned to lean and depend on God in indescribable ways. My faith has increased with every chance I have taken. I would not have traded my experiences with Him for anything!

> And without faith it is impossible to please God, because anyone who comes to him must believe that he exists and that he rewards those who earnestly seek him.
>
> Hebrews 11:6

Do you want to please God? Trust Him! Step out in faith! God wants you to experience Him in miraculous ways. If you fall, God will catch you. If God provides an opportunity, go for it!

Take chances and watch God come through every time. Don't miss out on the excitement and thrill of stepping out in faith.

Another way you can step out in faith is to think outside of the box. God created heaven and earth. He created you. He is the Author of creativity and innovation. He wants to inspire you. You need to let Him drop ideas straight from the throne of Heaven, creative ideas that have never been done before. God is limitless! Forget the old way or conventional thing, been there done that – pave a new road. Go where no man has gone. Wow! What an adventure that will unfold!

From the moment you were born, God gave you a unique and winning combination. He has given you everything you need to change your world. Your personality, talents, dreams, and desires are valuable treasures from on high. But it is up to you to develop these treasures as you journey through life. The journey is rewarding and exciting! Become teachable, study and learn God's Word, and develop your prayer life. Learn from your failure and step out in faith. God has given you treasures for a purpose - more importantly for HIS purpose. He has called you into ministry! Use your treasures for God's glory—there is nothing more fulfilling!

"My" Thoughts:

Are You Teachable?

Rate yourself on a scale from 1 -10 (1 being the least and 10 being the most), are you teachable? _____

Who has God placed in your life to learn from?_____
_____

The Word -

How can knowing God's Word impact and change your ministry?
_____
_____

What changes are you willing to make to improve?

Meditation _____   Memorize _____   Bible Study _____

Prayer -

Read the following verses: "Be joyful always; pray continually; give thanks in all circumstances, for this is God's will for you in Christ Jesus" (1 Thessalonians 5:16-18 ⁞ ⁞).

What does this verse mean to you? _____
_____

How can you pray continually?_____
_____

Failure -

As hard as it is, look back at a recent failure. Do you see how you could have done things a little differently to get a better result?_____
_____

Faith -

Do you remember the last time you took a risk? Describe it:

_____

_____

_____

_____

_____

_____

_____

_____

_____

_____

_____

_____

_____

_____

_____

_____

_____

_____

_____

_____

Personal Challenge:

Take a risk! Step up and try doing something crazy and awesome for God. Remember, faith pleases God!

chapter 16

THE TREASURE OF YOUR TESTIMONY

Suzanne Rentz

My family and I love to watch *Extreme Makeover – Home Edition* on Sunday nights. The best part of the show is always at the end, watching the surprised family's reaction when they unveil the new and much improved home. In one particular episode, there was a family that had their entire house blown up. The explosion was so bad that the front door flew over 40 feet. This family was obviously devastated. Many times after this catastrophe, they would sift through the dirt and debris trying to find mementos, whether it was a piece of a plate, the corner of a photo, or a scrap of material that used to be a curtain.

Not only did the *Extreme Makeover* team build them a brand new house, but they filled it with gorgeous furniture. There was one unique piece of furniture that stood out among all the others; it was located right in the entry. As the family walked into the house, they just broke down in tears when something caught their eyes. It was just a small, round table, nothing real grand, but it was decorated with the shattered remnants and pieces of their old home. It represented so many precious memories to this family. This table was truly special and they would treasure it for years to come.

This story is a perfect illustration of our wonderful miracle working God. God is a God of restoration; and, just like the goal of the *Extreme Makeover* team, one of His specialties is to take the shattered pieces and remnants of our lives and create something beautiful, a rare and unique treasure that is tailor-made just for us!

I am writing about a unique treasure which you may not even know you have. It is the treasure of your testimony, composed of your own personal experiences with God, the past joys as well as past hurts. This treasure is owned by you and you alone.

God desires to turn your tragedies into treasures. God wants to use what once held you captive to set others free.

The Great Escape

If you like to read exciting and suspenseful stories, turn in your Bible to the book of Acts. As you read about Paul and his miraculous jailbreak, pay attention to Paul's actions and what happened as a result of his actions.

Paul was arrested and severely beaten, then put in the inner cell and had his feet fastened in stocks. Paul and Silas were singing and praising the Lord and the other prisoners were listening. Suddenly, a violent earthquake took place and the foundation of the prison was shaken. All the prisoners' doors flew open, everybody's chains came loose. The jailer woke up and began to draw his sword to kill himself because he thought all the prisoners had escaped. But Paul shouted ….. "Wait - don't harm yourself, we are all here!"

The jailer then replied, "What must I do to be saved?"

Throughout the night, Paul was able to share Christ with his jailer's entire family and they all were saved and baptised! Paul and Silas were also ministered to; they were fed and their wounds were washed. The next day, the magistrates released them saying, "Go in peace!" (Acts 16:22-36.)

Wow! God supernaturally set Paul free, and he could have run from the jail escaping with his life but he didn't. He stayed. God used the very chains that had once held him captive to set others free; the jailer and his family were saved and baptized! As a matter of fact, this was the humble beginnings of the church in Philippi.

Regardless of the reason, some of us have been held captive by chains of sin. Not in a physical prison and not in iron chains but, instead, we have been held captive in the SPIRITUAL realm! Maybe you have been a slave and imprisoned to drugs, an abusive relationship, bitterness, shame, witchcraft, etc. The list goes on and on. It may have started out harmless, but, after a period of time, it started influencing your thoughts, your actions, and your choices. At some point, things started spinning out of control; you found it hard to just walk away.

My husband Mark describes it like this: "Sin always seeks out a victim." This is absolutely true! No matter if you choose to sin or even if you didn't have a choice, sin will try to steal from you and make you its prisoner. But God desires for you to be free and for you to walk in that freedom. For some of us, freedom and healing is a process and for others it can be a supernatural deliverance. Regardless, when you come to God, He always provides a way to set you free.

God's Word is very clear that we are to be careful not to go back into temptation. If you have struggled with a drinking problem, then being in a party-like atmosphere with alcohol is not the place for you. If you broke up with a deadbeat guy, then you should no longer be hanging out with him. We need to make a very clear break from the sin that entangled us in the first place so that we will not get tangled up all over again. However, in God's timing, God will use what once imprisoned us, and, just like Paul, He will use our testimony to make a difference in other people's lives.

I thank God for my past! I have seen, time and time again, God use my mistakes for His glory. I have written and spoken about this on many occasions. I have been able to speak into young women's lives who have gone through experiences similar to mine. The big difference is that, even though I was once in that bondage, I made it out! I know first-hand God's grace and His mercy. I have experienced His strength, and I know He can set others free just like He did me.

My close friend, Rebecca, struggled with anorexia, and God is using her testimony to expose His awesome truth. She knows firsthand what it is like to struggle with an eating disorder, and she knows what it can cost you. She was at a very dangerous point in her life when God turned things around. God set her free! Her story of God's healing and restoration is amazing! When she speaks at conferences and shares her testimony, there is not a dry eye among the crowd.

Recently on the news, I heard of a girl who started a "secret club" as a result of being raped, brutally shot, and left for dead. Her story is amazing and many other rape victims have been able to come forward and get help as a result of it. She named it the "secret club" because she knew all about the shame, and the pain, and the isolation that can come from being a rape victim. But, the prison of rape no longer holds her captive, and she uses that ugly, cold prison as a platform to encourage others to get help and get whole! This world is full of evil and bad things happen to good people. It breaks the very heart of God. Even though this girl would never have chosen this nightmare, God was faithful to bring healing into her life, give her the strength to face each day, and eventually turn things around in her life so that her story could bring healing to many.

> *And we know that in all things God works for the good of those who love him, who have been called according to his purpose.*
>
> *Romans 8:28* ⠿

When we trust Him, we will see God will work in and through all of life's circumstances and turn them around for our good. Regardless of our past, God wants to use the very thing that once held us captive for His glory. God is a God of restoration! He will take the ashes of our lives and make them into something beautiful that will glorify Him and impact the lives of others.

God's Keeping Power

There is another type of testimony that also is very powerful; it is the testimony of God's "keeping" power. If you have lived a sheltered life, you may have entertained thoughts like, *Who in the world wants to hear my boring and simple story?* If the truth be known, you may be afraid that you will even put people to sleep--that is if you can even think of anything to say! When I was younger, I actually looked at the ex-drug addict with envy in my heart thinking, *Wow! What a story of God's miracle working power! If only I could just have a story like that!*

The truth is that some of the most amazing testimonies are the ones that demonstrate God's incredible "keeping" power. Praise the Lord, everyone does not make life altering mistakes! And what a testimony to be able to share the blessings that come as a result of a life submitted to Christ--a life of commitment and devotion, void of consequences, scars, and regrets.

Daniel's Testimony (Look up Daniel 1:1-21)

This chapter sets the stage for Daniel's life. He was a young man who was committed and devoted to God in every way. The rest of the book of Daniel (chapters 2 – 12) goes on and on explaining all the exploits, visions, and favor he received as a result of his devotion to God.

When I read Daniel's testimony, it sends chills down my spine. Daniel is the one God rescued from the lions' den (chapter 6). Throughout his life, he never bowed to anyone but God! On every side, he faced pressure to conform; he could have easily compromised but instead he chose God. He chose to remain faithful and be committed to God. God gave him incredible wisdom, insight, and visions, favor with kings and kingdoms. God blessed his life. Daniel would have missed out on so much had he not been faithful to God all those years. Because of his faithfulness, God raised him up and Daniel's testimony impacted many lives.

If you have served God faithfully, don't withhold your testimony, but, instead, "shout it from the rooftops." In other words, share it with passion. You have cause to celebrate! We do not have to make bad choices and suffer the consequences to have a powerful story. God can be glorified through a life committed to Him.

You Have a TESTIMONY!

Your testimony is a very unique and special treasure that God has entrusted you with. Don't underestimate how valuable your testimony can be. You will influence lives! Your story could be the one thing that could make the difference between someone's victory and their defeat. Are you willing to share your experiences, your past hurts, and pain if it means others can come to know Christ as their ultimate Savior and ultimate Healer? Like Paul, are you willing to use the very chains and bars that once held you captive, to be a place where God is glorified? Many were saved because of Paul's obedience. There is no way of telling how many might receive their salvation and deliverance as a result of your obedience! Share your story of imprisonment to reveal God as the true prison-breaker.

If you have stayed true to God, then I want to personally thank you and implore you to share your story of God's amazing "keeping" power. Share the awesome truth so that others too can stay true to God and avoid the deep scars of pain and regret.

God has given you your personality, your talents, your desires, and a dream that only you are destined to fulfill. He has also given you the treasure of your testimony. Pursue Jesus, press in to God's Word and develop your prayer life. Take a leap of faith, and learn from your failures. Pursue Jesus, seek Him first and everything else will fall into place. Nothing will be more fulfilling than to live out your life with His purpose in mind! Use your God given treasures for His purpose and His glory and He will shine through you like never before. You, too, can make your mark in this world!

Develop Your Own TESTIMONY!

What has God done in your life? Sometimes, we don't see the fingerprints of God in our lives. We often don't see God's hand there gently guiding us along the way.

In the Old Testament, every time God did something extraordinary, they would stop and build an altar. This way, they would be reminded of God's faithfulness. This is done time and time again in the Bible, as they create a place of remembrance. Take a few minutes and look up Genesis 28:10-22. You need to see God's faithfulness in your life! Not only is this helpful in developing your testimony, but this is a very important step in your Christian walk.

Did God send someone along your path years ago who first witnessed to you?_____

Were you born or adopted into a home with two loving Christian parents?_____

Look back at your life, and then write down the times when God was faithful and the times when God showed you specific things.

_____
_____
_____
_____
_____
_____
_____
_____
_____
_____
_____
_____
_____
_____

SIGNIFICANT EXPERIENCES WITH THE LORD:

(In your testimony, include the answers to the questions that apply to your life.)

1. What were you like before you got saved? Were you struggling in any specific area (forgiveness, depression, drugs, etc.)? Did God immediately take that away or was it a process? Did you have to make hard choices afterwards?_____

_____
_____

2. Maybe you asked Jesus Christ into your heart when you were a little girl; if so, share that! What a great testimony that you were faithful to God._____

_____
_____

3. If you were saved as a little girl and you turned your back on God, what caused you to rededicate your life to the Lord?_____

_____

_____

_____

4. How did these things happen? Where were you? Explain the circumstances._____

_____

_____

_____

PEOPLE:

Ultimately, we know that it was the Holy Spirit that drew us to Jesus; but God also uses people, pastors, evangelists, neighbors, friends, etc. Who have been the biggest Godly influences in your life?_____

_____

_____

_____

BIBLE VERSES:

Write down at least one favorite Bible verse (maybe two or three). Why does that scripture(s) mean so much to you? How has it impacted your life?_____

_____

_____

_____

DESIRES, GIFTS, OR DREAMS:

We are all created with a purpose. Do you know that God predestined you? (For example, when a guy asks a girl to get married, he goes out and orders a ring. He takes a lot of time, picks the perfect diamond, a beautiful style, a gorgeous setting; the ring has to be just right. He wants it perfect!) Guess what? God created you; He predestined you for a purpose. He molded and created you better than any jeweler could make a ring. In His eyes, you are a work of art - a masterpiece. God did His job! Now your job is to start reflecting on dreams, desires, and gifts that He has given you, beginning from when you were a little girl. Do you see the same desires and dreams that you had as a little girl still resonating in your heart? If so, write them down! _____

_____
_____
_____
_____
_____
_____
_____
_____
_____
_____
_____

Be sensitive to who you are sharing your testimony with. You only need to share the part that relates to the audience or person. Too much sharing can be over-kill. Take your time writing your testimony, use the questions as a guide. Have your leader help you and give you direction. Memorize and look over your testimony. Share it with friends, your youth group, Christian clubs, etc. God wants to use your life. A testimony is a powerful way to witness. People can argue facts or religion, but they cannot argue your experiences with the Lord. Maybe someone listening might be able to relate to your story.

My Desire to Dance

Since I was a little girl, I knew I always had a strong desire to dance. I used to stand in front of the bathroom mirror and try to imitate the dance moves I saw on TV. Although it looked pretty funny, I would keep trying until I mastered the moves. Eventually, I would hear a knock and a yell at the bathroom door, telling me to get out of the bathroom. I grew up in a household where my dream to dance was never accepted. Alone in the bathroom, standing in front of that mirror, I would drift into another world, dancing for a make-believe audience. I would pray to God to allow me to be a song girl. I sought to follow my dream, but realized quickly, I had no support from my parents.

Losing hope on my dream to dance, I placed it upon a shelf and withdrew into a shy state. Growing up, I was the middle child of five kids, so it seemed there was never enough time for us all to get the attention we needed as kids. My father was very busy in ministry, and seemed to always have someone to minister to. During my teenage years, I had convinced myself I was fat and ugly. It seemed as the years passed, I became harder and harder on myself. I thought skinny people were the ones always getting noticed so I began to starve myself. Although I had blonde hair, green eyes, and only weighed 105 pounds, I felt no one would notice me. I felt fat and ugly and thought I still needed to lose weight. Something inside me drove me to hate who I was as a person.

At the young age of 16, I was kicked out of my parent's house. My father said I was too hard to live with. At 18, I was raped. After this traumatic event in my life, my self-esteem was gone. It seemed that every year that passed, things only got worse.

I did eventually get help for the anorexia and bulimia. I went to counseling and dealt with the feelings of rejection and with the fact that I was raped.

Could I ever be that young child dancing in front of the mirror again? It was not until I became an adult that I remembered dancing in front of the mirror. It seems I wasted so many years not knowing who I really was and how much God truly loves and cares for me. Unfortunately, I learned at a much older age how God really feels towards me. If I had felt this love at a young age, maybe I could have avoided all the hurt and pain that I experienced as a child.

Would I rewrite my life story? I now have confidence knowing I have a Heavenly Father who loves me so much. He enjoys, even when I was a young girl, watching me dance before Him. He reminds me that I am fearfully and wonderfully made (Psalms 139) and that dancing is a gift He gave me. He was with me all along, even though I didn't know it, encouraging me and cheering me on as I danced before that mirror as a little girl. He reminds me to never misuse this gift. Maybe, in some way, this will stir your heart, and give you hope that you will know God as I do now, and that your life can be completely different than mine was. We are all God's creations!

For some of you, relating to my story is not hard. Maybe the storyline or the names are different, but the feeling of worthlessness is the same. What if you could go back to the beginning? Be challenged to accept the love and plans God has for you. No story needs to be rewritten, for the Almighty Author knows the beginning and the eternal ending.

God is captivated by you! He leads the steps while your head is on His chest. As you perform, His eyes never leave you. You can feel His heartbeat next to yours. When you experience His love for you, you know there is nothing anyone can say or do to take away "who" you are in God's eyes. The confidence this gives you is unexplainable.

I now know that even as a young girl, God filled me up with love and talent! God wanted to use my gifts to perform for Him. He was pleased with me when I danced for Him. The Bible says in Jeremiah 29:11, 'For I know the plans I have for you,' declares the Lord, 'plans to prosper you and not to harm you, plans to give you a hope and a future' (NIV). There was a time Satan tried to taunt me with my past and rob me of my talents. Satan tried to put other obstacles in my life, such as a heart condition. After a season, God healed me of that heart condition too. I am so thankful for the plans and protection He places in my life!

For years now, I have been able to use my gift and work with an amazing dance team at my church. It has been so exciting to know God is using my talent for His glory. Being used by God to touch people's lives, is very fulfilling but today, my biggest joy is to sing and dance before an audience of One!

Linda

I treasure every opportunity
I have to Preach!

There are precious gifts the Lord has given me throughout my life. Gifts that are so vivid I can almost physically see the wrapping. The bows are big and beautiful and the gift-wrap is crisp and clean. They are so elegant I don't even want to open them, although I can't imagine my life without them. I look back and this opportunity was one of those gifts.

Humbled, I took my place on the dirt ground with dozens of African children. I was on a trip into "The Bush" (rural Mozambique Africa). The men had gone out to tell the community about the upcoming weekend church meeting. While they were gone, I (the only fair-skinned person) was asked to speak to the children in our small, open-air hut which we labeled a church. On the spot, I thought of a great children's story by Max Lucado that I had recently heard. I decided this would be the perfect story for these children to understand how special they were to the Lord. As I stood up and began to speak, I quickly realized my "translator" only knew about ten words in English. We spent more time trying to discuss the story, between the two of us, so she could understand. Finally, she "understood" and on we went to tell the story. Upon the end, she turned to me and said, "That's it?" I said, "Yes," with the obvious understanding that she did not comprehend any of the story, therefore, neither did the children. The overall point of the story was completely lost and the story ended with "That's it?" Humbled, I took my place on the dirt ground with the children.

As a person who has felt the call of the Lord to preach and teach since I was about ten years old, this was a moment I will never forget as the calm words ran through my head, "It's definitely not about me." There was nothing I could do or do better; it just was not about me.

Convinced the Lord had control of the situation, I found myself on a *chapa* (a small public transport) on the way to visit a new church plant. Bumpy was not the word to describe it; take the worst off-road terrain you have ever seen and put a falling-apart fifteen-seat van on it. Just as we flew over a bump and my head hit the ceiling, a pastor looked over at me and said, "I heard you are called by God.

You are preaching tonight." All of a sudden, I forgot the bumps in the road and my heart jolted out of place. Fear swept over my entire body. The confidence I once had in the Lord's control over my last experience, quickly went out the van window. My spirit began to panic! I couldn't do this! What would I speak on? Every insecurity began to seep out. The Africans had a deeper understanding of faith than I did. What could I teach them? Nothing! My confidence continually depleted until it transformed into anxious fear.

When we arrived at the church plant, everyone was in a one-room house wildly worshiping the Lord, "African style." I opted to sit outside on a small bench to prepare for speaking. I frantically flipped through my Bible wondering what to preach. My mind drew a blank and I couldn't remember anything. I felt like I was a little kid trying to do a book report on a book I had never even read. I froze! Tears began to sweep down my face. Just then, the only light bulb in the whole area went out. I sat in pitch blackness with a Bible, which I could no longer read. Tears were flowing like a river at this point. My body shook! The Lord then said sweetly to me, "Tell them what I have been teaching you."

That night I preached the second worst sermon I had ever preached. I cried three times. I had no outline, no preparation, and no practice. I stood with a pastor on either side of me holding up small candles so I could read my Bible. At the end, I forgot to pray, and, instead, awkwardly went to the last bench and sat down. And, again, the final words I heard were, "That's it?"

Humbled yet again and, even worse, now massively humiliated. I was sure this would be the last time I would be speaking, until the *chapa* ride back, when the same pastor turned to me and said, "Fifteen people got saved and a man delivered from substance abuse. You are speaking again tomorrow night at another church."

The phrase again penetrated my memory, "It's not about me." No matter how talented or how disastrous of a speaker I am, it's not about me. It's about Him! What a relief! What a gift!

Shiloh

God saved me for a purpose!

I know that God can heal! I believe He healed me and saved me for a purpose when I was a little girl. I had an allergic reaction to aspirin that caused my tongue to swell and I couldn't swallow. My body started to swell as well and I broke out in hives all over my body. I cried and I was scared because this had never happened to me. When my parents saw me, my mother's reaction was to immediately take me to the emergency room. As we were driving to the hospital I let them know that I was having difficulty breathing. Once there, my father picked me up and hurried me to the boys' restroom because I needed to vomit. I could see that my parents were frightened. The hospital staff let my parents know that there was no doctor available at the moment and they weren't immediately equipped with oxygen to ease my breathing. While in my father's arms, I stopped breathing and the staff began CPR and opened up a central line to combat the reaction from the aspirin, at least that is what my father told me afterwards! God showed up and performed a miracle in my life at the exact moment when I needed it. Because of Him I am still standing here.

I'm currently seventeen years old. One of my favorite scriptures is Ephesians 2:8; it says, "For by grace you have been saved through faith, and that not of yourselves; it is the gift of God" (NKJV). I believe that God saved my life and I consider it a gift! He has been there for me and my family in so many ways. I love Him and I want to serve Him.

Recently, I have been serving God at my church in children's ministry. It is so exciting to help lead the children's services, assist in planning and creating back drops, and praying with the kids. I love it and I am finding out that I am pretty good working with children. Who knows, I may just become a Children's Pastor!

I will always be thankful that God showed up at that hospital and rescued me. Just when things were at their worst, God intervened. Jesus Christ saved me and I owe Him my life. Now, I have a chance to show my love for Him by loving His kids.

Jessica

Section VIII

"... that's because she's 'on fire'..."

"What do they have that I don't?"

Let's get this PARTY started!

"I will love Jesus like that someday..."

"Maybe if I fake it, they will think I know Jesus like they do."

Sharing my faith

I grew up going to church, learning Scripture and more about who God is. My life and my walk with God seemed normal until I reached middle school. At first, I did not even want to consider a public high school simply because I had only experienced private schools. It took me several months to realize that it does not really matter what I want, but what matters is what God wants. In the end, I chose to attend a public school because it was where God wanted me to go.

It was not long after I had adjusted into high school that my parents told my sister and me that we were going to move. Again, I wanted to go to the private school at my new church, but I wanted to make sure that it was what God wanted me to do. I prayed about it for a couple months until I finally felt God telling me to continue going to a public school.

Since then, I have been so happy that I know I am doing God's will. At my old high school, I never truly felt like I was making an impact for God. I hate to think that people did not even know that I was a Christian. I regret hiding myself and my relationship with Christ, but there is no way to go back now. Who knows how many lives I might have changed if I had tried?

God is good and He gave me a second chance. Now I have been able to build new relationships and start a new reputation. People at my school know who I am in Christ. It has become much easier to share Christ with my friends because they know where I stand.

One opportunity that I had to share my faith came, unexpectedly, during my first period History class. Every morning we share a warm-up with a buddy and this particular morning, mine came into class crying. At first, I did not know what to do, but then I thought about what I would do in that situation—pray! So I asked my teacher if I could step into the hall with my buddy. It was awkward, at first, but God gave me the words to say. I was able to encourage her and share God's love with her. At the end of our discussion, I even prayed with her. It was so amazing! I never thought that I could make that much of a difference in someone's life!

I think that I would not have been able to do that if it were not for all of the positive influences in my life. People continued to tell me, "You can make a difference in the lives at your schools!" My pastors would say, "We aren't permitted to preach on school campuses, but you guys are on that mission field every day." I never really thought about this until after I moved, but I realize, now, how much of a difference I can make. There are some people at my school who are never around many Christians, but I have a great opportunity to reach out to them. How cool is that! I love going to my school because I know that every day is a new chance to reach out with God's love and witness to my friends.

Kelsey

chapter 17

THE INVITATION
Shiloh Harrison

In the summer of 2004, I went to Mozambique, Africa, to work in an orphanage. A twenty-two year old guy had traveled to come share his story with us. This boy had been raised at the orphanage. He now had the opportunity to attend college in South Africa. He began to tell us about the beautiful things the Lord had done for him throughout his life. He was so grateful. The smile on his face ran from ear to ear. There was an intimacy he had with the Lord that everyone in the audience could see. He told us about an amazing miracle; the Lord kept multiplying one pot of chili, which was made to feed four people, into enough to feed 127 orphans. He told us about miracles of things we as Americans often take for granted, like being able to, for the first time, taste fresh water or feel the soft touch of a band aid. The boy continued praising the Lord as he told story after story of God's beauty. Eyes welling up with tears, he spoke softly with these soul cementing words, "If you do not feel invited by God, something is wrong."

A man was giving a big dinner, and he invited many; and at the dinner hour he sent his slave to say to those who had been invited, 'Come; for everything is ready now.' But they all alike began to make excuses. The first one said to him, 'I have bought a piece of land, and I need to go out to look at it; please consider me excused.'

Another one said, 'I have bought five yoke of oxen, and I am going to try them out; please consider me excused.'

Another one said, 'I have married a wife, and for that reason I cannot come.'

And the slave came back and reported this to his master.

Then the head of the household became angry and said to his slave, 'Go out at once into the streets and lanes of the city and bring in here the poor and crippled and blind and lame.'

And the slave said, 'Master, what you commanded has been done, and still there is room.'

And the master said to the salve, 'Go out into the highways and along the hedges, and compel them to come in, so that my house may be filled. For I tell you, none of those men who were invited shall taste of my dinner.'

Luke 14:16-24

Every invitation I have ever received has been to a party, an exciting event, a holiday get together, but never to something negative. I have never opened up my mailbox and seen the words, "You are invited to DETENTION!" My heart would sink. Invitations are not for disappointment. Why do we respond in this same way to Christ's invitation to us? There seems to be a sense of disappointment, that our fun is being taken away, or that we are heading into punishment.

The Bible uses the parable of the banquet story to show us a small picture of the kingdom of God (the piece of Heaven that reigns through His Spirit on this earth, otherwise known as Christianity). In this story, God throws a massive party. He makes up these awesome invitations and sends them out. The Bible says that each of us has been given an invitation to the party. We are each invited into the kingdom of God, never forced, but welcomed with excitement. When we grab the envelope out of our mailbox, we read it, get excited, and then have the opportunity to R.S.V.P.

When I send out birthday party invitations, it is exciting to receive R.S.V.P. calls. I remember one call very well, "Of course, I will be there. You're my best friend. I wouldn't miss it for the world!" I got all excited that my closest friend would be coming to celebrate with me.

The day arrived and people began to show up, but after waiting awhile, I gave up hope that my best friend would come. My party became a haze as I contemplated that deep feeling of rejection that came when I realized I valued my friend more than my friend valued me. It was a hard thought to accept. Instead of a celebration, it was a day of fighting back tears because of my dearest friend's absence. How this friend treated me, many times, is how we treat the invitation of Christ.

A lot of us look at others who are excited about their faith in Christ, and we wonder why we, as Christians, still feel like we are missing out on part of Christianity. How else can we get it? The missing piece is we have all received an invitation and many of us have R.S.V.P.'d telling the Lord something like this, "Of course, I will be there. You're my Best Friend! I wouldn't miss it for the world!" We are so excited about going to the party, but soon that excitement wears off; we sit staring at other Christians, wondering what it is that they have that we don't. Maybe the difference is simply this-- you R.S.V.P.'d to the party, but have never shown up.

"My" Thoughts:

1. How would you feel if your best friend never showed up to your party?_____
_____
_____
_____
_____
_____
_____
_____
_____
_____
_____
_____
_____

2. How do you think the Lord feels when you don't show up to His party?_____
_____
_____
_____
_____
_____
_____
_____
_____
_____
_____
_____
_____
_____

3. Tell the Lord what you want to do about that._____

_____

_____

_____

_____

_____

_____

_____

_____

_____

_____

_____

_____

_____

_____

_____

_____

_____

_____

_____

_____

_____

_____

_____

_____

_____

_____

_____

_____

_____

_____

_____

_____

_____

_____

_____

_____

_____

Being a Missionary on my Campus

Growing up in a Christian home, I have always known who God is. At a young age, I accepted Jesus as my Lord and Savior. I began learning all the Bible stories and memorizing countless passages of Scripture. Still, it is a daily struggle to live in God's will. Knowing that I am His servant, called to reach out to His children, is a huge responsibility! Yet, in all my experiences so far, I have definitely found that being in His will truly is the best place to be.

Having felt called to missions when I was in the seventh grade, I and my parents have made many decisions based upon this path. I attended a small private school from kindergarten to eighth grade. My parents were concerned about where they would send me to high school. They had heard some negative things about the local public high school but were hesitant to send me to another private school. After much prayer and discussion, we finally decided that I should go to the public high school in our neighborhood, viewing it as my first missions ground. Because of my relatively shy nature, leaving the small school I had previously attended to go to a large high school where I knew no one was very difficult. I found it hard to make friends, and my initial dream of making an impact on my school became a small priority. However, I eventually began to develop relationships with both students and faculty, and by my junior year had earned a good reputation and had made many connections within the school and the school district.

I became a Campus Missionary with the Assemblies of God, making a commitment to reach my school for Christ. During my second year of high school, I began a prayer group at my school and met with several of my friends every Monday morning to pray for our school. I sincerely feel that prayer is an incredibly powerful weapon in the fight for our schools, and I continued to pray and to build relationships with my peers and teachers. My involvement on my campus and my creation of the prayer group even earned me the Campus Missionary of the Year award from the Oregon district Assemblies of God in 2003.

However, my faith was tested one year ago when my family was uprooted from my lifelong home of Milwaukee, Oregon, to follow my dad's calling as a children's pastor. I struggled with feelings of anger toward God, questioning why this was happening to me. I could not understand why He would put me through something so difficult at such an important stage in my life. I was so frustrated that,

just as I was beginning to make an impact on my school, I was taken away from everything I had ever known. For months, I struggled with feeling like I would never be able to build back what I had earned — the relationships, the influence, and the reputation — and my hope of changing my school for Christ diminished.

Through this time, I had to learn complete reliance on God, and it ultimately brought me closer than ever to Him. At a youth camp during the summer after I moved, I was challenged to lead a life of significance, and our ever-faithful God once again gave me the determination to change my school. I became more involved in the campus club at my new school and discovered that, with God's help, I really could have an influence. I created new relationships with classmates and teachers and, again, earned a good reputation, as someone who is committed to following Christ.

Now instead of wondering why it happened, I am able to believe that God brought me here "for such a time as this." He has a purpose, regardless of whether or not I know what it is. I have always had a passion for reaching those who are hurting and desperate and are without the assurance of Christ's love. I have begun to see how God is using me to touch people I otherwise would have never encountered. As I finish my senior year at my new high school, I look forward to all the ways God will continue to use me for His glory. I strive daily to fulfill this purpose that God has given me, trusting in His ultimate plan for my life and knowing that there is no better alternative!

Lara

chapter 18

BEING STOOD UP

Shiloh Harrison

After about an hour, I remember calling my best friend to ask her where she was. My parents had thrown a surprise 18th birthday party for me, and my best friend was nowhere in sight. Over fifty other people had shown up. Some were childhood friends, others drove hours to attend, but my one best friend had better things to do. When I called her, the phone just rang and rang. No one picked up. My heart yearned for an answer. I hoped there would be some logical reason why she wasn't there. I wanted to make every excuse for her. There may be a lot of reasons why we R.S.V.P. to the Lord, but we never show up to His party.

We Label...

After my first mission trip to Africa, I was overflowing with a joy from the Lord. When I returned home, the Lord told me churches would be calling me to speak about what the Lord had shown me. I remember speaking at one church in my hometown. The room was large and a little bit chilly. Huddled between two round tables was a total of 12 teenagers. That night I hadn't really prepared, but I felt the Lord softly guide my enthusiasm as I told stories of my experiences and humbling lessons the Lord had taught me while I was away. Feeling it was time to finish, I closed by thanking the Lord for His gracious blessing to us. Later that week, a friend of my mother, who attended that church, told me she spoke with the youth pastor and his wife. The conversation ended with a statement similar to this, "We need more 'on fire' teenagers like her in the world."

Although that was supposed to be a compliment, my heart sank. At that point, I had been labeled. 'On fire' was the term which set me apart. This was the term which stripped the entire message from the sermon. You see, the moment we label someone, they lose a piece of reality. In history, we labeled Martin Luther King Jr., Michael Jordan, Princess Diana, Mother Teresa, Rosa Parks, Joan of Arc, and Abraham Lincoln. Each was labeled differently, but each was labeled. The danger of a label is that it takes away the personal challenge of movement. It puts the person on a pedestal and freezes us in the status quo.

When we label others, we rid ourselves of the small desire inside us which spurs us on towards greatness. We push these people out of our reach. Labels move us from, "Wow! I want to love people like Mother Teresa did!" to "Well, she is not the average person; she had an amazing calling by God." Labels hold us back from doing the impossible and paralyze us into living stale. When we label people as 'on fire,' we take away the personal inspiration to know God in that same way. My question is, Why is being 'on fire' abnormal? Why isn't everyone 'on fire'? Why is it just the few and far in between?

We have labeled those in the party as 'on fire.' We see them as having experienced more of Jesus than we have and that scares us. If we let the scare do what it is supposed to, it will move us out of our comfort zone and into a new exciting place with the Lord. If it scares us too much, we quickly label and release that pressure. By labeling, we are missing out on the party.

The Cost...

There are a few of us, at this point, who realize we have never really entered Christ's party. We have become real with ourselves and have stopped trying to pretend. We have come to a place where we know, but are not yet sure, if we are ready to show up. We know the cost but we are not sure if we want to lay everything down.

In Luke 14, when God calls His friends to remind them about the party and asks them where they are, each friend has a practical answer. In our terms, the first friend was scheduled to work a shift at Starbucks, the second was being responsible doing homework and doing her chores as her parents asked, and the third was spending time with her family. The Lord is not saying that these things are wrong. What He is saying is that His party, His kingdom and His pizza are so much better! The Lord is showing us that He should be first place in our lives, not only because He is God, but because His party is better!

Many of us know that we have not entered the party. We even know exactly what has been keeping us from entering. We know. We just have not decided how important it is to us. We can tell people that we are Christians until we are blue in the face, but until we actually step into the party, we will never truly know what being in love with Jesus is like.

The Lord is not implying that the practical things (i.e. responsibilities, family, school, chores, etc.) in life are not important. What He is saying is that whatever you value most in this life, should be surpassed by 1,000 percent with your love and devotion for Christ. If it isn't, it may be a good sign that you have never tasted God's pizza. Your Christianity might taste like stale crackers right now. Pizza is sounding pretty good. If you had tasted the Lord's pizza, you would have been sold on the first bite and your devotion would surpass everything else this world has to offer.

Taste and see that the ⸬⸬⸬ *is good.*

Psalm 34:8 ⸬⸬

Some Day...

When I was in high school, I really admired my youth pastor's passion for the Lord. After watching his passion direct him for years, I remember thinking, *Someday I am going to be like him.* Although I never asked Him a question, the Lord quickly responded, "Why someday? Why not now?" I mumbled in my heart, "What am I waiting for?" I couldn't think of an answer.

Years later, I found myself wandering through the streets of England with some friends. We had opened an outreach center for youth in the inner city. Our aim for wandering was to fall into conversation with other teens like ourselves and randomly invite them to the center. This day we ran into a young girl and her hunched grandfather. As we brought up the subject of the youth center, he looked up from his cane and questioned, "It's just for youth?" I responded by letting him know that, although it was designed for youth, anyone was welcome. To this he replied the truthful, yet, strangely, piercing words, "That's the problem... youth is wasted on the young."

Energy, enthusiasm, life, opportunities, and passion lie within youth, within being young. Youth is held by the young. The old man was ultimately saying that, if he had his youth back, and knew the things he knew now, he would have used more of that energy, enthusiasm, life, opportunity, and passion to live life to the fullest. He would have risked a little more.

> *Remember your Creator in the days of your youth, before the days of trouble come and the years approach when you will say, "I find no pleasure in them."*
>
> *Ecclesiastes 12:1*

Everyone puts very low expectations on us as young people. We are not expected to do much. They expect us to wake up when the alarm sounds, get ready, go to school, listen, go home, do homework, eat dinner, sleep, wake up and do the same the thing day after day. If we can do this relatively well with no massive interruptions, we have fulfilled their expectations. Why is it that their expectations are so low? Maybe it is because that is all we expect of ourselves.

Why do we say, "Someday?" Why don't we break these expectations and live for Christ now? What is stopping us from being who we want to be today?

> *Don't let anyone look down on you because you are young, but set an example for the believers in speech, in life, in love, in faith and in purity.*
>
> *1 Timothy 4:12*

We Fake It...

The most common reason we don't show up to the party is we fake it. We tell everyone we LOVE the party and they should come join us at the party. We say things like "God is good," "Praise the Lord," "I will pray for you," and "Honk, if you love Jesus," all with a mask on. We have played the religious game so long that we fool even ourselves.

The scene begins to look something like this: You hold in your hand the cherished (mint condition) invitation. How exciting it is that you have been invited! You hold it in your hands as you walk through the halls in school. You hold it carefully because you are so proud. All day you randomly have that exciting thrill rush through your veins as you sit in your classes. You have been invited! At moments, you just want to get up and shout, "I HAVE BEEN INVITED!" but you don't because people would think you are weird. Between classes, you saw your best friend, so you showed her your invitation. Your excitement spilled over on to her.

Finally, the day arrives for this party. Still holding your invitation, you pull up to the house. And as you put your car in park, you take a moment to breathe out the excitement. You look out your window and see people walking under the night sky into the party. Still filled with excitement, you can't seem to focus on opening the car door and stepping towards the party. But, finally, you do because you know that's the only way to the party. As you begin to walk toward the house, you hear the music blaring and see the colorful lights through the mansion's windows. Through those same windows, you also see the people dancing, eating, and laughing. You might even recognize some faces.

You get lost in the party while you dance the night away. Your favorite music is playing, and the lights are playful and life-giving. You know, beyond a shadow of a doubt, that this is the best party you have ever been to. Lost in the movement of the evening, you begin to feel people bumping into you or you bumping into them. Suddenly, you hear someone yell, "Hey! Watch where you are going!" Suddenly, with a jump of shock, you are confronted with a group of people staring strangely at you as they continue to walk into the party. Through the snickers of laughter, you hear someone whisper, "Look, she thinks she is in the party." Embarrassed, you slow your dance, and the fuzzy clouds lift from your eyes. It is at that moment that you realize that you never entered the party but were dancing alone, outside, while being entranced looking through the window. The party looked amazing from the window, but was nothing compared to the fun and awe of actually being inside at the party. Everyone else knew you weren't in the party; it was only you who was confused.

Just then you remember thoughts that had run through your head as you were dancing outside the party, *Why does everyone else look like they know something I don't know? Why does it look like they are having more fun at this party than me? What are they tasting that I am not tasting? Maybe this party isn't all it's cracked up to be, I could throw a better party than this.* But, you push those thoughts out of your head as much as you can because people told you it's not "O.K." to question or doubt. You thought maybe you weren't having as much fun because you weren't trying hard enough, so, you put on a bigger smile, dance faster, and yelled louder, "This party is so cool!", the whole time having feelings of emptiness sweep through you.

Humbled, you break back into reality and find yourself still standing outside that window. That window, that was once so inviting, is now cold and unwelcoming. The door now holds in the warmth. As you watch, the crowds make their way into the party, and you are faced with a reality check, "What do I do now?"

"My" Thoughts:

1. Which reason do you feel best explains why you have not shown up to the Lord's Party?

   A. You have labeled others.

   B. You have other things that are more important.

   C. You are waiting for "someday."

   D. You faked yourself out.

2. Explain to the Lord why you have done this and tell Him what you would like to do instead.

_____

_____

_____

_____

_____

_____

_____

_____

_____

_____

_____

Changing my World through Missions

A few friends and I hopped off the subway and went walking down the streets of Cairo, Egypt. A small, beautiful Egyptian boy came nudging alongside of us, begging us to buy a travel size Kleenex from him. Because there were beggars all around, and being the "good" Christian people we were, we tried to shoo him away; however, he did not want to relent.

We ducked into a café for coffee and to spend some time with God. The small boy stood outside the large windows of the café, waiting for another victim. I was intrigued as I watched him. All of a sudden, he looked around mischievously and quickly dropped to the ground to pick up something. Taking one more look around to make sure no one was looking, he gobbled the mysterious object. My heart felt like an elephant was jumping up and down on it. I just kept thinking how beautiful that little one was.

The little boy and I began to make faces at one another through the window. Then, I ran outside, past the boy, to a grocery store, bought a bag full of groceries, went back out into the scorching heat, and placed it at the boys feet. Then, I pulled out my favorite grocery item, a Snickers bar, and placed it in his hands. His face lit up with a smile. I went back inside the cafe and sat by the window and watched him run off, swinging his bag of groceries with joy.

Just as the story seemed to end, it began again. The boy came back, after about a half-hour, empty-handed. We continued our face-making fun, as the waiters of the café tried to shoo the boy away, again. In between begging from one stranger to another, he would look through the window again and make faces at me. The elephant came back, trampling my heart again. Tears and frustration filled my soul, and, then, I realized this child had probably never been given the opportunity to be a child. He had a job to do everyday...beg! Possibly, he might even have been punished if he had come home without anything in his hands. This child probably never had the opportunity to feel assured of the next meal. All of a sudden, a thought began to torment my mind, *What if this child were my little brother?* Fury raged in my heart as people continued to walk by him. Scars on his face and, probably, his tummy grumbling and no one even stopped!

At that moment, I looked out the window, and, to my astonishment, a twin brother appeared. Immediately, I walked outside past the six waiters who were keeping watch to make sure the kids didn't crowd their guests, and went over to the boys. I grabbed both their tiny, dirty hands and walked them right past the line-up of annoyed waiters and into the cafe. I sat them down at our table, pulled out markers and paper and ordered big strawberry juices with lots of whipped cream and straws for them. I could not change a life forever, and there was no way they would both fit into my carry-on luggage, but, for one moment, these children would actually be treated like children.

The next day, as I walked out of a store, a woman, wrapped from head to toe in Islamic clothing, grabbed my hand and began to kiss my cheeks, over and over and over. Teary eyed, I realized, this must be "my" boys' mother. Apparently, she had not been offended, but was deeply touched and blessed that one human would treat her children to a moment of joy, something all mothers long to do for their children. Seconds after her arrival, she disappeared.

Humbled, I realized how much we, as Christians, wait for some huge excuse to love the hurting people around us, even though, most of the time, we just over-look those in need. I usually find myself with this self-righteous excuse rattling through my head, "I am not going to give to someone who begs; it just perpetu-ates more begging. I would rather pick at random an unsuspecting person and support them, with no strings attached. This seems to me to be the wisest road." Then, that still small voice, the Lord, quietly whispered, "You beg from Me every day, and I never turn you away..." Then, as I looked into the big brown eyes of each little beggar, I saw the reflection of myself.

The twin boys' names were "Allah" and "Mohammed" how ironic. In Matthew 25:40, it says that whatever we do to the least of these we do to Him!

Shiloh

chapter 19

PARTY CLOTHES

Shiloh Harrison

When I was in my last year of college, my father flew to southern California to be my "Valentine." We went to the movies and out for dinner. The most exciting part of our date was when he took me to the Los Angeles Staples Center to see the NBA All-Star Slam Dunk Contest. Sitting high in the stands, I watched every guy in uniform from the NBA take his turn competing. There was no confusion as to who was on which team. Each player had their own team's uniform on.

It's the same way in life. Our clothes show to whom we belong. In high school, at lunch, I could walk through the quad and know exactly who belonged to which group by the clothes they wore: the rockers, the rapper, the skater, the surfers, the band, the football players, the cheerleader, etc.

The 'banquet' story is told in the Bible a few times. When Matthew tells it, he adds another portion of the story we did not hear from Luke.

> *Those slaves went out into the streets and gathered together all they found, both evil and good; and the wedding hall was filled with dinner guests. But when the king came in to look over the dinner guests, he saw a man there who was not dressed in wedding clothes, and he said to him, 'Friend how did you come in here without wedding clothes?' And the man was speechless. Then the king said to the servants, 'Bind him hand and foot, and throw him into the outer darkness; in that place there will be weeping and gnashing of teeth.'*
>
> *Matthew 22:10-13*

The party was a wedding. This adds to the history. Reading the Biblical story may make readers wonder why the Lord would be so harsh as to throw someone into hell just for having on the wrong outfit. Back in the time when the Bible was written, the wedding customs were different than they are today. When a guest would R.S.V.P. for a wedding, they would be fitted for a wedding outfit. Every guest would have a custom-tailored wedding outfit to match the wedding party. This was not only an honored gift from the wedding party, but also a design which showed which party everyone was a part of. For that particular day, you were a part of that family.

In the NBA, you can't play for the "Kings" and wear a "Lakers" jersey. You wear the uniform of the team you belong to. In the same way, when going to a wedding, if you were not wearing wedding clothes, you were saying to the wedding party that you wanted to enjoy all the benefits of the party but you didn't want to have relationship with the family, much less have anyone on the outside even know you were at the party. By not wearing the wedding clothes offered, you would essentially be telling the person that you were embarrassed to be called their friend.

Often we have this same problem. We want to enjoy all the blessings God gives, but when it comes to living life for Christ, we are embarrassed to say we are a Christian.

What you wear, also, shows what is important to you. We spend hours picking out the perfect outfit for the party. It is the BEST! Or, so we think. Until we realize there is something better. We have clothed ourselves with the right attitude, the right smile, the right heart, the right job, the right friends, the right goals, the right TV shows, the right music, and even the right guy. What we clothe ourselves with is what is most valuable to us. This is the best party outfit we could find, until we find that the Lord has something better.

It's time to go shopping for a new outfit! The moment you R.S.V.P.'d to the party, the Lord took your measurements and began to make you an outfit that fit you perfectly. It looks best with your eyes, and even makes your hips look just right.

Rather, clothe yourselves with the Lord Jesus Christ, …

Romans 13:14

What does it look like (practically speaking) when you put on the party clothes Christ made especially for you?

Simply put, if you're not willing to take what is dearest to you, whether plans or people, and kiss it good-bye, you can't be my disciple.

Luke 14:33

We have to love living in the clothes of Christ so much that everything else we would put on begins to fade into the background. You have to become so fed up with living a half-hearted Christianity that in desperation you are ready to do anything to have a life more fulfilling. If you have ever thought to yourself, *There has to be something more*, you're right. Stop faking it and go after it!

… since you have taken off your old self with its practices and have put on the new self, which is being renewed in knowledge in the image of its Creator.

Colossians 3:9-10

When entering the party, we must wear "His" party clothes. Before we can put on new clothes, we must decide we want better clothes than the ones we have on. We need to make a decision to put on the new clothes. Before we can enter the awesomeness of the kingdom of God, we must die to ourselves and put on His self, because His ways, His party, is much better than ours. Taste and see for yourself!

…No eye has seen, no ear has heard, no mind has conceived what God has prepared for those who love Him.

1 Corinthians 2:9

God can do anything, you know—far more than you could ever imagine or guess or request in your wildest dreams! He does it not by pushing us around but by working within us, his Spirit deeply and gently within us.

Ephesians 3:20

He does it, not by pushing us around, but by a beautiful and exciting invitation into a new life!

You are a specially invited guest to the Lord's kingdom. When you sense His tug on your heart, that is His beautiful reminder to come to His party. To be a Christian is exciting! He has called you, not to strict adherence of rules, but into a life more than your wildest dreams could ever imagine! You have made a lot of excuses-- excuses why you have not really lived a life after Christ. You have labeled other people as "on fire" so that you wouldn't have to be challenged by their passion, and in turn you missed out. You have decided that the cost is too great, that you value the things of this world more than the things of God's world, and in turn you have missed out. You have put it off for "someday," because you are young and will have time for that "Jesus stuff" later, and in turn you have missed out. You have faked yourself out, while trying to fake everyone else out, and in turn you have missed out. You have missed out on Jesus! You have missed out on the beauty of the life your Creator intended for you to live!

Taking off your old clothes requires surrendering to the Lord. It requires laying down the things most important to you and saying, "Jesus You are worth more than all of that!" It means surrendering the sin which has kept you from an extravagant life in Christ. It's time to not only put on a new outfit but put on that special outfit that our God made perfectly for you! To clothe yourself in Christ is to walk in obedience. It is reading and obeying the Word. To live in Christ is not to question why you are wearing the King's clothes and smelling like "His" pizza! Today is the day to choose to enter His Party!

...choose for yourselves this day...

Josh 24:15

"My" Thoughts:

1. What have you clothed yourself in?_____

_____

_____

_____

_____

_____

_____

_____

_____

_____

2. What do you feel the Lord wants you to clothe yourself in? _____

_____

_____

_____

_____

_____

_____

_____

_____

_____

3. Write to the Lord. Tell Him where you think you have been, where you want to be, and what your next step is. _____

_____

_____

_____

_____

_____

_____

_____

_____

In Conclusion...

Wow! You persevered and you read thru this entire devotional. I am so proud of you! As you turned the pages, I hope God's love for you jumped right off the pages, landing smack dab in your heart!

Even though we've never met, I feel as though I know you. You see, you have been in my thoughts and prayers. Matter-of-fact, I and a group of authors wrote this book with you in mind! It is our prayer that God's powerful truths will forever impact your life and your future.

God loves you in a sweet and intimate way. He knows everything about you (the good and the bad); He will never stop loving you. No matter what challenges lie ahead; God will be with you, and you will make it.

So do not fear, for I am with you;
do not be dismayed, for I am your God.
I will strengthen you and help you;
I will uphold you with my righteous right hand.

Isaiah 41:10

What a powerful scripture! God will be your strength, your help, and He will hold you up with His powerful, strong and mighty hand. You have an amazing future to look forward to with God on your side!

On a final note, I want to leave you with a letter my husband, Mark, wrote when we first started dating. I have saved it through the years because I feel it really reflects the very Father heart of God!

God loves you and so do I, my sweet friend!

Suzanne

To My precious daughter…

I stood in awe the moment I laid eyes on you.

I knew you would be beautiful but words cannot describe the moment you were born. It was as if time stood still.

There you were, my fragile innocent baby girl.

I was so proud; my heart just skipped a beat. The angels, well they could hardly contain themselves, dancing and singing as they marveled at your beauty.

Yes, you were My creation and, now that I brought you into this world, I had to stand back and allow you to grow.

Looking ahead, I see the painful times that you will encounter and I want to ensure you that your tears will not fall silent.

I see and feel each one.

Even if you stop believing in yourself, I will never stop believing in you.

This cold world, so full of evil, will try and steal your very soul, but I will be your refuge and true defender.

In all of creation, there is no one else like you.

My timing is perfect; you were created for such a time as this!

You have a plan and purpose; this is your time to fulfill your destiny!

Love,
Your Heavenly Father

Daughters of Heaven Ministries

"Inspiring a generation to experience God's love and true intimacy for life."

Take advantage of our resources! If you are a youth leader, pastor, parent or anyone investing in the lives of young people, we would love to partner with you to reach this generation for Christ.

Daughters of Heaven Conferences

Are you interested in hosting a Daughters of Heaven Conference or other special event? Daughters of Heaven conferences engage young women in a conversation about what it means to be loved by the Father and how to  discover His unique plan for their life. Dynamic speakers encourage an atmosphere of expectancy for young women to dream big with God whether they are beginning their walk of faith, renewing their commitment or going deeper. Break out sessions—or "chat rooms"— encourage connection in a smaller setting and address the needs of this generation.

Topics include Breaking Free (hope & restoration), dating relationships, purpose & personality, among other things. We have been holding conferences since 1995 and can provide you with the tools to plan, promote and host a dynamic one or two day conference in your community.

Wholly Devoted Conferences

Do you want to include young men in your conference experience? Wholly Devoted Conferences were developed by Mark Rentz to delve further into topics connected to relationships, dating and sex. Young people are daily confronted with lies in our media-saturated society, so we unapologetically present the truth about God's design for sexuality. Our "guys only" and "girls only" chat rooms provide forums for them to wrestle with their own values, give feedback and ask candid questions about the "why?" and "how?" of sexual purity. An opportunity to make a formal commitment brings the conference to a powerful conclusion. We pray young people will be captivated by His love and resolve to live wholly devoted to His purposes.

Daughters of Heaven Speakers

If you are looking for someone to speak at your event, we can help! Our Speakers share from God's word the insights that have guided them through their own journey, and each has a unique and dynamic way of connecting with the younger generation. If you are looking for someone to speak at your conference or other event, or if you would like a copy of their bios, please contact us.

Mentoring Program

Do you want to extend the impact to your youth of the conference? T2 is a mentoring program based on Titus 2 which encourages the older to instruct the younger. Because we have only a brief time with your young people, we encourage the development of mentoring relationships within your community of faith and will provide tools to get started. If you would like to include this in your conference weekend or would like more information about mentoring, please logon to our website.

DVD Series

Available in 2012... we will be launching our brand new DVD series entitled "life: connected" designed to use in conjunction with this devotional. Geared with today's youth in mind, this 9-week series will address the major issues young women face. This format is perfect for any small group setting. Go to: daughtersofheaven.org for release date and additional information.

Suzanne Rentz

Contact Us:
www.DaughtersOfHeaven.org
or Call 866.381.3882

Do You Need Help?

Contact any of these ministries and they will be a great source of help and support to you!

Are you Pregnant?

Contact: Alternatives Pregancy Center

2628 El Camino Ave. Sacramento, CA 95821

916-972-0367

alternativespc.org

Contact: Sydna Masse

Ramah International

1-866-807-2624 (EST)

http://ramahinternational.org

Considering Adoption?

Contact: Bethany Christian Services Adoption

Agency National Office

901 Eastern Ave NE

PO Box 294 Grand Rapids, MI 49501-0294

Phone: 616-224-7610

info@bethany.org

Issues with your sexuality?

Contact: Unspoken Ministries

6051 S. Watt Ave. Sacramento, CA 95829

Phone: 916-798-3307

Email: **cblair@agncn.org;**
Charsblog.com

Have you had an Abortion?

Contact :Truth Ministries

P.O. Box 1763 Manteca, CA 95336

(209) 825-5822

truthministries.us

Contact: Surrendering the Secret

3910 Northdale Blvd., Suite 210 Tampa, FL 33624

813-931-1804

surrenderingthesecret.com

Battling Drug, Alcohol, or other Addictions?

Contact: Teen Challenge

PO BOX 1015 Springfield, MO 65801

(417) 862-6969

tcusa@teenchallengeusa.com

and/or

Contact: Mercy Ministries

MercyMinistries.org

Do you want to find out more about MINISTRY opportunites? Do you want to start a Campus Club or become a Campus Missionary?

Contact: Jeff Devoll—My Campus Ministries

5449 East Levee Rd. Sacramento, CA   95835

Office: (707) 333-9089

Visit our website at: **jeff@mycampus.org**

Do you have a love for Sports?

Contact: Fellowship of Christian Athletes

FCA World Headquarters

8701 Leeds Road Kansas City, MO 64129

Toll free: 800-289-0909

e-mail: **fca@fca.org** or web: **www.fca.org**

Do you want to get involved in Missions?

Contact: Global Passion Ministries

100 Anderson Road Napa, CA 94558

Phone: 707-252-9725

admin@globalpassion.net

or

Contact: YWAM

Youthwithamission.org

About the Author

Suzanne Rentz

As a young child growing up in Eureka, California. Suzanne had a deep love for God and a dream to one day stand before women and share the message of His love and acceptance. It was nearly twenty years later before that dream became a reality, but in 1991, Suzanne discovered the joy of following her heart. After marrying her husband, Mark they began serving as youth pastors as Calvary Assembly in Milpitas.

Then in 1995, Suzanne teamed up with a group of women, Valeri Noonan, Jennifer Davis, Silvia Alvarez, and Anna Ruiz. All of them had a desire to make a difference in the lives of young women in their community and they put together the very first Daughters of Heaven Conference. That year in San Jose, California more than 180 girls attended a weekend Daughters of Heaven Conference designed specifically for them. Witnessing the life-changing presence of God wash over the girls as they discovered his great love, forgiveness and restoration profoundly impacted this group of women. It was out of this humble beginning that Daughters of Heaven Ministries was birthed, since then several conferences have been held throughout the United States and thousands of young women have been encouraged with life-changing results.

Suzanne Rentz is the President of Daughters of Heaven Ministries. She is the author of Daughters of Heaven, Lessons in Life, published by Harrison House. She has been the keynote speaker for Daughters of Heaven Conferences as well as other Conferences, church events, and Women's Meetings. She has spoken to the youth at Summer Blitz at Kenneth Hagin's Camp meeting, conducted sessions at Assemblies of God Church Camps, taught Bible Studies, and instructed leaders at the Northern California Assemblies of God Leadership Summit.

Suzanne's best friend, and most significant partner in life, is her husband, Mark. Mark is an ordained minister with the Assemblies of God. He is an anointed writer, worship leader and gifted speaker. Together, Mark and Suzanne have co-taught at several of the Daughters of Heaven Conferences, Wholly Devoted Conferences, and several other conferences and functions. They reside in Sacramento, California, along with their four children, Luke, Andrew, Elijah, and Gabriella. Between sports, homework, & church, there is never a dull moment in the Rentz Household.

Suzanne's true passion is to help young women discover God's love and acceptance, understand that they are created in His image, and uncover His incredible plan for their lives. Suzanne communicates a message from her heart that is crucial for today's generation. Her message is 'strong and clear'; if young women truly know their value and incredible worth to their Heavenly Father, then they can live their life to the fullest: full of purpose, love, adventure, and most of all, full of Him!

About the Contributing Authors ...

Rebecca Harris

Rebecca was licensed with the Assemblies of God in 2004 and served as the children's pastor of River City Community Church for five years before returning to university to pursue graduate work in the area of biblical studies. She recently completed her M.A. in biblical interpretation at Regent University. Rebecca plans to continue her studies and would like to teach at the university level. She currently works as a research assistant. Rebecca and her husband live in Huntington, WV, and together they lead the children's church program at their church.

Shereen Christian

Shereen is a Speaker and Writer with a heart to see all women enjoy healthy, whole lives. She lives in Rocklin, CA with her husband, Gary, their three daughters, Jessica, Jordyn and Jaclyn Grace, and her yorkie Princess Bella. If you're interested in having Shereen speak at your event, you can contact her through Daughters of Heaven Ministries.

Jamie Aleman

Jamie is a licensed minister of the Assemblies of God and has worked in youth ministry many years as a youth leader, adult leader and currently along side her husband, Ron who is a youth pastor. Ron and Jamie have been married 8 years and have 3 wonderful boys~ Ronnie 7, Ryan 4 and Robbie 2. Jamies passion is to see the Lost come to Jesus and the Church become like Jesus.

Heidi Bents

Heidi and her husband Stuart, graduates of Oral Roberts University, were ordained through their local church and served on staff for 10 years as Associate Pastors of Prayer/Evangelism. Heidi is the devoted mother to seven fantastic children, aged five to twenty-two at present. Sharing her testimony of the Redemptive Power of Jesus Christ is a personal passion. A speaker, singer and author, she has led various in-depth ladies' Bible Studies, mentored many precious women, and served as key-note speaker with Daughters of Heaven Ministries Conferences for over a decade. She assists her children with leading in-home mentorship groups focusing on the study of God's True Word. Heidi is currently authoring a book about her near death experience during the miraculous birth of their son Braeden. Stuart and Heidi have recently launched a new company, "Lion Gear" founded upon Revelations 5, which promotes the Salvation Message of Jesus Christ through offering a line of high quality athletic apparel. "Join The Tribe"@www. LionGear.com; Heidibents@Liongear.com

Shiloh Harrison, M.P.A.

Shiloh is currently an Admissions Counselor at William Jessup University. She is a speaker and missionary to Africa. She attended New York University, MPA in Public and Nonprofit Management, Policy, and International Economic Development; Vanguard University, BA in Pastoral Leadership/Religious Studies.

Angela Hansen

Angela & her husband, Ken have been married for over eight years. They have a daughter named Isabella and a baby on the way. They live in northern California & they serve in various ways at Origin Community Church in Rocklin.

Char Blair

Char Blair is a gifted communicator. Her witty sense of humor and willingness to speak truth from God's Word in to real life situations is just the beginning of her many God-given talents and abilities. Char is the founder of Unspoken, a ministry that is designed to encourage those struggling with life altering problems. She is a credentialed minister with the Northern California & Nevada Assemblies of God District Council and a graduate of William Jessup University, receiving her degree in Psych/Counseling and Biblical Theology.

Sheena Souza

Sheena is a graduate of Vanguard University, with a BA in Psychology. She has been leading worship since she was 14, and is very passionate about seeing other experience the tangible presence of God. She is now 25, and co-labors with her husband and his ministry at the Rock of Roseville church. Sheena is also a music teacher, and has three beautiful daughters.

Kathy Holt

Kathy is a graduate of Bethany University in Scotts Valley, CA. She is married to Christopher Holt. Christopher is currently a part time media minister at Harvest Church in Elk Grove. Kathy is the devoted mother of four children. Her passion is worshipping and knowing Christ more intimately.

Angela Germolus

Angie attends Family Christian Center in Patterson, Ca Where she and her husband Daniel are actively involved in Children's ministry and Youth Ministry. Daniel and Angie have been married 4 years! Angie has a passion to see lives changed from the inside out and to Show people that they are not victims of their circumstance but Victors!

Emily Mills

Emily is currently a student at Maysville Community and Technical College, and she will be transferring to Eastern Kentucky University this fall to pursue a B.A. in Cultural Anthropology and a B.A. in English with a focus in Literature. Afterwards, she would like to pursue a M.F.A. in Creative Writing with a focus in Poetry. When she was 14, Emily wrote a teen devotional and, in 2009, revised it. It has not yet been published, but Emily feels that it is important for young people to understand and apply the gospel of Jesus Christ. She is currently involved with children and young women at her church, Victory Christian Center, where her parents, Byron and Rhea Mills, are Senior Pastors.

Kristine Ives

Kristine is a mental health therapist and volunteer victim advocate specializing in children, adolescents, and survivor's of sexual violence. She recently adopted and eleven year old boy named Nick and they keep busy in Denver, CO playing all kinds of sports - especially hockey and snowboarding.

Marian Large

Marian is a graduate of Rhema Bible Training Center. Marian is currently involved in the ministry of helps, doing funeral luncheons and meals for shut-ins. Marian and her husband, Jim, have been Altar Care leaders at Rhema Bible Church in Tulsa, oK, for over 20 years. They, also, conduct Altar Care/Prayer Worker Seminars around the country. They can be contacted by email - jbmearge@windstream.net.

Roxanne Marie Mattheis

Roxanne will have 7 years clean July 29, 2011. She wishes to thank her son Charlie, her parents Chuck and Jay Lynn, sister Rachelle and her wonderful husband and Charlie's step dad Brian and family for their never ending love and support. Also special thanks to Teen Challenge and Calvary Ranch for taking me off the broken road and leading me on God's path. Charlie now lives with his mother and Brian full time and attends Foothills Christian HS. Most important all glory be to God. Thank You Lord for forgivness and thank you Charlie for being my earthly savior.

Jessica Arvizo

Jessica is married to Kris Arvizo. Both Jessica and Kris have been attending Third Day Church. Jessica just recently found out she is pregnant with Twins. She is currently attending school to become a medical assistant. God has been so faithful as she has walked with Him and there have been many blessings throughout her life. She loves God with all her heart wants to share the happiness and joy she has experienced with others around her.

Tiwalola Abogunrin

Tiwalola currently attends the University of California, Merced and is pursing a B.A in Sociology with a minor in Writing. Upon graduating, she plans to pursue a career working with troubled teens and adults in the California Corrections system as a probation officer. She continues to write and share her personal experiences with others.

Nicky Moore

Nicky has a degree in Human Development & Family Studies which has proven helpful for many of lifes' endeavors. Currently, she manages a successful sales team in Fort Collins, CO. She implements teamwork at home in raising three children-Jadon, Lauren, and Rachel. She and her husband attend Timberline Church, it has been their home-a place of tremendous growth in the last decade. Keeping steadfast on Christ's purpose for her life is of utmost importance.

Linda Robinson

Linda and her husband have been in full time ministry pasturing for over 20 years together. They have been involved in Ministries such as Jr. High, to College and now oversee all Creative Arts Ministries at Cathedral of Faith in San Jose Ca.Linda's heart is to help young ladies overcome addictive behavior brought on by some form of abuse.Linda's most fulfilling role is being a mother and wife to her 2 sons Matthew and Ricky and husband Rick.

Lara Pagh

Lara is the Assistant Children's Pastor at Harvest Church in Elk Grove, CA. She has been blessed to serve at Harvest for the past two years and recently received her pastoral license from the Assemblies of God. She graduated from Asuza Pacific University in May 2009 with a bachelor's degree in mathematics. Lara has a passion for discipling children, expressing God's love for them, and teaching them how to show their love for God through worship.

Kelsey Pagh

Kelsey is completing her Bachelor's degree in Theology and French at Whitworth University in Spokane, WA. She will begin seminary in the coming year in order to receive a Master of Divinity degree. God has called her to full-time ministry abroad. Eventually, she hopes to teach Bible or theology classes for national church pastors and leaders.

Additional Contributing Authors:

Jordyn Rentz

Clare Holt

Jessica Rentz

Britni Bersin

Angelica Vasquez

Rebecca Reagan Harrison

Erin Simmons

Ada Tajadeen

Debbie Evans

Jacquelyn Porter

Prayer of Salvation

God loves you—no matter who you are, no matter what your past. God loves you so much that He gave His one and only begotten Son for you. The Bible tells us that "...whoever believes in him shall not perish but have eternal life" (John 3:16 NIV). Jesus laid down His life and rose again so that we could spend eternity with Him in heaven and experience His absolute best on earth. If you would like to receive Jesus into your life, say the following prayer out loud and mean it from your heart.

Heavenly Father, I come to You admitting that I am a sinner. Right now, I choose to turn away from sin, and I ask You to cleanse me of all unrighteousness. I believe that Your Son, Jesus, died on the cross to take away my sins. I also believe that He rose again from the dead so that I might be forgiven of my sins and made righteous through faith in Him. I call upon the name of Jesus Christ to be the Savior and Lord of my life. Jesus, I choose to follow You and ask that You fill me with the power of the Holy Spirit. I declare that right now I am a child of God. I am free from sin and full of the right-eousness of God. I am saved in Jesus' name. Amen.

If you prayed this prayer to receive Jesus Christ as your Savior for the first time, please contact us on the Web at **www.harrisonhouse.com** to receive a free book.

Or you may write to us at

Harrison House • P.O. Box 35035 • Tulsa, Oklahoma 74153

OTHER BOOKS YOU MAY ENJOY...

Destined to Reign
by Joseph Prince
978-160683-009-3
$14.99

Discover the secret of reigning over every adversity, lack and destructive habit that is limiting you from experiencing the success, wholeness and victory that you were destined to enjoy. Find out how it is not about what you have to do, but what has already been done. It is not about what you must accomplish, but what has been accomplished for you. It is not about using your will power to effect change, but His power changing you. Start reigning over sickness, financial lack, broken relationships and destructive habits today.

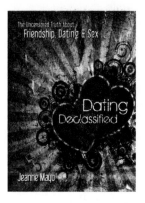

Dating Declassified by Jeanne Mayo
978-160683-001-7
$14.99

Jeanne Mayo, renowned youth culture expert, talks bluntly about topics that most don't have the guts to address. Inside *Dating Declassified* you will find hard hitting feedback on dating, friendship, falling in love, masturbation, determining your future, sex. Homosexual struggles, and more. Avoid the pitfalls. It's your life. It's your choice. It's worth getting the facts.

Confessions of a Non-Barbie
by Kinda Wilson
978-160683-008-6
$10.99

This book is all the things someone should really tell you about what girls go through. This book takes a candid look at beauty, rejection, singleness, dating and breakups. The author shares the things she has learned plus some good advice from a few others. This is your chance to look inside the minds and journals of teen girls and pick up a few tips!